The Myth of a Racist
Criminal Justice System

Contemporary Issues in Crime and Justice Series
Roy Roberg, Louisiana State University: Series Editor

Crime and Justice: Issues and Ideas (1984)
Philip Jenkins, Pennsylvania State University

Crime Victims: An Introduction to Victimology (1984)
Andrew Karmen, John Jay College of Criminal Justice

Sense and Nonsense about Crime: A Policy Guide (1985)
Samuel Walker, University of Nebraska at Omaha

The Myth of a Racist Criminal Justice System (1987)
William Wilbanks, Florida International University

Hard Time: Understanding and Reforming the Prison (1987)
Robert Johnson, The American University

The Myth of a Racist Criminal Justice System

William Wilbanks
Florida International University

Brooks/Cole Publishing Company
Monterey, California

Consulting Editor: Roy Roberg, Louisiana State University

Brooks/Cole Publishing Company
A Division of Wadsworth, Inc.

Printed in the United States of America

10 9 8 7 6 5 4 3 2

Library of Congress Cataloging-in-Publication Data

Wilbanks, William, [date]
   The myth of a racist criminal justice system.

   Bibliography: p.
   Includes index.
   1. Criminal justice, Administration of—United
States.   2. Discrimination in criminal justice
administration—United States.   3. Race discrimination
—United States.   4. United States—Race relations.
I. Title.
HV9950.W55   1986   364'.973   86-13443
ISBN 0-534-06816-2

Sponsoring Editor: **Claire Verduin**
Editorial Assistant: **Linda Ruth Wright**
Production Editor: **Fiorella Ljunggren**
Manuscript Editor: **William Waller**
Permissions Editor: **Mary Kay Hancharick**
Interior and Cover Design: **Sharon L. Kinghan**
Typesetting: **Linda Andrews, Ashland, Oregon**
Printing and Binding: **Malloy Lithographing, Inc., Ann Arbor, Michigan**

Credits continue on p. 209.

To Mrs. Wilma Wilbanks Hander, my mother, who instilled in me a passion for knowledge and truth

and

To Dr. Michael J. Hindelang, my major professor in the Ph.D. program at the School of Criminal Justice, State University of New York at Albany, who taught me the skills and joy of research and writing. His untimely death in 1982 at the age of 36 greatly diminished the discipline of criminology.

Foreword

The Contemporary Issues in Crime and Justice Series introduces important topics that until now have been neglected or inadequately covered to students and professionals in criminal justice, criminology, law, psychology, and sociology.

The volumes cover philosophical and theoretical issues and analyze the most recent research findings and their implications for practice. Consequently, each volume will stimulate further thinking and debate on the issues it covers, in addition to providing direction for policy formulation and implementation.

Is there systematic racial discrimination throughout our criminal justice system? William Wilbanks observes that tremendous differences of opinion exist between black and white Americans, as well as among criminal justice practitioners, on this question. He suggests that although most blacks believe the police and courts do discriminate against them, a sizable minority of whites believe that the criminal justice system actually discriminates in favor of blacks in an attempt to react to charges of racism. In order to address the issue of racism, Wilbanks has conducted a comprehensive review of the available research on formal decisions made by personnel throughout the criminal justice system. As a result, he concludes that although individual cases of racial prejudice and discrimination do occur, at this point there is insufficient evidence to support a charge of systematic racism against blacks in the U.S. criminal justice system.

In reaching the conclusion that a racist criminal justice system is a myth, Wilbanks takes a hard look at some critical issues surrounding the "discrimination thesis." He points out that when the "accusers" of a racist system define racism, they implicitly suggest that the term applies only to whites; in other words, blacks generally are not, or cannot be, racist. He cites numerous examples of "double standards" throughout the system that either are ignored or go unnoticed by the accusers. The types of examples the accusers cite, Wilbanks suggests, indicate that the public (both black and white) has been socialized to

see racism from only one perspective—that is, only whites can be racist
—thus, the double standard.

   In general, the evidence analyzed by Wilbanks with regard to the
issue of racism in the police, prosecution, sentencing and prisons, and
parole system indicates that support for a discrimination thesis is
sparse, inconsistent, and frequently *contradictory.* In his work, the
author has taken an important first step toward defining the parameters
of racism in the criminal justice system, as well as reviewing and interpreting the current research on this topic. It will now be necessary for
other criminal justice and criminology researchers to critically examine
both the premises and the research on which Wilbanks's book is based
and either support or refute the conclusions drawn by the author. Let
the debate begin.

Roy Roberg

Preface

Popular opinion and some textbooks—such as *The Criminal Justice System and Blacks,* edited by Georges-Abeyie, and *Race, Crime and Criminal Justice,* edited by McNeely and Pope—maintain that the criminal justice system in the United States is racist. Other writers, however, have opposite views about specific parts of the system. Gary Kleck of Florida State University, for example, concluded in a 1981 article in *The American Sociological Review* that there is no systematic discrimination at the point of sentencing.

About the same time that Kleck's article was published, I was reading the works of Thomas Sowell, W. J. Wilson, and W. E. Williams. Sowell attributes ethnic behavior, including crime, to cultural legacies rather than to discrimination or opportunity. Wilson has written *The Declining Significance of Race,* and Williams is the author of *The State against Blacks,* a book that disputes the view that racial discrimination is pervasive in employment. Each of these authors challenges the idea that racial discrimination is pervasive at this point in American history. This is all the more interesting because Sowell, Wilson, and Williams are black.

This controversy intrigued me, and in December 1983 I began research for a book that would summarize the existing literature on racial discrimination across the various points of the criminal justice system. I wanted the book to be suitable as a supplementary text for undergraduate and graduate survey courses (for example, Introduction to Criminal Justice) and as a primary text for more specific courses on race, crime, and criminal justice. The edited volumes now available for classroom use on this issue use only a small fraction of the relevant articles and, in my view, have an ideological bias that determined the selection of "pro-discrimination" studies.

At the same time, I wanted the book to be available to those who work in the criminal justice system and often hear the charge that the system is racist. Those practitioners need a single, readable volume that summarizes the evidence on this issue. I hope that the book will also be of interest to general readers interested in the question "Is the criminal justice system racist?"

Two years of research went into this book. The extensive bibliography attests to that research effort. I believe that the literature search and review have been comprehensive. I do plan a revised edition of this volume in two years or so, however, and I solicit suggestions from readers about sources and points that should be discussed. Attribution will be given in the revised edition to those who suggest new arguments or raise important issues. In short, I hope that this volume will stimulate further thinking, investigation, discussion, and dialogue.

I wish to express my gratitude to the reviewers of the manuscript for their constructive criticism. They are Bill Allen of Belleville Area College, Roy L. Austin of Pennsylvania State University, William Feyerherm of the University of Wisconsin, Milwaukee, and Carl Pope, also of the University of Wisconsin, Milwaukee.

I also wish to express my appreciation to Claire Verduin and Roy Roberg for deciding to publish a controversial book, to Fiorella Ljunggren for her contribution as production coordinator, and to William Waller for his excellent editing job, which greatly improved the manuscript.

William Wilbanks

Contents

1

The Myth Examined   1

2

Defining Racism   13

3

Why Do Blacks and Whites Disagree?   31

CONTENTS

4

Difficulties of Proving Discrimination 40

5

The Police and Racial Discrimination 57

6

Prosecution and Racial Discrimination 84

7

Sentencing and Racial Discrimination   103

8

Prisons, Parole, and Racial Discrimination   126

9

Conclusions and Recommendations 142

Appendix 149

Racially Disproportionate Incarceration Rates:
Are They a Product of Cumulative Discrimination
by the Criminal Justice System?

Bibliography 172

Name Index 201

Subject Index 205

1

The Myth Examined

White and black Americans differ sharply over whether their criminal justice system is racist. The vast majority of blacks appear to believe that the police and courts do discriminate against blacks, whereas a majority of whites reject this charge. In Dade County (Miami), Florida, for example, a poll by a television station found that 97 percent of blacks believed the justice system to be racist and that 58 percent of whites rejected this charge.[1] This disparity in views between blacks and whites also appears to exist among those who work in the criminal justice system. A supplemental study for the National Advisory Commission on Civil Disorders in 1968 found that 57 percent of black police officers but only 5 percent of white officers believed that the system discriminated against blacks.[2]

Some black critics have suggested that the criminal justice system is so characterized by racism that blacks are outside the protection of the law.[3] Furthermore, many blacks believe that when whites speak of wanting justice, they really mean "just us" (blacks).[4] Another critic finds the criminal justice system to be more criminal than just.[5]

A sizable minority of whites, in contrast, believe that the justice system actually discriminates *for* blacks in "leaning over backward" for them in reaction to charges of racism from the black community, liberal white politicians, and liberal elements of the news media.[6] White police officers have reported often ignoring criminal activity by blacks out of a fear of criticism from the department, the black community, or the media. Since officers are rarely criticized for inaction, they find themselves tempted to overlook a situation that might lead to physical conflict and subsequent criticism.[7]

There is also evidence that some whites who work in the system may favor blacks because of the psychological tendency to fight off their fear that they might be prejudiced.[8] It is as if white practitioners were attempting to prove that they are not prejudiced against blacks by giving them the benefit of the doubt in marginal cases or actually being more lenient. Though there has been no research on the question, one might speculate that introspective whites (who question their own behavior) and white liberals (who presumably are sensitive to the criticisms of racial prejudice) would be more subject to this psychological phenomenon of reverse discrimination.

These contrasting perceptions by whites and blacks of the fairness of the criminal justice system have at least four important consequences. *First,* research indicates that blacks may turn to criminality or engage in more crime because of a perception that the criminal law and its enforcement are unfair and even racist. Davis suggested in 1974 that the belief by black men that the criminal justice system is racist or unfair produces a "justification for no obligation" to the law.[9] It is as if some blacks were saying, "I don't respect a system that is racist, and so I don't feel obliged to abide by the laws of that system."

The connection between a belief that the system is unjust and a denial of personal responsibility for breaking the law is sometimes made specifically by black authors. One black lawyer, for example, in suggesting that justice is a "skin game," wrote that "people steal because they have to; there are no other palatable choices."[10] Thus the suggestion is made that since the economic and justice systems are unfair and racist, blacks are justified in breaking the law. Another illustration of this view is the assertion by another black author that "racism is the single most damaging reality of the criminal justice system—a reality that is responsible for the disrespect, distrust, and fear that black people hold for the law."[11] Thus some blacks receive the message that they are not actually offenders when they commit a crime but victims of an unjust system. Certainly such a belief, whether true or false, is criminogenic.

Second, it is well known that many "civil disturbances" (or "riots" or "rebellions," depending on one's political views) are caused by a perception that the system is unfair and unjust.[12] A riot in Miami in 1980 grew out of a protest over a verdict of acquittal for white police officers who had beaten a black motorcyclist to death.[13] The Kerner commission, which investigated the civil disturbances in American cities in the 1960s, found a widespread belief among blacks that the criminal justice system was racist and concluded that this perception was one of the major causes of the violence.[14] If such perceptions exist, surely there is a need to critically examine their validity.

A black psychologist contends that the Miami riot, which resulted in the death of 17 people, was based on an incorrect view of the acquittal verdict.[15] The psychologist, Marvin Dunn, says that newspaper and television coverage left the impression with the public that the prosecution was certain to win and that the verdict came as a shock to both blacks and whites. Blacks then took to the streets to protest what they perceived as an obvious whitewash by an all-white jury in Tampa, where the trial was held. Dunn maintains, however, that most lawyers who observed the trial believed that because of inconsistent testimony the state had failed to prove its case. He says it is unlikely that the presence of blacks on the jury would have made a difference, since there was clearly a reasonable doubt about the guilt of the officers. As he also notes, however, the presence of black jurors would have reduced the perception of an unjust verdict.

A black leader may even suggest to blacks on occasion that they have no control over their actions because the "fact" that the economic and criminal justice systems are unjust and racially discriminatory will inevitably lead to rioting. The head of the Urban League in Miami was quoted in the *Miami Herald* as suggesting that the "white power structure" had created an atmosphere of violence in the black community and that expecting riots not to occur was "too much to ask of any human being."[16]

Third, there is some evidence that the black view of the criminal justice system as racist and of the police as brutal and prejudiced has created hostility toward police officers, which has led in turn to reactive hostility by them. One author suggests that the reciprocal images of the two parties ("niggers" and "pigs") often cause simple encounters to become violent.[17] It is as if two gunslingers were approaching each other in a Western town, each expecting the other to be ready to shoot and therefore keeping his finger on the trigger.

This mutual expectation of violence does not always result in violence. But as Chapter Five indicates, demeanor is an important predictor of whether someone is arrested for a minor offense. The demeanor of many young black males is hostile (and, one might argue, for good reason) and thus subjects them to a greater likelihood of formal action by the police. The point is that the view of the criminal justice system (especially the police) as racist has produced hostility, which has in many cases resulted in police behavior that then justifies the racist label. In other words, the police behavior that blacks fear and expect is produced in part by that expectation.

Fourth, the recent white backlash to civil rights programs such as affirmative action and racial quotas may be due in part to a white perception that blacks complain about racism in a society that actually practices reverse discrimination (that is, favors blacks through affirmative action and quotas). The view of many whites that the criminal justice system actually treats blacks more favorably needs to be critically examined. Later chapters will mention several studies that appear to document instances of more favorable treatment of blacks.

In view of these important consequences of the sharp contrast in perceptions between whites and blacks, it is amazing that so little research has been done to examine (1) the origins of and reasons for the contrasting views, (2) the validity of the views, and (3) their consequences. Though volumes have been written on the topics of racism and crime, the literature examining the connection between the two is sparse. Of the three topics listed above (origins, validity, and consequences), only validity has been addressed by a large body of research. Unfortunately, the research reporting on tests of possible racial discrimination in decisions by the police, the courts, and the prisons is found only in academic journals and remains unknown to the general public. Those who wish to become informed on the validity issue will find the studies reported in the literature to be difficult to understand, given their statistical content and given the lack of consensus among the researchers.

The public often views academics as irrelevant because of their tendency to write about topics of interest only to other academics. The public has little interest in reading, for example, about tests of subcultural theory or a validity check for self-report surveys. Rather, it is interested in data that would confirm or deny the charge that police activities and court decisions are racist. But for some reason academics have been reluctant to address topics that deal directly with the racial aspects of crime.

For example, academics often chastise the white public for fearing an unfamiliar black person, since "everyone knows" that crime is intraracial and thus whites have more to fear from fellow whites than from blacks. Though the "fact" of intraracial crime has been assumed, little research has been conducted to test this assumption. A recent article, however, found that black offenders were more likely to select whites than blacks as victims in violent crimes.[18] The author expressed surprise that this finding had not been reported since the data were readily available (though "hidden" by the format of tables in the annual crime-victimization survey by the U.S. Department of Justice). It would appear that academics have little interest in exploring the racial aspects of crime. The public view that black areas are more dangerous for whites (or blacks) is viewed as prejudice by many criminologists, and yet research on the validity of such perceptions is almost nonexistent.

Perhaps criminologists are more out of touch with their lay audience than anyone realizes.[19] The theories that are the focus of most criminological texts—that is, conflict theory, labeling theory—are precisely those that students find unimportant or invalid. Many students leave criminology classes with their original views unaltered, since the views about cause that they are likely to espouse (permissiveness, poverty, mental illness, lack of faith in God) are not critiqued in class or in texts. They may come out of these classes knowing about anomie, differential opportunity, and so on, but their views of the causes of crime are unaffected by listening to and parroting back the theories that interest academics.

The research agenda of criminologists would be very different if the issues in the mind of the public were given priority. Surely the first priority in a "consumer-based" criminology would be to find out what issues were of greatest concern to the public. Though the public might not see any need to do research into "facts" that are known through common sense (for example, blacks might argue that any fool could see that racism permeates our society, including the criminal justice system, and whites might argue that any fool could see that affirmative action proves reverse discrimination), the public does appear to be vitally interested in certain issues whether or not it sees those issues as needing validation through research. Some of those issues would probably impinge on the connection between race and crime. For example, the following might appear near the top of the public's research agenda:

1. Are decisions by those in police, judicial, and corrections agencies racist? If so, would the infusion of more black police officers, prosecutors, judges, and wardens affect decision making? Do black police officers make racist decisions? Do black judges?
2. Is the white fear of black neighborhoods unfounded? Are whites more likely to be attacked in black neighborhoods than in white ones? Are blacks more likely to be attacked in white areas or in black areas?
3. Is an individual white more likely to be victimized by an individual white or by an individual black? Is an individual black more likely to be victimized by an individual black or by an individual white?

This book is written in the belief that many aspects of the question "Is the criminal justice system racist?" have not been addressed by criminologists and that the issue as a whole has not been addressed in a manner designed for consumers. Both laypersons and those who work in the criminal justice system can find nothing in the current literature to guide them in determining whether the system is racist. This book is intended to fill that void.

Thesis of the Book

I take the position that the perception of the criminal justice system as racist is a myth. Since this assertion can be interpreted in many ways, it is necessary to specify what it means and does not mean.

First, I believe that there is racial prejudice and discrimination *within* the criminal justice system, in that there are individuals, both white and black, who make decisions, at least in part, on the basis of race. I do not believe that *the system* is characterized by racial

prejudice or discrimination against blacks; that is, prejudice and discrimination are not "systematic." Individual cases appear to reflect
racial prejudice and discrimination by the offender, the victim, the
police, the prosecutor, the judge, or prison and parole officials. But
conceding individual cases of bias is far different from conceding
pervasive racial discrimination.

Chapter Four ("Difficulties of Proving Discrimination") and subsequent chapters argue that the evidence at most decision points fails
to show any overall racial effect, in that the percentage outcomes
for blacks and whites are not very different. There is evidence, however, that some individual decision makers (for example, police officers, judges) are more likely to give "breaks" to whites than to blacks.
It appears, however, that there is an *equal* tendency for other individual decision makers to favor blacks over whites.[20] This "canceling-
out effect" results in studies that find no *overall* racial effect. It is
important to note that though racial discrimination has occurred in
numerous individual cases against blacks and whites, there is no *systematic* bias *against* blacks.

Second, the question of whether the criminal justice system is
"racist" cannot be discussed until the term *racist* is defined. As Chapter Two ("Defining Racism") points out, some appear to see any
black/white disparities as prima facie evidence of racism. Thus if
blacks outnumber whites in prison at a ratio of 8:1 (this is the rate
ratio, controlling for the fact that blacks make up only 12 percent
of the U.S. population), that disparity is viewed as racism. By that
definition the criminal justice system is racist, since that 8:1 disparity
does in fact exist.

If one defines racism as a conscious attitude or conscious behavior by
individuals that discriminates against blacks, however, there is little or
no evidence that most individuals in the system make decisions on the
basis of race. In short, the definition of racism often predetermines
the answer to the question "Is the criminal justice system racist?"

Furthermore, it should be noted that the research discussed in this
volume is concerned primarily with formal *decisions* (for example,
arrest, conviction, sentencing) made by those in the criminal justice
system. To argue that there is no systematic bias against blacks in
formal decisions does not speak to the issue of whether the police
are more likely to "talk down" to black citizens or to show them less
respect. The fact that a police officer may call a 40-year-old black
man a "boy" does not necessarily mean that the officer will be more
likely to arrest that man (or, if he does, that his decision is based
primarily on the racist stereotype). As two authors state, "Harassment
of minorities by system personnel, less desirable work assignments,
and indifference to important cultural needs could exist, but not
be systematically reflected in formal processing decisions."[21]

The focus in this book on formal decisions by the criminal justice system that affect blacks should not be construed to mean that informal decisions (as suggested above) are not important. But the charge of racism is generally directed at the formal decisions that can result in the deprivation of liberty, and thus I will focus on those decisions. Also, researching the informal decisions (harassment, talking down) is much harder and is subject to personal biases by observers.

Third, the assertion that the criminal justice system is not racist does not address the reasons why blacks appear to offend at higher rates than whites even before coming into contact with the criminal justice system.[22] It may be that racial discrimination in American society has been responsible for conditions that lead to higher rates of offending by blacks, but that possibility does not bear on the question of whether the criminal justice system discriminates against blacks.

An excellent illustration of how racial discrimination may have led to a greater likelihood of blacks' being involved in criminal activity can be found in the book *Brothers and Keepers,* an account of how two black brothers chose different directions. The author obtained a Ph.D. in English; his brother, Robby, received a life sentence for murder.[23]

No way Ima be like the rest of them niggers scuffling and kissing ass to get by. Scuffling and licking ass till the day they die and the shame is they ain't even getting by. They crawling. They stepped on. Mize well be roaches or some goddamn waterbugs. White man got em backed up in Homewood and he's sprinkling roach powder on em. He's steady shaking and they steady dying. You know I ain't making nothing up. You know I ain't trying to be funny. Cause you seen it. You run from it just like I did. You know the shit's still coming down and it's falling on everybody in Homewood. You know what I'm talking about. Don't tell me you don't, cause we both running. I'm in here but it's still falling on me. It's falling on Daddy and Mommy and Dave and Gene and Tish and all the kids. Falls till it knocks you down [p. 152].

He blew it. Not alone, of course. Society cooperated. Robby's chance for a normal life was as illusory as most citizens' chances to be elected to office or run a corporation. If "normal" implies a decent job, an opportunity to receive at least minimal pay-off for years of drudgery, delayed gratification, then for Robby and 75 percent of young black males growing up in the 1960's, "normal" was the exception rather than the rule. Robby was smart enough to see there was no light at the end of the long tunnel of hard work (if and when you could get it) and responsibility. He was stubborn, aggressive, and prickly enough not to allow anyone to bully him into the tunnel. He chose the bright lights winking right in front of his face, just beyond his fingertips. For him and most of his buddies "normal" was poverty, drugs, street crime, Vietnam, or prison [p. 220].

Thus the question of whether the criminal justice system is racist must not be confused with that of whether blacks commit crimes at a higher rate than whites because of discrimination in employment, housing, education, and so forth. It may be that racial discrimination produces a gap in offending between blacks and whites but that this gap is not increased as black and white offenders move through the criminal justice system. (That will be the position set forth in later chapters.) If the gap does not increase after the point at which offenses occur, the system cannot be held responsible for the gap that results at the end of the system (prison).

Universities in the United States are sometimes accused of being racist because their student enrollment or faculty does not have the numbers of blacks one would expect given the proportion of blacks in the population. Those universities so accused often respond that they are not responsible for the failure of prospective black students or faculty members to meet admission criteria. Though one can argue that society as a whole is responsible for inferior schooling for blacks that has resulted in their being "less qualified" for admission as students or faculty, surely it would be unfair to blame the universities for this problem. In my view the university is responsible, assuming good faith and effort in student and faculty recruitment, only for the treatment of minorities once they enroll or join the faculty. Likewise, the criminal justice system is not responsible, with respect to the charge of racism, for differing levels of offending by blacks and whites. It is responsible for differential treatment once offending occurs.

Fourth, the assertion that the criminal justice system is not racist does not deny that racial prejudice and discrimination have existed in or even been the dominant force in the design and operation of the criminal justice system in the past. There is evidence suggesting that racism did permeate the criminal justice system in earlier periods of American history, especially in the South.[24] The evidence regarding northern cities, however, does not support the discrimination thesis. Roger Lane, perhaps the most prominent historian of U.S. criminal justice, found no evidence of systemic racial discrimination in the criminal courts of nineteenth-century Philadelphia "or indeed for those in any northern city in the same period."[25] But the question today concerns whether the operation of the system *at this time* is characterized by racial prejudice and discrimination. I believe that there is insufficient evidence to support the charge that the system is racist today.

Fifth, I am not suggesting that the nondiscrimination thesis has been proven by the existing literature. But surely the burden of proof rests on those who hold that the system is racist. Though I do believe that the weight of the existing evidence supports the nondiscrimination thesis (NDT) rather than the discrimination thesis (DT), I do not believe that the case for the NDT has been proven. The belief that the criminal justice system is racist is a myth in the sense that there is insufficient evidence to support this position.

Organization of the Book

The following chapters address whether the criminal justice system is racist. Chapter Two explores the varying definitions of *racism* and how that term overlaps with *prejudice* and *discrimination*. The chapter also examines the extent to which blacks can be considered to be as racist as (or even more racist than) whites. It argues that the term *racist* is used and interpreted in so many different ways that a better approach is to abandon it and replace it with *racial prejudice* (an attitude) and *racial discrimination* (a behavior).

Chapter Three explores the origins of the contrasting perceptions by blacks and whites regarding racism in the criminal justice system. Both views—that the system is racist and that it is not—are "ignorant" in that both are based on nonscientific samples of cases and on cultural traditions that are part of the ideology of blacks and whites.

Chapter Four examines the difficulties that arise in trying to "prove" either the DT or the NDT. The public is generally not aware that social scientists have great difficulty in "proving" either thesis. The discussion of problems inherent in proving either position serves as an introduction to the chapters that follow, on the alleged practice of racial discrimination by the police, prosecutors, and so on.

Chapter Five explores whether the police practice racial discrimination in deployment patterns, in arrest statistics, in individual officers' bias, in police brutality, and in the use of deadly force. For each of these five areas of concern involving possible racial discrimination by the police, the claims will be stated along with the supporting rationale and evidence supporting each charge. Each claim is followed by a number of arguments against it that suggest that the DT is more problematic than the NDT.

Chapter Six examines the extent to which the system of prosecution displays racial discrimination in the bail decision, the charging process, plea bargaining, the providing of legal counsel, the selection of jurors, and convictions. Again, for each of these processes the DT claim is stated, along with supporting rationale and evidence, and critiqued.

Chapter Seven focuses on the sentencing decision of the judge. It presents arguments suggesting that the claim of racial discrimination in sentencing is a myth. The evidence presented in this chapter involves the decision whether to incarcerate, the length of sentences, and the death penalty.

Chapter Eight examines the claims that prison and parole officials are guilty of racial discrimination in classification, treatment, discipline, and parole. This chapter also explores the extent to which racism (both white against black and black against white) exists among prison inmates.

Chapter Nine draws conclusions from the previous chapters, poses challenges to the DT, and attempts to suggest "where we go from here" with respect to research.

An appendix studies the processing of all felony defendants in two states, California and Pennsylvania, from arrest to final disposition. This rather technical study, which is referenced at several points earlier in the book, is included to demonstrate the lack of cumulative discrimination across decision points of the criminal justice system.

Next is a lengthy bibliography on race, crime, and criminal justice. Most of the books and articles are cited in the text. The bibliography is indexed by topic (for example, all citations labeled "J" refer to race and jail/prison) to make it easy to locate all the sources that relate to that topic.

Summary

There is a sharp disagreement between blacks and whites over whether the criminal justice system is racist. The nearly unanimous perception of blacks that the system is racist is important in view of the evidence that this perception has (1) generated more criminality, (2) caused civil disorders, (3) led to hostility by blacks against the police and reactive hostility by the police against blacks, and (4) led to a white backlash that perceives blacks as claiming racism in the face of facts that indicate favoritism for blacks.

The thesis of this book is that the criminal justice system is not racist. First, there is no doubt that there is racial prejudice and discrimination *in* the criminal justice system, in that there are individuals, both white and black, who make decisions partly on the basis of race. But the *system* is not characterized by racial discrimination against blacks. Second, the view that the criminal justice system is racist is problematic in view of the myriad definitions of the term *racist* and is valid only if one accepts the view that racism is proven simply by blacks' being disproportionately represented at arrest through prison.

Third, the assertion that the *criminal justice system* is not racist should not be confused with the issue of whether blacks commit more crimes at a greater rate than whites because of discrimination by the *sociopolitical system.* Fourth, the denial of a racist justice system at the present time does not deny the existence of systematic racial prejudice and discrimination in the past in designing and operating the system. Fifth, the assertion that the belief in a racist system is a myth does not suggest that the opposite thesis (the NDT) has been proven. This book suggests that neither thesis has been proven. The DT is a myth in the sense that evidence for this thesis is lacking and that the DT is more problematic than the NDT given the existing evidence.

Notes

1. Reported by WPLG-TV in Miami on April 29, 1981.
2. The study was by Rossi et al., "Between White and Black: The Faces of American Institutions in the Ghetto," and is quoted in Jacobs and Cohen (1978, p. 172).
3. T. Jones, 1978, p. 357.
4. The quotation "just us" is from Richard Friar as cited in a speech by Sterling Johnson at an Urban League symposium. See Johnson, 1977, p. 161. In a similar vein, a black police officer is quoted by Johnson (1977, p. 164) as having said that "justice is a statue in Foley Square that the pigeons shit on."
5. Wright, 1984a, p. 205.
6. Porter and Dunn, 1984, p. 176.
7. Porter and Dunn, 1984, pp. 177, 184.
8. Dutton and Lake, 1973, p. 95. They hypothesize "that if a white man thinks racial equality is desirable and racial discrimination is not, he probably wants to think of himself as a person whose behavior is consistent with these values. When such a person finds himself in an interpersonal situation with a member of a minority group whom he perceives as having been discriminated against, then any failure on his part to comply with the requests of this minority group member may carry with it cues of an underlying prejudice which will prove threatening to the values or self-image of this person. . . . The white's desire to avoid these threatening cues from his behavior may result in his treating the minority group member more favorably than another white in the same situation" (p. 95).

   Dutton and Lake (1973) concluded in a study of giving to white and black panhandlers that the white subjects who were threatened with the possibility that they might be prejudiced behaved more altruistically toward black than white panhandlers. "Reverse discrimination, then, is viewed as an attempt by whites who think racial prejudice is undesirable and who are threatened by the possibility that they themselves might be prejudiced to prove to themselves through their behavior toward a black that they are not prejudiced" (p. 99).

   Kluegel and Smith (1982) found that belief in widespread reverse discrimination is related to people's perception of their own opportunity, to their ideology of stratification, and to feelings of relative deprivation.

   Lewis, Balla, and Shanak (1979) found some evidence of white clinicians' "leaning over backward" to give preferential treatment to black juveniles. Owens (1980), a black author, agrees that some whites may lean over backward "to convince themselves or others that they are not prejudiced" (p. 74).
9. Davis, 1974.
10. Moore, 1973, p. 11. Though there appears to be no literature attempting to replicate or expand on Davis's thesis ("justification for no obligation") there is considerable literature on internal versus external locus of control for blacks and whites. Some have suggested that because of discrimination blacks may believe that they "don't have a chance," that they are thus "pawns" of the socioeconomic system, and that they are simply the product of their environment. However, Farley and Sewell (1975) found that black delinquents were not more external in perceived locus of control than black nondelinquents. But there appears to be some support for a class link to internal versus external locus of control; that is, those who are poor are less likely to believe that they control their environment. See Farley and Sewell, 1975, pp. 391–392; and Langer, 1983.
11. The quotation is from D. Georges-Abeyie in an introduction to comments by a black judge. See Crockett, 1984, p. 195.

12. Justice, 1969.
13. Porter and Dunn, 1984.
14. National Advisory Commission on Civil Disorders, 1968.
15. Porter and Dunn, 1984, pp. 198–199. Dunn made more explicit observations as a guest lecturer in my class at Florida International University in May 1985. He said that if all the members of the jury had been black and devoted members of the NAACP who judged the case on its merits, they would have returned a verdict of not guilty, since it was clear to anyone involved with the trial that there was reasonable doubt.
16. Wilbanks, 1984b.
17. The quotation is from Stark, 1972, p. 98. On the danger of mutual stereotypes, reciprocal images, and the self-fulfilling prophecy see Toch, 1969, 1975; Foster, 1974; and Shaver, 1983, pp. 134–137.
18. Wilbanks, 1985a.
19. One criminologist suggests that the consumer has fared poorly from the services of the criminal justice system and that criminologists and the system need to be more sensitive to their needs. See Wilkins, 1984.
20. See Gibson, 1978, and the discussion and notes on the canceling-out effect, in Chapter Four of this text.
21. The quotation is from Zimmerman and Frederick, 1984, p. 327. On this point see also Reiss, 1980, p. 277.
22. A survey of explanations for this apparent gap is given by Wolfgang (1977) and Wolfgang and Cohen (1970).
23. Wideman, 1984.
24. There are numerous discussions of the design and operation of the criminal justice systems in the South after the Civil War to subjugate blacks under a new type of servitude (that is, the prisons). See Adamson, 1983; Hindus, 1976; Brown and Steiner, 1969; Carper, 1964; Cahalan, 1979; Mancini, 1978; Rafter, 1985; and Sellin, 1976. A fuller discussion of leasing in southern prisons is given in Chapter Eight of this text.
25. Lane, 1986. In Chapter Three, "On the Uses of Criminal Statistics: Philadelphia Justice, Black and White," Lane also says that the criminal courts in Philadelphia, New York, and Boston actually gave shorter sentences to blacks than they did to whites toward the end of the nineteenth century. Lane also found that in Philadelphia blacks were less likely than whites to be convicted of interracial homicides and that, until the very end of the century, blacks were far less likely than whites to be hanged for murder. The studies he cites are all Ph.D. dissertations: Steinberg, 1983 (a study of Philadelphia); Epstein, 1981 (a study of Philadelphia); Kuntz, 1978 (a study of New York, Boston, and Philadelphia); and Naylor, 1979 (a study of Philadelphia). Chapter Nine of this text suggests that the failure to find evidence of the DT in the criminal justice systems of nineteenth-century northern cities when there was evidence of racial discrimination in society is problematic for those who maintain today that there must be racial discrimination in the criminal justice system since there is discrimination in society.

2

Defining Racism

Though it is quite common to see charges of racism in the media and in the academic literature, it is rare to see the term defined.[1] Those who make such a charge assume (and often state) that demands to define the term are simply a diversion from the issue, because "everyone knows what racism means." Those who deny the charge of racism generally do so without even having attempted to determine just what the accuser meant by the use of the term *racism* in the charge. It is as if those denying the charge were saying, "Whatever it means, I don't do 'it.' I'm a fair-minded person." Those who deny being racists may think of racists as members of the Ku Klux Klan, and they know they are not "that kind of person."

Discussion of this issue can never be "educated" until both those who make the charge of racism and those who deny it recognize each other's definition of that term. The confusion begins with the failure to differentiate among three words: *prejudice, discrimination,* and *racism.* The dictionary definitions of these are:[2]

> *prejudice*—"an adverse judgment or opinion formed beforehand or without knowledge or examination of the facts," or "irrational suspicion or hatred of a particular group"
>
> *discrimination*—"an act based on prejudice"
>
> *racism*—"the notion that one's own ethnic stock is superior"

Thus, according to the dictionary, prejudice is a bias against a particular group. That bias may or may not arise out of a racist belief that one's own group is superior. Racism is a type of prejudice and, at least by definition, has no necessary relationship to any act of discrimination. Racism is (according to the dictionary) a belief and not an act.

The dictionary does not necessarily contain a correct or official definition of a word, however. It represents only what the editors view as a consensus definition. The usages of the terms *racism* and *racist* range widely and often differ markedly from the dictionary definition given above. Such usages are not necessarily wrong; they simply have not achieved consensus. Some people appear to equate the term *racism* with racial prejudice or bias and thus suggest that any prejudgment or bias against another ethnic group constitutes racism.[3] Others suggest that racism occurs only when the racial bias is accompanied by an act, and thus they appear to equate racism with racial discrimination.

Still others suggest that racism can occur without a conscious decision to discriminate against an ethnic group.[4] If the effect of a decision is that blacks are placed at a disadvantage, for example, then the decision may be racist regardless of the intent. If blacks are more likely to fail a literacy test given to high school students as a requirement for graduation, the use of the test may be viewed as racist, not because the intent was racist but because the effect was racist. This is an example of institutional racism, which suggests that procedures of institutions reflect racism if their effect is that blacks are overrepresented in negative outcomes.[5] It also appears that some even use the term *racism* to apply to decisions treating blacks *less* harshly than whites, since this leniency is viewed as being the result of paternalistic racism. (See the section in Chapter Four entitled "Is Leniency Discrimination?" for a discussion on this topic.)

One writer goes beyond the concept of institutional racism to suggest an even broader concept, "cultural racism."[6] Cultural racism involves the dominance of the white culture in the economic and social spheres, with the result that blacks must sacrifice elements of their own culture to be successful financially and socially. The dominance of the Protestant Ethic in American society represents cultural racism, since "black people in this country as a group show less preference for delayed reinforcement than do whites. This fact alone accounts for some portion of the disadvantage experienced by blacks in America."[7]

Thus definitions of racism range from a conscious attitude by an individual to an unconscious act by an institution or even to the domination of society by white culture. The usages vary so widely that it should be clear that no effective communication can take place between two persons or groups without specifying the definition of the term that each is using.

It appears at times that the term *racism* is used more as a political strategy than as a word intended to describe a state of mind of the "accused." Though it is incorrect to assert that the charge of racism is used only as a ploy to put someone on the defensive, this would often appear to be the case. The ABC television program "Nightline" conducted a debate in January 1984 over the wisdom of building more prisons. An advocate of community alternatives suggested that the backers of building prisons were motivated by "subtle racism." It is difficult to argue with anyone who accuses you of subtle (or unconscious) racism, since that term is never defined. And if one argues that there was no intent to place blacks at a disadvantage, the "accuser" might argue that the intent was unconscious or subtle.

Thus the term *racism* is sometimes used to accomplish some political goal (for example, defeat of a prison construction bill). The use of the term as a strategy is similar to the use of anger to place someone on the defensive and thus to gain compliance with one's wishes. In a recent book Tavris has argued that aggression is a strategy, not an instinct, and that people learn to use anger to control others.[8] This is not to say that everyone who lodges a charge of racism is simply using a ploy to gain a political advantage. But it is clear that this charge is sometimes used as a strategy. One test to determine the sincerity of such a charge is to ask the accuser to define the term *racist* and to explain how that term is applicable to the issue at hand. If the accuser will not or cannot define the term and refuses to explain its applicability to the issue, it is probably being used as a political ploy.

Since the term *racism* is generally introduced by those who claim that the system is racist (the "accusers"), that "side" has defined the term in a manner that best suits its position. The defining of terms by only one side in the debate has been unfortunate, because the more problematic aspects of the definition have not been addressed. Two questionable aspects of the term *racism* as it appears to be defined by accusers are its limitation to whites (the double standard) and its equating of racial effects with racism.

The Double Standard

The use of the term *racism* by accusers implicitly suggests that the term applies only to whites (that is, that blacks are not generally or cannot be racists). In short, there appears to be a double standard. Let us note some examples of this double standard of racism:

1. A killing by a white police officer of a black youth is often termed racist, whereas the killing of a white police officer by a black is rarely so designated. It is often pointed out that approximately 50 percent of the victims of police killings are black and that this fact alone presents a prima facie case of racism. But it is seldom pointed out that more than 50 percent of the police officers who are killed are victims of blacks.[9] Why does this fact not represent a prima facie case for black racism against police officers? Defenders (those who deny that the killings of police officers by blacks are racist) would argue that blacks may kill officers out of fear for their lives and not because of racism.[10] But the police would argue that they kill a disproportionate number of blacks out of fear for their lives, since blacks are more likely to threaten them. Why don't the police who shoot blacks receive the same benefit of the doubt as the blacks who shoot police officers?

Black police officers have been shown to use deadly force against other blacks more often than white officers do.[11] Does this finding prove that black officers are more biased against blacks than are white officers? The explanation, instead, lies in the tendency to assign black officers to "high-crime" (that is, black) areas, where they are more likely to encounter blacks who threaten them. But that explanation is similar to the one the police make in trying to defend the disproportionate shooting of black victims by white officers (that is, that blacks are more likely than whites to threaten white officers). There appears to be a double standard of racism in that whites are seen as guilty when blacks are disproportionately shot by officers, whereas blacks are not guilty (of racism) when officers are shot by blacks.

2. When police officers (mostly white) close ranks and refuse to "fink" on their fellows in cases of police misconduct, the closing of ranks is considered racist if the victim of the misconduct is black. If the black community closes ranks and refuses to fink on another black who has committed a crime against a white, however, that action is not considered to be racist. After the 1980 Miami riot mentioned in the previous chapter, an elderly black woman stepped forward to testify at two trials against several black youths who had beaten whites to death. As a result of her testimony she received threats on her life, was constantly accused by blacks of being a "traitor," and eventually had to move out of the community. To my knowledge no one has called the behavior of her black neighbors racist. But why not? Is this not a double standard? One might ask whether a white citizen would be harassed and threatened for testifying against a white mob that had victimized a black.

3. In my criminal justice class on the nature and causes of crime I show a film in which several sex offenders in a state program explain the reasons for their offenses. In the discussion that follows I always ask the students if they have seen any suggestion of racism in the film. Rarely does anyone suggest that the film is racist, because all of the approximately twenty sex offenders are white. I then ask the students what their answer would have been if all the sex offenders (or even the majority) had been black? Some students respond that they would have argued that the film was racist, since the suggestion would have been that sex offenders are largely black. But arrest figures in the FBI's *Uniform Crime Reports* of 1984 indicate that approximately 50 percent of those arrested for sex offenses are black. Is not the suggestion of a film that all or most sex offenders are white then incorrect and even racist, in that it presents a distortion of the character of sex offenders with respect to race? In this case it appears that white students, who make up approximately 80 percent of my classes, have been so socialized to see racism in terms of blacks as victims that they fail to see that whites can be viewed as victims of racist imagery as well.

In a similar vein, a study of the characteristics of criminals on television dramas found that blacks were underrepresented with respect to their numbers in the general population and among arrest figures.

Although blacks were found to have been written into television programs roughly in proportion to their distribution in the actual population (that is, 10 to 12 percent of all characters), they made up only 10 percent of the perpetrators of violent crime (though in "real life" blacks account for 46 percent of all arrests for such crimes) and only 3 percent of TV killers.[12] Does this "distorted" view of real black (and white) criminality represent racism, in that whites are unfairly represented as being more likely to kill than are blacks? And since such decisions may be conscious or unconscious and involve individuals (writers, producers) and institutions, perhaps such a distortion represents institutional racism against whites.

4. A recent book on rape-prevention strategies by Bart and O'Brien[13] utilizes a double standard of racism. The authors are apologetic in their presentation of black-on-black rape and remind the reader that many feminists believe it is racist to report black rapists to the racist police. They even had a black female psychiatrist review the section of their book dealing with black-on-black rape to see if their discussion of this topic was racist. And yet the authors completely ignore the problem of black-on-white rape. Though no direct figures are given, it appears that more than 50 percent of the white women were raped by blacks. The authors evidently do not consider this fact relevant to the issue of racism even though the pattern is interracial. One wonders how the authors would characterize rapes of black women if more than half were by white offenders. It would appear that simply *talking about* black criminality is, in their view, racist, whereas *actual offending* by blacks across racial lines is not racist. Surely this represents a double standard of racism.

5. The term *racist* is often used when discussing the manner in which the death penalty is imposed in the United States. The *Dallas Times Herald* conducted a study of the imposition of the death penalty from 1977 to 1984 in the United States, but especially in Dallas County and the state of Texas.[14] The reporters concluded that their data indicated the presence of a "subtle racism" in the use of the death penalty in Texas and most other states.

They noted racial disparities in probabilities of receiving the death penalty. The study found that 11.1 percent of the killers of whites in the country were sentenced to death, compared with 4.5 percent of the killers of blacks. The authors concluded that this pattern was racist in that it demonstrated that white life was viewed as more valuable than black life. They did not mention the fact (though the data are found in their tables) that white killers were actually more likely than black killers (11.1 percent to 7.3 percent) to receive the death penalty. Obviously, the racial disparity that favored black offenders was ignored, and the disparity that disfavored black victims was made the focus of the article.

Furthermore, the newspaper did not point out (though the data could have been obtained from its tables) that whites who had killed whites were more likely than blacks who had killed whites (11.5 percent to 10.4 percent) to be on death row. Their tables also indicate, though they fail to mention, that whites who killed blacks were more likely to reach death row than blacks who killed blacks. The double standard of racism is clear: disparity that disfavors blacks is indicative of racism, and disparity that disfavors whites is not.

6. Pekkanen chronicles the case of a white woman who reported having been raped by a black man in Washington, D. C.[15] The jury comprised ten blacks and two whites, and the defense attorney reminded the predominantly black jury of many incidents in the past involving the "railroading" of black men accused of having raped white women. After the jury had acquitted the defendant, one black juror told the prosecutor that pressure had been put on two black jurors who were holding out for a guilty verdict. Two other black jurors were said to have shouted "traitor" at these two, and eventually the holdouts switched to acquittal.

If the above case had involved a white defendant, a white jury, and a black victim, many would have accused the defense attorney of a "racist" appeal to the prejudices of the jury and would have characterized the verdict as racist. But I doubt if many would call the verdict in this case racist. Doesn't this failure constitute a double standard of racism? Wasn't this verdict based on race? Then why wasn't the verdict "racist"?

7. In December 1984 Bernhard Goetz shot four black youths on a New York City subway car and became known nationwide as the "subway vigilante." The defense attorneys for one of the wounded youths have suggested that Goetz was racist, in that he shot the four because they represented some type of "black peril" and perceived all black youths as menacing and threatening, even though these youths were only asking for money. This stereotype of young black males as likely robbers is said to have led to Goetz's belief that his life was in danger; thus his perceived need for self-defense was based on a racist stereotype. This may be true, but no one—including Goetz, since his stereotype may be unconscious—will ever know if race played a part in his actions.

It is interesting, however, that no one has asked similar questions about the reasons for the actions of the four youths. Why did they choose Goetz as their target for harassment and possible robbery? Out of the many people on that subway car they chose Goetz. Maybe this was because he was physically isolated from the rest of the passengers or because he looked like the kind of person (that is, a wimp—and his TV appearances do suggest this) who would submit to them. But it is also possible that they enjoyed harassing whites, since by ganging up on a white they could reverse the traditional dominant position of whites over blacks and make this particular white "squirm." In short, it may be that they enjoyed playing this "intimidation game" on whites. If this is the case, were their actions racist? (One should keep in mind that the four black youths chose Goetz, he did not choose them. He did react to them.) It would appear that many people are more interested in exploring the conscious and unconscious motivations of Goetz than those of the four youths who chose him. Does this represent a double standard of racism?

8. A recently published article indicates that in the violent crimes of assault, rape, and robbery black offenders in the United States select white rather than black victims more than 50 percent of the time.[16] By contrast, white offenders choose white rather than black victims in more than 96 percent of their criminal attacks. Before the publication of this research criminological texts had stated that violent crime was primarily intraracial. It appears that this is not the case from the perspective of choice of victim by black offenders. And yet it is doubtful that anyone will suggest that black offenders are racist in selecting white victims. But if the research had indicated the opposite (that is, if white offenders had been found to select black rather than white victims) there would have been a multitude of public statements suggesting that white criminals were racist. Why is such an outcry not heard now with respect to black offenders? The answer is that the public (both black and white) has been socialized to see racism as a one-way street (the double standard).

It is not surprising that black offenders choose white victims in robberies, since whites are more likely to have money. But it is difficult to understand why black offenders are more likely to choose white victims in assault and, especially, rape. The literature of rape suggests that rapists violate women sexually to humiliate and degrade them rather than for sex.[17] If this is true, the motivations of black rapists need to be reexamined since for some reason these men are more likely to humiliate and degrade white women than black women. Could this be because they are striking out at both women and white society when they choose white victims? And is there any doubt that white rapists would be termed racist if they were more likely to select black women as victims? Then why are not black rapists viewed as racists? The answer seems to be that in our society the term *racist* is reserved for white actors—thus the double standard.

The data showing black offenders to be more likely to choose white victims have been "hidden" for ten years by the format of tables in the reports from the National Crime Survey. If the data had indicated a tendency for whites to victimize blacks, is there any doubt that this fact would have been discovered and published ten years ago? I think not. I am not suggesting that the Department of Justice intentionally hid these data, but I am suggesting that the "mind set" with respect to interracial crime is limited to acts committed by whites against blacks.

9. Press coverage and academic studies of riots are often character-ized by a double standard of racism. In the 1980 Miami riot, eight whites were attacked by black mobs. The whites were beaten, muti-lated, burned, run over by cars, and killed.[18] Five blacks were killed by the police or private security guards in the same disorders, and three blacks were killed by white citizens firing from a pickup truck. The shootings by the whites have often been termed racist, since the occu-pants appear to have been driving around shooting into crowds of blacks. Likewise, it is not uncommon to hear the killings of the blacks by officers characterized as racist.

Seldom if ever, however, have I heard the attacks by the black mobs termed racist. And yet it would appear that these whites, innocently driving through a black area, were simply at the wrong place at the wrong time. They did nothing to provoke the mobs. They were killed because they were white and because blacks were attacking whites. How can such killings be termed anything but racist? And yet many would resist calling those killings racist because, we are told, the mob was simply reacting to racism (that is, an unjust verdict in the trial for the killing of a black by police officers). Surely the term *racism* is more appropriate to describe those killings of the whites than the killings of the blacks (by whites), but the term was more often heard to describe the killings by the whites in the pickup than those by the black mobs. This represents a double standard of racism.

Killings of whites by blacks in riots are probably not what the Cali-fornia legislature had in mind when it enacted a 1978 law creating a special category of murder for "racist" killings.[19] And yet since anyone who killed someone because of his or her race would be committing this new capital offense, the law would surely apply to interracial kill-ings during riots. The law was intended to cover Ku Klux Klan types who kill blacks out of racial hatred, but were not the riot deaths in Miami caused by black mobs just as reprehensible? The fact that the California legislators did not have such killings in mind is evidence of the extent to which the double standard of racism permeates our society.

A similar bill was introduced in the U.S. House of Representatives in 1985.[20] It would require the federal government to collect data on crimes of violence that were "committed to manifestly express racial, ethnic, or religious prejudice." The bill was written to deal with such crimes as church and synagogue desecrations and cross burnings. It does not seem to have occurred to the authors that "hate crimes" might include the considerable number of black-on-white crimes dis-cussed earlier.

10. In September 1983 a white woman was attacked by a crowd of black males after her car stalled in a black area of Miami. A white man

saw the attack and attempted to intervene. Although his jaw was broken, he succeeded in rescuing the woman. The rescuer was widely hailed as a hero for having braved the hostile crowd to save a stranger.

Two weeks later, however, a white Unitarian minister suggested in an article in the *Miami Herald* that the incident was racist, not because a black mob had attacked a white woman but because the rescuer had somehow been racist in trying to protect white womanhood. She also contended that the newspapers and television stations were racist in focusing on a black-on-white incident and that the president of the United States was racist in that he had telephoned congratulations to the white racist rescuer.[21] The author did not suggest that the black mob was racist for having attacked a white woman and her rescuer. One can only speculate whether the author would have suggested a racial motive if a black had been attacked by a mob of whites. In the view of the minister, racism is something whites do to blacks. Certainly this represents a double standard.

11. A final illustration of the double standard of racism involves the tendency of members of one group, whether ethnic, political, or religious, to assign deterministic causes to the failures of its own members ("us") and nondeterministic causes to the failures of groups and individuals who are viewed as adversaries ("them"). Patterson cautions against the suggestion that black problems such as crime are really a "white problem," in that white action and inaction are responsible.[22] Such deterministic explanations (that behavior is determined by others rather than chosen) may have immediate political gains but serve as a two-edged sword.

> If the high crime rate among Blacks and all the other problems of the group can be explained away in deterministic terms, then equally, the pronounced crimes of Whites against Blacks, both past and present, can and must be explained in deterministic terms. Sauce for the goose is sauce for the gander. . . . To excuse one's actions on deterministic grounds while condemning similar actions on the part of one's oppressor on morally autonomous grounds is both ethically unacceptable and, of itself, morally contemptible. It is unacceptable in the categorical sense that to accept a standard of judgment for oneself which is not applicable to others is morally irrational, since it is so patently unfair. . . .
>
> Determinism, then, leads its black supporters into a trap from which there is no escape. To be consistent one must accept the fact that Whites too are products of their environment and, as such, their exploitation of you and their racism can be explained away and excused in much the same way that black criminality and failure can be explained away and excused. In rejecting consistency and opting for the cheap righteousness of retributive condemnation, one accepts one's moral inferiority.[23]

The above illustration of a double standard in the assigning of causes for group and individual behavior serves as an introduction to a later section in this chapter, "A New Definition of Prejudice."

Equating Racism with Disparity in Outcome

As mentioned earlier, some people use the term *racism* to describe situations in which there is a disparity in outcome by race though there may be no evidence of an intent to produce that effect. This usage of the term is generally called institutional racism. When blacks fail a high school competency test in disproportionate numbers, for example, the result is often attributed to institutional racism. The term *institutional racism* is problematic for several reasons. First, use of the term involves a double standard. No one suggests that a disproportionate number of blacks on a high school basketball team would represent institutional racism against whites (though one Texas judge did mandate that whites be added to an all-black high school team at an integrated school).[24] Moreover, the majority of rapes in prison are black on white,[25] and yet no one has suggested that the prison system is guilty of institutional racism against whites in that they are disproportionately victimized by blacks. Why is it that the term *institutional racism* is applied only when the negative outcomes affect blacks? One answer to this question is that a charge of racism or discrimination is an "ethical judgment made about disproportionality: discrimination is disproportionality that is not considered justifiable."[26]

Racial effects can be produced by a multitude of causes. Granted, racial discrimination is one of those possible causes; but it is not the only one. Disproportionate representation of blacks on basketball teams and failure lists could also be due to differential ability, differential interest in the activity, differential experience, differential cultural attitudes toward the activity, and so on. To claim that black overrepresentation on failure lists rather than basketball teams is due to racial discrimination is to beg the question. The use of the term *institutional racism* assumes what one should be attempting to prove (that is, that racism has produced the racial disparity in outcome).

The use of the one term *racism* to apply to attitudes, actions, and results is confusing. It is like using the term *love* for friendly affection between friends, devotion to family, physical desire for the opposite sex, and devotion to God. Languages other than English have different words for each type of love. We should discontinue using the term *racism* for any attitude or action that might be viewed by anyone as being disadvantageous to blacks regardless of intent. What is needed is a new definition of prejudice that does not involve a double standard.

The term *institutional racism* has led to public policies that are problematic in that they are based on the assumption that racism created the problem and thus that government should intervene to protect the rights of minorities. Quotas and affirmative action goals in hiring and promotion became commonplace in the late 1960s[27] but are less common today. The shift away from quotas cannot be attributed just to the conservative trend in the political climate and to the policies of the administration of President Ronald Reagan. The shift has come in part because of the problematic nature of quotas. Quotas assume that disparity in outcome is the product of institutional racism and can thus be overcome only by government intervention. But quotas create a new kind of racial discrimination (that is, against white males), and it is difficult to determine when they are an appropriate remedy (that is, when institutional racism is so ingrained that no other remedy will work). Furthermore it is argued that most blacks do not support quotas[28] and that lower-class blacks may be more harmed than helped by them.[29]

The difficulty in knowing when to impose quotas to remedy institutional racism can be seen when they are applied to the criminal justice system. Many support the idea of quotas in the hiring (and perhaps even the promotion) of minorities to work in the justice system but would certainly balk at the idea of the imposition of racial quotas for the clients of the system. A black Yale sociologist has suggested that institutional racism (and sexism and ageism) is responsible for creating social conditions that produce different levels of criminality for blacks and whites, the two sexes, and different age groups and for the differential treatment of these groups by the criminal justice system.[30] Thus he proposes that "admission" quotas be established so that the prison population would reflect the same race, sex, and age distribution as the general population.

This proposal obviously begs the question, in that it assumes what should be proven (that institutional racism has produced the racial distribution of the prison population). But if one believes that the criminal justice system is characterized by institutional racism, surely one should advocate quotas to overcome that racism. And if the proposal of the Yale sociologist is too radical, why not establish quotas for prison on the basis of the percentage of blacks who are arrested? This proposal makes sense only if you believe that institutional racism is pervasive in the criminal justice system. It makes the error of all quota systems: it assumes that disparity in outcome is caused only by discrimination and ignores the causal importance of differential values, interests, abilities, cultural preferences, and other factors.

A New Definition of Prejudice

A more balanced view defines racial prejudice as the attribution of negative traits and motives to other ethnic or racial groups. Attribution theory is a branch of social psychology that studies the process by which people assign positive traits and motives to themselves and their groups (their family, ethnic group, sex, country, and so on) and negative traits and motives to "them" (the other sex, ethnic group, country).[31] People see their own (and their group's) *good* behavior as being the product of positive traits and motives but view their own (and their group's) *bad* behavior as being the product of external pressures or circumstances.

By contrast, when "they" (those we view negatively or are biased against) do something good, we are reluctant to attribute good traits to them. But when "they" do something bad, we attribute that act to a basic character flaw. Thus if we or our group does something bad, we tend to excuse that behavior as the product not of evil motives or traits but of pressures that made us act in an uncharacteristic fashion. On the other hand, if "they" do something bad, we attribute evil motives or traits to them, since we have prejudged their character as bad.

Let us take this view of prejudice in the context of attribution theory and apply it to the views of blacks and whites with respect to the alleged racist character of the criminal justice system. Blacks see killings of blacks by the (largely) white police force as being indicative of racism (an evil motive or trait attributed to the out-group). Though many reasons for the killing of a disproportionate number of blacks could be given (for example, blacks are more likely to attack the police; to be involved in violent confrontations with the police; or to provoke the police), the negative motive (racism) is chosen because it illustrates or confirms the negative view held of the out-group (the police are racist). Unfortunately, this reasoning is circular, since racism is inferred from the acts to be explained (why so many blacks are killed by the police).

On the other hand, the disproportionate killing of police officers by blacks is viewed as being the result not of a negative motive (racism or hatred of the police) but of a more positive one (blacks are simply reacting to provocation by the police or to pent-up hostility against the police generated by a racist society or police force). Why do we give the benefit of the doubt to "our group" and attribute evil to "them"? That is the nature of the human attribution process. We extend our projection of beneficent motives to "others like me" but project negative motives to "them." Thus a particular racial group is racially prejudiced to the extent to which other ethnic groups are viewed as "them." Because blacks have been discriminated against for hundreds of years, they have developed a strong view of other groups as "them," and thus the attribution process by blacks is characterized by attributing negative motives and traits to those in out-groups (for example, whites).

Another way of looking at the attribution of causes for the good and bad behavior of the in-group and the out-group is to compare two schools of criminological theory. The "Classical" school has traditionally argued that people *choose* to be criminals and that such choices are made by weighing the costs and benefits of crime against those of legitimate activities. The "Positive" school has argued that the behavior of criminals is "determined" by psychic or environmental factors and that freedom to choose is illusory. Thus in-groups take a Classical view of their own good behavior ("we" chose to be good and have the trait of "goodness") and of the bad behavior of the out-group ("they" chose to be bad and have the trait of "badness"). On the other hand, in-groups take a Positive view of their bad behavior ("we" did wrong only because of external pressures, and such behavior does not indicate bad traits) and of the good behavior of the out-group ("they" may do good, but such is not indicative of "goodness"). Racial prejudice is nothing more than the tendency of a racial group to take a Positive explanation for its bad behavior and a Classical explanation for the bad behavior of the opposite race.

In my view the tendency to see other ethnic groups as having negative motives and traits is more pronounced among blacks than whites, and thus blacks are more (racially) prejudiced against whites than whites are against blacks. Though research on the relative extent of racial prejudice among blacks and whites is rather limited, there is some evidence that blacks are more likely to assign negative traits to whites than whites are to blacks.[32] The black tendency to see racism as the motive for acts of whites is so pronounced that one author has characterized this bias as a type of social paranoia (they are out to discriminate against me) or "hypersensitivity."[33]

One of the best explanations for racial prejudice by blacks is by Porter and Dunn in their book on the 1980 Miami riot.[34] Though they do not term the black actions racist or prejudiced, their description below fits the definition of racial prejudice I have given with respect to one ethnic group looking on another as "them" and being anxious to believe the worst of that group.

> It is the willingness, even eagerness, with which blacks generally believe the worst of the police that provides the emotional thrust behind the violence. Deep down, the crowds do not react to what the police are doing in the current situation as much as they react to what the police have done in the past—to what they "always" do in a given set of circumstances. . . . It often matters little whether the police act responsibly in a particular situation or not; the crowd has already condemned them because of their actual or alleged misconduct that has occurred before. In this sense, riots are caused not so much by the precipitating events as they are by a general pattern of perceived oppression. The precipitating spark merely provides an occasion for blacks to try to "get even" [pp. 181-182].

Surely the prejudice described above is "racist" in that it is racial in origin. One might argue that the prejudice of blacks toward the police is actually "blue racism," in that the bias is more against the white officers because they are policemen than because they are white (black officers sometimes face this "blue racism" by other blacks). Furthermore, one might argue that the police also are biased against blacks and are anxious to believe the worst about them; that is, "blue racism" is two-sided. And yet the fact remains that the black community has a racial prejudice against the police. The tendency for blacks and whites to be anxious to believe the worst about the "other group" is what racial prejudice is all about.

Furthermore, it would appear that over time white prejudice has been declining,[35] whereas black prejudice has been on the increase. Several writers, in attempting to explain the riots in the cities in the 1960s and 1970s, have commented on the "generation gap" among blacks in general and among the black leadership.[36] Younger blacks, and especially better educated blacks, are simply less willing than their parents to accept manifestations of racial prejudice. There is a definite trend toward more antiwhite (that is, racially prejudiced) attitudes among young blacks.

At one time there were certain "bounds" that were not crossed, in that blacks might have antiwhite attitudes but not act on those attitudes. It has even been suggested that the killings of whites by blacks in the 1980 Miami riot was indicative of a "turning point in race relations in the United States,"[37] since once that "boundary" has been crossed, it is more likely to be crossed again. The abandonment of the historical social prohibition by the black community of attacks on whites is also indicated by the rise in recent years of black-on-white crime. Thus it would appear that black rage and prejudice against whites have intensified and "come out of the closet." Charles Silberman in his classic 1978 book, *Criminal Violence, Criminal Justice*,[38] called attention to the growing tendency for blacks to directly express rage against whites:

> After 350 years of fearing whites, black Americans have discovered that the fear runs the other way, that whites are intimidated by their very presence; it would be hard to overestimate what an extraordinarily liberating force this discovery is. The taboo against expression of anti-white anger is breaking down, and 350 years of festering hatred has come spilling out.
>
> The expression of anger is turning out to be cumulative rather than cathartic. Instead of being dissipated, the anger appears to be feeding on itself: the more anger is expressed, the more there is to be expressed [p. 153].

The view that the expression of anger is not "cathartic" but "cumulative" (that is, that the expression of anger does not reduce anger but simply makes a similar response more likely in the future) is the consensus view today.[39] Thus it would be difficult to find scientific support for the view that the expression of rage (as in a "race riot") somehow relieves the pressure and reduces the sense of rage. It appears to do just the opposite.

Critics of the view that blacks are more racially prejudiced (or "racist") than whites contend, however, that such research is misleading, for two reasons. First, blacks may have a negative view of whites, but such a view is based on a history of discrimination and thus is not paranoia. But isn't that position like that of the white bigot, who says his dislike of blacks is based on "facts" and thus is not prejudiced? It may be that many whites have a "good reason" to dislike blacks (perhaps a relative was murdered by a black), but we do not justify anti-black views on this basis. Second, it can be argued that blacks may have a negative view of whites but that they are not generally in a position of power to act on those prejudices. In short, blacks may be racially prejudiced but cannot be racist, since they are powerless to act on those prejudices.

But there are many situations in which blacks do have power over whites. In many prisons blacks are the majority and often select less powerful whites as victims of rape and assault. In fact, some authors suggest that black-on-white rape predominates in prison because blacks see sexual assault as a way to get back at white society in a situation where the power relationship between the races is reversed.[40] And perhaps the black offender in assault, rape, and robbery chooses white victims more often because he is the person with power and can now act out antiwhite views previously held in check.

Summary

The definitions of the term *racism* vary so widely that it should be abandoned in favor of the terms *prejudice* (the attitude or belief) and *discrimination* (the behavior). Furthermore, the terms *racism, prejudice,* and *discrimination* have generally been used only to refer to the attitudes and behavior of whites. Because this double standard of racism is so common, a new definition of prejudice is needed to eliminate it.

Racial prejudice is defined as the attribution of negative traits and motives to other ethnic or racial groups. Thus a particular racial group is racially prejudiced to the extent that other ethnic groups are viewed as "them" and assigned negative traits and motives and "we" are assigned positive traits and motives. By this definition blacks are more racially prejudiced than whites. In recent years the negative attribution process (prejudice) has decreased among whites but increased among blacks. Finally, the tendency for blacks to assign negative traits and motives to whites (but not to blacks) is largely responsible for the black perception of the criminal justice system as racist.

Notes

1. It is significant that Gordon Allport in his classic book *Prejudice* did not even mention the term *racism*. The confusion over the term is due to the refusal of some authors to distinguish it from the terms *prejudice* and *discrimination*. For example, Sedlacek and Brooks in *Racism in American Education* refuse to define the term, since their purpose "is to define a process operationally, without worrying much about the semantics of the terms. Understanding the process is more important than the particular label" (1976, p. 39).

2. *American Heritage Dictionary of the English Language*. Boston: Houghton Mifflin Co., 1970. Lewis Carroll in *Through the Looking Glass* eloquently expressed the "slippery" nature of definitions and how one might use a term such as *racism* to one's own advantage: " 'When I use a word,' Humpty Dumpty said in a rather scornful tone, 'it means just what I choose it to mean—neither more nor less.' 'The question is,' said Alice, 'whether you can make words mean many different things.' 'The question is,' said Humpty Dumpty, 'which is to be master—them or all.' "

3. Nettler (1984, pp. 269–270) argues that a stereotype of an ethnic group does not constitute racism, since it is impossible to think of persons and groups without categorizing. He also argues that stereotypes are not necessarily inaccurate, because they sometimes lead to more accurate information about others than does detailed information about each individual. On the accuracy of stereotypes see also Mackie, 1972/1973. Likewise, J. M. Jones (1972, pp. 60*ff*) argues that an opinion or stereotype about a group or person is not a prejudice unless it is held in disregard of the facts. For writers who seem to equate stereotypes and prejudice see Feldman, 1972; Guichard, 1977; Duncan, 1976; and Gaertner & McLaughlin, 1983.

4. The term *institutional racism* is most commonly used when accusers charge that racism can exist without conscious intent.

5. Jones (1972, p. 131) says that racism exists when "racist consequences accrue to institutional laws, customs, or practices, . . . whether or not the individuals maintaining those practices have racist intentions." Sedlacek and Brooks (1976, p. 44) argue that when they use the term *racism*, they are focusing on "results, not intentions. . . . Because racism continues to have adverse effects, we are not especially concerned about the reasons why."

   For a criticism of the use of the term *institutional racism* see Kleck, 1981, pp. 784–785. Kleck also gives six different definitions of racism that have been part of the "charge" against the sentencing process and points out the difficulties in attempting to validate them.

   A variation on "unconscious" racism is the term *subtle racism*, which suggests that the racist motive may be only partially recognized. See Henderson and Taylor, 1985, for the use of this term.

6. J. M. Jones, 1972, pp. 155–167.

7. J. M. Jones, 1972, p. 165.

8. Tavris, 1982, pp. 155, 191*ff*.

9. Matulia, 1982, pp. 42, 64.

10. Banks, 1975, p. 26.

11. Matulia, 1982, p. 59.

12. Lichter and Lichter, 1983, pp. 22–24.

13. Bart and O'Brien, 1985.

14. Henderson and Taylor, 1985.

15. Pekkanen, 1977, pp. 177, 197, 270.

16. Wilbanks, 1985a. One might argue that the fact that black offenders choose whites as victims more than 50 percent of the time is not surprising given that more than 80 percent of the potential victims in the United States are white. However, the same logic could not explain why only 14 percent of black victimizations are by whites (who constitute over 80 percent of potential offenders). Note that the most recent victimization report (Bureau of Justice Statistics, 1985) includes two tables on intraracial versus interracial violent crime. Table 44 presents the percentages from the perspective of the victim, and Table 45 from the perspective of the offender.

17. Brownmiller, 1971. She argues that rapists are not motivated by mental conflicts and illness but are part of the subculture of violence and are simply venting their aggression on women as sexual objects.

18. Wilbanks, 1984c. Information on the participants and circumstances involved in all of the 17 deaths that occurred during the riot are given in the appendix of this book. Descriptions of the killings can also be found in Porter and Dunn (1984, pp. 71-72). It is interesting to note that Porter and Dunn call the killings of whites "antiwhite" (pp. 173, 178) but do not term these killings "racist." But the term *racist* is used often to describe white-on-black events (that is, police brutality) preceding the riot.

19. *Newsweek*, Feb. 23, 1981, p. 80. (This is the story of a white who killed a black child and was charged with a racist murder.)

20. House Bill 1171, Feb. 20, 1985.

21. Wilbanks, 1983.

22. Patterson, 1973, pp. 53-54. For other examples of "reverse racism" in the impugning of motives for "them" versus "us" see the speeches of two black judges (Crockett, 1984, pp. 195-204, and Wright, 1984a, pp. 205-218) and Hines (1984).

23. Patterson, 1973, p. 54.

24. In a syndicated column by James J. Kilpatrick, *Miami Herald*, Jan. 6, 1981, p. 7A.

25. Carroll, 1977; Lockwood, 1980; Scacco, 1975; Davis, 1968; Duffy, 1985.

26. Zimmerman and Frederick, 1984, p. 316. On the difference between discrimination and disparity see Parisi, 1982.

27. For a history of the ideas that led from equality of opportunity to equality of results (that is, numerical quotas) see Eastland and Bennett, 1979; Glazer, 1983; and Sowell, 1984.

28. Glazer, 1983, p. 177.

29. Sowell, 1984; Sowell, 1978.

30. Bell, 1983.

31. For a description of attribution theory see E. E. Jones and Nisbett, 1971, and Lillyquist, 1980, pp. 48-67 (in a chapter entitled "Attribution of Responsibility for Crime"). On the role of in-group and out-group differences in the causal attribution of behavior see Stephan, 1977.

32. Research supporting the view that blacks are at least as racially prejudiced as whites includes Foley and Kranz, 1981; J. M. Jones, 1972, pp. 77-80; L. Wilson and Rogers, 1975; Stephan, 1977; Moe, Nacoste, and Insko, 1981; Carroll, 1982; Patchen, 1983; and Ugwuegbu, 1979.

33. Helmreich, 1982, p. 60. Many might argue that the belief that racism is pervasive is not paranoia but reality. One black actor said, "Any black man in America who is not paranoid must be sick" (Wright, 1984a, p. 206).

34. Porter and Dunn, 1984.

35. Condran, 1979; Banks, 1970.

36. Porter and Dunn, 1984, p. 191.
37. Porter and Dunn, 1984, p. xiv.
38. Silberman, 1978, p. 153.
39. Tavris, 1982.
40. Lockwood, 1980, p. 37. (He reviews several explanations for the predominance of black-on-white rape.)

3

Why Do Blacks
and Whites Disagree?

There is little doubt that the correlation between race and belief in the DT is strong. This is not to say that all blacks believe the criminal justice system to be racist or that all whites do not, but it is clear that most blacks assert that the system is racist and most whites deny it. Why this disagreement?

One might even argue that it is highly unlikely that so many blacks could be wrong about discrimination in criminal justice, so there must be a "kernel of truth" to the belief. The fact that many people believe in something, however, is certainly not evidence of the validity of that belief. Most Americans strongly believe in the deterrent effect of the death penalty and in the effectiveness of rehabilitation, though research has failed to confirm these "common-sense" views. In a similar vein most police officers and an even greater majority of psychiatric nurses believe that the full moon "brings out the weirdos" and that there are more acts of violence during the full moon than at any other time. But the best scientific evidence finds absolutely no validity in such beliefs.[1]

To understand the divergence of opinion between blacks and whites over whether the criminal justice system is racist we need to address four questions:

1. Why do blacks believe that the system is racist?
2. Why, according to blacks, do whites deny that the system is racist?
3. Why do whites deny the black charge that the system is racist?
4. Why, according to whites, do blacks charge racism?

Why Do Blacks Believe
that the System Is Racist?

First, blacks are aware of the discrimination and oppression to which they have been subjected for hundreds of years in this country. Though they believe that overt discrimination has decreased, they are also likely to believe that discrimination exists in all aspects of American society (including the criminal justice system), though perhaps in a more subtle way than in the past. Much of the literature by blacks on this issue focuses on what is seen as a shift from individual to institutional racism, which is "less overt and more subtle than individual racism."[2] Thus the long history of racial discrimination against blacks is not viewed as "history" but as "current events." In short, racial discrimination is often viewed as having changed only in form (from individual to institutional), not in intent or effect.

Second, in response to this history of discrimination blacks have developed a negative view of whites that attributes evil motives and traits to them. Black culture is characterized by an attribution process (see Chapter Two) that sees whites as an out-group intent on denying blacks equal rights and opportunities. This cultural bias has led to a tendency to look for "facts" to confirm this negative view of whites. When an incident occurs that is subject to several causal views (for example, a white police officer strikes a black suspect), the black is likely to choose the possible cause that confirms this negative view of whites (for example, all white officers are racist). Alternative explanations for the officer's having struck the black citizen (for example, the officer was attacked first or provoked) are rejected, since such explanations do not conform to the negative view of whites, especially white officers, that blacks generally have.

Third, the negative view of whites that blacks have developed over centuries of racial discrimination is supplemented by a liberal ideological bias, which sees human conduct as being more the result of external (social, economic, and political) forces than individual effort (or lack of effort). This liberal belief is in part an inevitable result of centuries of racial discrimination, since it has always been abundantly clear to blacks that just "trying harder" will not improve their economic or social position in society. Those who have historically been more successful (such as whites) tend to be more conservative, in that they generally impute their success to skill and effort rather than to luck or social, economic, and political advantage.[3]

The liberal ideological bias of black culture is also seen in explanations given for the disproportionate numbers of blacks in the criminal justice system. Whereas conservatives attribute criminality to individual moral failure, liberals see it in terms of social influence. Samuel Walker describes the liberal outlook this way: "People do wrong because of bad influences in the family, the peer group, or the neighborhood or because of broader social factors such as discrimination and the lack of economic opportunity."[4] Furthermore, liberal ideology tends to see the criminal justice system as being characterized by a "pattern of irrational decision making. The entire system treats the 'respectable' offender with kid gloves but reserves the harshest treatment for the poor, especially the young, black poor. . . . Class and race bias pervade the entire administration of justice."[5]

Fourth, the black leadership and black media are almost unanimous in asserting that the criminal justice system is racist, and blacks hear few voices of dissent to make them question the DT. Furthermore, blacks hear many (liberal) white leaders express a belief in the DT and thus are led to believe that "honest" white leaders see the obvious truth in the view that the system is racist. Since black leaders are generally liberal, it is rare to hear one express a view other than the DT. There was a time when white society would not let a black leader emerge who expressed liberal (or "radical," in the white view) opinions.[6] Today, however, the situation has been reversed, in that most black leaders attempt to stifle any dissenter to their liberal views.[7] A conservative black, Clarence Pendleton of the U.S. Civil Rights Commission, is denounced by the traditional black leadership as an "Uncle Tom" and is accused of selling out to the Reagan administration for personal advancement.[8] Conservative black writers such as Thomas Sowell, W. J. Wilson, and W. E. Williams are alternately ignored or denounced by black leaders. Thus black voices questioning the DT are seldom heard, and the black community is left with the impression that its leaders unanimously endorse the DT.

Some blacks who work in the criminal justice system reject the view that the system is racist. But these practitioners are reluctant to express views that are likely to lead to charges that they have been co-opted or are Uncle Toms. And even the expression of such dissenting views is not likely to have much impact on the black leadership or the black community, since these dissenters are viewed as being deluded by a desire to see their actions and those of the system in which they work in a positive light. In short, these dissenters are believed to have a vested interest in denying the racist nature of the system, since to admit it would mean that they worked for and were a part of such a system.

Fifth, many blacks see the criminal justice system as racist because of personal experience. Many blacks have been stopped by the police and "hassled" simply because (in their view) they were black.[9] One study reports that one in every four adult blacks in Detroit claimed to have been stopped and questioned by the police without good reason. One in five claimed to have been searched unnecessarily.[10] Such personal experiences tend to confirm what people commonly hear in the black community (for example, that the police are racists). Thus blacks often express the view that they do not need (statistical) "proof" of racial discrimination, since they have experienced it. Many blacks have been "radicalized" by personal encounters with the police. Before the negative encounter they might not have believed all they had heard about the police and might have been willing to give the police the benefit of the doubt. But a negative experience radicalized them.

Radicalization may occur when a family member encounters the system rather than through a direct experience. John Wideman in *Brothers and Keepers* tells of how his mother was radicalized after another son's arrest and incarceration for robbery and murder.

> In spite of all her temperamental and philosophic resistance to extremes, my mother would be radicalized. What the demonstrations, protest marches, and slogans of the sixties had not effected would be accomplished by Garth's death and my brother's troubles. She would become an aggressive, acid critic of the status quo in all its forms: from the President . . . on down to bank tellers. . . . A son she loved would be pursued, captured, tried, and imprisoned by the forces of law and order. Throughout the ordeal her love for him wouldn't change, couldn't change. His crime tested her love and also tested the nature, the intent of the forces arranged against her son. She had to make a choice. On one side were the stark facts of his crime: robbery, murder, flight; her son an outlaw, a fugitive; then a prisoner. On the other side the guardians of society, the laws, courts, police, judges, and keepers who were responsible for punishing her son's transgression.[11]

Sixth, blacks know that whites have racist stereotypes of blacks and thus assume that whites in the criminal justice system must act on those stereotypes in making discretionary decisions. It is assumed that if you don't like blacks, you are bound to discriminate against them. Though this might seem like a common-sense view, there is considerable evidence that prejudiced persons do not necessarily discriminate against the persons whom they view negatively. A conservative white male, for example, might admit that he has stereotypes of liberals, blacks, and women but maintain that he does not necessarily discriminate against them. He may consciously guard against the tendency to discriminate or may "lean over backward" and actually favor the stereotyped group. Blacks certainly have stereotypes of whites (and Hispanics, women, and others), but few would admit to acting on those stereotypes so as to discriminate. Furthermore, some research maintains that we do not even know when our judgments are prejudiced (that is, based on stereotypes),[12] and thus we would have to admit (if prejudice inevitably results in discrimination) that we often discriminate even when we are unaware of our prejudices.

Seventh, blacks overestimate the extent of overt racial prejudice in the white population and appear to assume that the Archie Bunker character is widespread among whites.[13] Thus the reasoning by many blacks seems to be that most whites are bigots, most of those who work in the criminal justice system are whites, most bigots discriminate in their actions, and thus the criminal justice system is racist.

Why, according to Blacks, Do Whites Deny Racism?

First, whites have always denied the existence of racism in this country. Though whites generally believe that racial prejudice and discrimination have been a part of our history, they are reluctant to admit that racism exists today. This reluctance is due, in the black view, to a refusal to face up to current discrimination, since to admit that it existed would require that an effort be made to eradicate it.[14] By denying discrimination whites can maintain a system that discriminates against blacks while protecting the vested interest of whites and yet not feel guilty for doing so. In short, the denial by whites of a racist criminal justice system is a defense mechanism to maintain a self-image of fairness while at the same time benefiting from the unjust system. The United States is an "unequal society that would like to think of itself as egalitarian."[15]

Second, since whites predominate among those who work in the criminal justice system and blacks predominate among defendants in that system, it is only natural (according to attribution theory) that whites are more likely to identify with the white practitioners than the black defendants. Blacks believe that the white citizenry identifies with whites who work in the system, since whites are prejudiced for whites and against blacks. Thus when asked to "choose sides," whites naturally choose the white view over the black view.

Whites are viewed by blacks as being reluctant to interpret negative behavior by whites toward blacks as reflecting racial prejudice. Whites are seen as tending to identify with those whites who work in the system and thus to attribute to them (as an in-group) motives other than racism. Thus in the situation of a white officer's striking a black citizen, whites are more likely to attribute some rational or positive reason for this behavior, since the officer is "one of them." In other words, whites are prone to explain away or excuse negative behavior (brutality, verbal abuse) against blacks because of white racial prejudice for whites and against blacks.

Why Do Whites Deny the Black Charge of Racism?

First, many whites see blacks as being prone to interpret all behavior by whites as the result of racism. A joke that is sure to receive nods of approval and boisterous laughter among many whites is the story of the black who is stopped by a white officer after an armed robbery and a 100-mile-per-hour chase in which several cars are damaged. On his way to jail the black protests to the officer that he is being arrested only because he is black. In short, many whites see blacks as attributing their ill fortune to racial discrimination instead of to their own behavior. Therefore whites see the claim of discrimination as an attempt by blacks to deny responsibility for their actions ("you are treating me this way because of who I am—a black—not because of what I did"). It is not an exaggeration to suggest that these whites view the black claim of racism as paranoia.

Second, many whites see the black claim of a racist system as a political ploy to place white society and the criminal justice system on the defensive and to divert attention from the behavior of the black defendant. Though it may be thought that many black defendants do sincerely believe the system to be racist and to be "stacked against them," it is also thought that many use that charge to win preferential treatment from those in the system who do not want to be seen as racist.

Third, whites generally identify with those whites who work in the criminal justice system, and since they believe themselves to be nondiscriminatory, they tend to project that egalitarian motive onto the whites who work in the system. The white citizen thus seems to reason that the practitioner is someone like himself who wants to be fair and attempts to be fair.

Fourth, whites perceive the level of criminality by blacks to be far higher than that for whites (as evidenced by the term *high-crime area* to refer to black areas) and thus believe that the accumulation of black defendants in the criminal justice system is simply the result of the greater tendency of blacks to commit serious crimes.

Fifth, though most whites have had no opportunity to directly observe the contact of blacks with white police officers and court personnel, they tend to form their view of the character of this contact from what they have observed of white/black contacts in other areas. Many whites have worked in settings where job discrimination has been claimed by blacks and are likely to believe that such claims are spurious. In fact, most whites see blacks as being discriminated *for* through affirmative action programs and quotas.[16] Thus, many whites carry over their perceptions from the workplace to the criminal justice system, where they have little opportunity for direct observation, and disbelieve the charge of racism there.

Why, according to Whites, Do Blacks Charge Racism?

First, whites are often heard to say that blacks are being misled by their leaders' constant focus on racial discrimination as being responsible for black ills. They argue that black authors and leaders have "brainwashed" the black citizenry with assertions that black lack of progress in housing, employment, education, and the criminal justice system is due to discrimination, not to any individual or cultural trait of blacks. This white view is even expressed by some black authors, such as Thomas Sowell.[17] Sowell suggests that black culture, which was created in response to past discrimination, has deficiencies that make it difficult for blacks to take advantage of opportunities. Other authors contend that deficiencies in educational skills are retarding black progress more than race.[18]

Whites suggest that blacks are living in the past because they are still responding as if racism permeated American society, when in actuality race has little significance today. But black leaders will not give up the focus on racial discrimination as the cause of black ills and thus (many whites believe) have convinced the black citizenry that things have not really changed (that is, discrimination is just as real and pervasive today but is more "subtle"). The push for quotas is seen by blacks as being necessary to redress subtle racism, but it is viewed by whites as being unnecessary, since what is needed (in the white view) is improvement in "qualifications" (better educational and job skills).

Second, many whites see the black claim of a racist criminal justice system as the product of reverse racism. They believe that blacks find discrimination in the actions of whites within the criminal justice system because that is what they are looking for. Thus they view blacks as being prone to attribute evil motives to white practitioners and good motives to black citizens who come into conflict with the system. This racial bias is seen as fed by black leaders who repeatedly suggest to blacks that such attributions of evil motives to whites represent reality.

Third, single cases involving obviously unjustified behavior by whites against blacks are viewed by black citizens as being typical, whereas whites view those cases as being atypical. For example, the 1980 riot in Miami was sparked by an acquittal verdict in the fatal beating of a black motorcyclist by white policemen. Blacks saw this case as being representative of the way white officers treat black citizens. Most whites viewed the case as not being representative of the way that officers routinely deal with blacks. Most police officers (and probably most white citizens) saw race as incidental rather than as *the* cause of the fatal beating. They traced the beating to the victim's defiance of authority (he fled and then allegedly resisted arrest by striking the arresting officers) and to "rotten-apple" policemen who were unrepresentative of the police. Though white officers and citizens might admit that race played a role, the racial factor is not viewed as being a primary cause of the police reaction. Thus blacks tend to see individual cases such as this fatal beating as typical of a racist system, and whites are likely to see it as an aberration or the result of a few bad (and unrepresentative) officers. Again, the perception on the part of both blacks and whites predetermines the view of "the facts."

Are Beliefs about a Racist System 'Ignorant'?

It is interesting that both blacks and whites see the view of the "other side" as being based on prejudice and a distortion of "the facts." But it would appear that neither blacks nor whites have based their views on "the facts." Both sides are quite ignorant of facts that would tend to confirm or deny their opposite views. The research on alleged discrimination is almost totally unknown to the average black or white person. Views formed in this "information vacuum" are thus "ignorant" (lacking in knowledge of the facts). It is unlikely that either side would suddenly change its view if presented with incontrovertible facts contradicting that view.

The purpose of this book is to present certain "facts" with regard to the presence or absence of racial discrimination in the criminal justice system. Specifically I will suggest that when one examines studies of decision making by the criminal justice system in the United States, it is difficult to argue that racial discrimination is pervasive. I will suggest that the facts that can be gleaned from research into this issue are inconsistent with the DT.

Summary

Discovering why blacks and whites disagree involves learning the reasons (1) why blacks believe that the system is racist; (2) why, according to blacks, whites deny that the system is racist; (3) why whites deny the black claim that the system is racist; and (4) why, according to whites, blacks believe that the system is racist. The literature addressing these four questions is almost nonexistent. It is clear, however, that both "sides" see the view of the other side as being based on prejudice and a distortion of the facts. It appears that neither blacks nor whites have based their views on "the facts," in that both are ignorant of the research evidence that does exist on this issue. Thus both black and white views are formed in an information vacuum and are based largely on personal and cultural ideology.

Notes

1. Rotton and Kelly, 1985.
2. Peirson, 1977, p. 107. Tunteng (1976) argues that the focus of American black

culture on individual and institutional racism is not found in all black cultures. He maintains that Africans focus on economic discrimination under colonialism.

3. Jencks, 1972, p. 227.
4. Walker, 1985, p. 10.
5. Walker, 1985, p. 13.
6. Akbar, 1984, pp. 16-20.
7. Loury, 1984, 1985.
8. "Official: Blacks," 1984.
9. See, for example, Watts, 1983. Also, since Alpert and Hicks (1977) found that prisoners' attitudes toward the legal system were markedly negative, the black community's view of the legal system may be affected by significant numbers of former inmates. However, Berman (1976) argues that though black parolees reported more negative views of the justice system than did white parolees, there was no racial difference when the black and white parolees were asked about their personal experiences with the system. He goes on to suggest that the more negative black view of the system may be due to "pluralistic ignorance," not personal experiences with the system.
10. Reiss, 1980, p. 278.
11. Wideman, 1984, pp. 70-71.
12. Hepburn and Locksley, 1983.
13. Brigham and Giesbrecht, 1976, p. 70. It is interesting to note that though blacks in rural areas are less likely to view the criminal justice system as racist, empirical evidence indicates that discrimination is more often found in rural and suburban areas than in urban areas. See Zimmerman and Frederick, 1984. On the other hand, blacks in urban areas are more likely to believe that the system is racist, though little evidence of this belief has been found in studies of urban systems. In short, there appears to be little correlation between strength of belief in racism in the system (between rural, suburban, and urban areas) and empirical evidence on actual discrimination by area of a state.
14. See, for example, Peirson, 1977, p. 107.
15. Gans, 1973, p. xi. See also Ryan, 1981, pp. 37-40. Ryan's description of the Marxist concept of "false consciousness" could easily be applied to the white belief about opportunities for blacks. False consciousness "is a belief system that reflects, not reality as it actually is, but the illusions that provide a justification for the interests of a particular class that has gained a dominant position in society. . . . The assumptions of such a belief system, it must be emphasized, are held at a very deep, almost unconscious level. If thought about at all, they are considered to be obvious realities rather than hypotheses or premises. Although usually unverifiable, if not demonstrably erroneous, they are not regarded as subject to verification or requiring proof" (pp. 38-39).
16. On whites' beliefs about blacks' opportunities and reverse discrimination see Kluegel and Smith, 1982, and Smith and Kluegel, 1984.
17. Sowell, 1981, 1984.
18. See W. J. Wilson, 1978, 1981; W. E. Williams, 1982; and Akbar, 1984.

4

Difficulties of
Proving Discrimination

The public may be surprised to learn that despite a considerable amount of research, no consensus has developed on whether discrimination has been "proven" to exist either at individual points in the criminal justice system or for the system as a whole. If so much research has been done, why hasn't the issue been resolved? Why can't we prove to fair-minded people of both races that discrimination either exists or does not exist? Several problems that partly explain the failure of past research to resolve this issue are discussed in this chapter. There are problems with (1) researcher bias, (2) the nature of direct proof, (3) determining whether leniency is discrimination, (4) spurious relationships that are often described as causes, (5) the interpretation of the black/white variation after controls, (6) reliance on statistical significance as a measure of importance, and (7) the canceling-out effect. The chapter closes with a summary of problems associated with direct proof and proposes that the DT be tested via indirect proof.

Problems Associated with Researcher Bias

The public biases with respect to the question of discrimination in the criminal justice system were described in Chapter 3. Researchers are not immune from bias either, and that bias may influence them in the choice of the topic for study, the methods used, and the interpretation of the results. Any suggestion that social science is value free and that its researchers are not influenced by ideology or emotion is as naive as the belief that Supreme Court judges simply interpret the law and are not influenced by political ideology.

Perhaps a couple of examples will help clarify this point. Sometimes the ideology and public stance of an organization may influence the type of research done and the interpretation of results. A literature survey of the police use of deadly force was recently completed for the International Association of Chiefs of Police (IACP).[1] Not surprisingly that study concluded that racial bias was not a significant factor in the police use of deadly force. On the other hand, the National Urban League also recently completed a survey of the same literature and concluded that racial discrimination was a major factor in the decision of the police to use deadly force.[2]

How can two studies that surveyed the same literature come up with such contradictory conclusions? Perhaps both were looking for evidence to confirm what the sponsors already "knew" to be the "truth." It is obvious that the ideologies and public stances of the IACP and the Urban League are contradictory. Either the two organizations chose researchers who shared their bias, or the researchers consciously or unconsciously interpreted the literature in a manner that was consistent with their funding agency's views. Would you expect the National Association for the Advancement of Colored People to publish research indicating that blacks were not discriminated against by the application of the death penalty? Would you expect the National Association of District Attorneys to publish results suggesting that there was racial discrimination in the prosecution of death penalty cases?

The problem of bias is not limited to those who fund or publish research. On the one hand, radical criminologists tend to study and write about "crime in the suites" (white collar crime) rather than "crime in the streets" (robbery, burglary, and so on) and are concerned with abuses of government power (such as police brutality). On the other hand, conservative criminologists are prone to focus on violent crime by the poor rather than on abuses of power by corporate or government officials. Radical criminologists are also critical of their colleagues who stress quantitative methods (the manipulation of numbers and statistics) at the expense of the qualitative methods (observations, examination of single cases in more depth) needed to delve into white collar and governmental crime.[3]

Researchers' interpretations are often biased by the thesis they are attempting to prove. Kleck[4] points out that though several comprehensive reviews[5] of the impact of race on sentencing have found *at best* a "modest" relationship between race of defendant and sentence when some controls are applied, the rather cursory reviews of this literature in textbooks often state the opposite—that racial disparity is great and widespread. He suggests that this erroneous conclusion is due to the "cumulative effects of a number of pernicious but common practices found in short summaries of research and evidence."[6] In his view those who are biased toward the discrimination thesis often engage in selective citations (that is, cite only studies that agree with their position); present figures indicating racial disparity with the suggestion that "the evidence speaks for itself" (that is, fail to suggest explanations other than discrimination for the disparity); and maintain a "magnanimous neutrality," writing that the literature is "ambiguous" or "inconclusive" when the weight of evidence is largely against the discrimination thesis.

It should be noted that both "sides" in this debate engage in these "pernicious and common practices." For example, some texts maintaining that discrimination is not pervasive tend to "overselect" and discuss studies that have found no discrimination and to slight those that have found evidence of discrimination.[7]

Problems Associated with Direct Proof

The research process whereby any issue in criminal justice is "proven" in a scientific sense is much more difficult than the public would imagine. The public is likely to think that we can simply research the issue and prove one side or the other. But many pitfalls are encountered in any attempt to prove whether discrimination exists at a particular point in the criminal justice system. Let us go through the process by which information on such a question is gathered and interpreted to see why so little "proof" seems to be obtainable.

If we decide to study a particular decision point such as sentencing, we must first decide what research methods to use. The layperson might suggest that researchers simply go into the courts, observe the sentencing process, and talk with judges, prosecutors, defense attorneys, and defendants. Unfortunately, observational research is highly prone to researcher bias, because the investigators tend to select "facts" that confirm their thesis. If one is convinced that racism is pervasive in sentencing, for example, one may fix upon participants' statements that affirm this thesis, as when the defendant or his attorney assures the researcher that racial prejudice was the basis of the sentence. Or the researchers may observe that a white judge refers to a 40-year-old black defendant as "boy" and then sentences him to ten years in prison. The observers, especially if they believe in the DT, may assume that the sentence was given *because* the defendant was black. It may be, however, that such a sentence either was less than one would expect for the crime or was "average" and that the comment was only incidental to the sentence. There is no way to determine by simple observation what the "going rate," or sentence, is for a given defendant type (exclusive of race) and crime or the "cause" for the sentence. In short, observation does not allow for the control of relevant variables in the decision process.

After reading a paper (the one included in the Appendix of this book) at an academic conference in 1985 I was told by a black criminologist who critiqued the paper that such quantitative research was invalid in that more qualitative research was needed to detect racial discrimination in the criminal justice system. The critic went on to explain that one had only to observe the sentencing process to find examples of racial discrimination. The example of a white judge giving a black defendant a long prison term after calling him "boy" was given as the type of proof one could glean from such qualitative or observational research. Since this criminologist was convinced that racism was pervasive in the system, would you consider valid the results of such observational research? I might add that neither would I credit the proof of no discrimination obtained by the observations of a white conservative judge with twenty years' experience on the bench. As discussed in Chapter Two, the attribution process is such that one "observes" what one is looking for.

In short, good social science does not attempt to prove the existence or nonexistence of racial discrimination in the criminal justice system by the "anecdotal" method, that is, by citing a case that "proves" the thesis. Social science approaches research into the DT by statistically analyzing large numbers of cases involving blacks and whites decided at a particular point in the criminal justice system.

Since I have studied the disposition of all murder cases in Dade County, Florida, for 1980,[8] let us take this study as an example and look at the problems involved in studying racial discrimination at the sentencing stage. To determine if judges discriminate on the basis of race in sentencing, we must first gather information on a large number of cases in which sentences have been handed down. There were 269 arrests made in the 569 homicides that occurred in Dade County in 1980. One hundred forty-nine people were convicted of murder or manslaughter, with 83 of this total being black and 66 being white (including Hispanics). But any attempt to determine if the resulting sentences were based on racial discrimination faces several problems. Those problems will be listed and discussed in turn.

Is Leniency Discrimination?

First, as I mentioned earlier in defining discrimination, lenient as well as harsh sentences may represent racial discrimination. If a judge considers murders of blacks to be less important than murders of whites, he or she may sentence the killers of blacks to lesser terms than the killers of whites. Since murders are predominantly intraracial (black on black and white on white) the more permissive attitude toward the killing of blacks would result in more lenient sentences for black killers. Thus it is not clear what would constitute racial discrimination, in that in some cases a lenient sentence might be based on racial discrimination. To make the matter more complex it is asserted by some that leniency for black-on-black crime may actually contribute to more black victimization, since the message from the judiciary would appear to be that one will not be punished as severely for killing other blacks as for killing whites. Blacks are encouraged by a lenient sentencing policy to take out their aggression on other blacks.[9]

Discrimination might also involve leniency if the killer (because of racial prejudice) is viewed as being less rational, more impulsive, and thus less "responsible."[10] Juveniles and women are often given lesser sentences when judges view them as being less able to control their impulses and emotions. Surely racial prejudice can result in more lenient sentences when judges through racial prejudice see black defendants as less rational and in control and thus less responsible.

One author critiques six different explanations for a pattern of lenient treatment that he found was given to black murder defendants in the United States.[11] These explanations included the devaluing of black murder victims by whites, so that the black offender is considered less of a threat to society; white paternalism (for example, the view that blacks are childlike and thus not as responsible); and white compensation for unconscious prejudice. Thus one might assert that evidence of discrimination has been found even when more lenient treatment is given to blacks. One study of racial discrimination at the point of arrest proceeded to "prove" this point by demonstrating that arrests of blacks were less likely to result in convictions (thus indicating that the black arrests were more likely to be based on flimsy evidence).[12] Thus leniency at one point in the system was proof to this researcher that discrimination had occurred at an earlier stage. Since both higher and lower conviction rates for blacks have been interpreted as evidence of racial discrimination, it is difficult to determine what type of evidence would refute the discrimination thesis.

Spurious Relationships

Second, difference in outcome is not equivalent to racial discrimination unless that difference cannot be accounted for by "legal" factors related to the offender or the offense. For example, suppose we found that the 83 blacks sentenced for 1980 Dade County homicides had received an average term two years longer than the 66 whites but that this difference could be accounted for by the greater prevalence among the black offenders of a prior record and by their greater involvement in robbery-related, as opposed to domestic, killings. In other words, when we controlled for prior record and type of homicide, the racial disparity in sentences would disappear and the original relationship between race and length of sentence would be found to be spurious.

In simpler words, although it might initially appear (before controls were introduced) that the two-year difference in average sentence between blacks and whites was caused by race, it would become obvious when controls were introduced that the difference in sentences was actually the result of prior record and type of homicide. That is, blacks were more likely than whites to have had a prior record and to have been involved in robbery-related killings and thus to have received a longer average sentence.

The process of controlling for other possible "causes" of longer sentences for blacks involves both identifying possible factors that may influence the sentence (that is, control factors) and using various statistical techniques to separate the effects of race from the effects of the numerous control factors. Several control factors that immediately come to mind are prior record, type of murder, type of attorney (whether public defender or private), relationship of victim to offender, race of offender and victim, socioeconomic status of offender, characteristics of judge (whether conservative or liberal, black or white, male or female), and characteristics of the jurisdiction (for example, urban or rural).

Perhaps a couple of examples will illustrate how an initial relationship between race of offender and disposition disappears when a control variable is introduced. A recent study in a Georgia city found that blacks who drove after drinking were more likely than white drunken drivers to be arrested in lightly patrolled areas.[13] What appeared to be racial bias disappeared, however, when the socioeconomic status of the drivers was considered. In other words, black drinking drivers who were blue collar workers were no more likely to be arrested than white drinking drivers of the same class. The real "cause" of higher arrest probabilities was socioeconomic status and not race. The fact that more blacks were blue collar workers (the status with the highest probability of arrest) made the "average" probability for blacks higher than that for whites, who were largely white collar workers.

Another study found that black police officers were more likely to shoot and kill citizens than were white police officers.[14] But when the researcher controlled for type of precinct patrolled (high-crime or low-crime) and for whether killings were off duty or on duty, there was no indication that black officers were more likely to kill.

It should be noted that the addition of control variables does not always reduce the initial race effect. It is quite possible that the introduction of controls can increase the race effect. For example, one study of the decision to prosecute found no race effect until strength of evidence was introduced as a control variable.[15] Once strength of evidence was constant, there was a statistically significant race effect, in that race of the victim, but not the defendant, had an impact on whether prosecution was pursued. In other words, if the evidence was equal, cases with white victims were more likely to be prosecuted. Thus strength of evidence suppressed the race effect.

Another methodological difficulty arises when one argues that the original race effect disappears after controlling for other variables. Several researchers have argued that in a real sense one cannot separate

the race effect from control variables.[16] Some studies find a race effect
on outcome, for example, but then find that when one controls for
demeanor and type of attorney, the relationship disappears. But since
one's demeanor is partly a function of race and since blacks are less able
to afford a private attorney, is it fair to suggest that one can separate
race from these variables? One might argue that to be black in the
United States is to be poor and angry and thus that it is rather silly to
suggest that one can (statistically) separate race from these variables.
Thus it is argued that race affects outcome *indirectly* through demeanor
and type of attorney but that this still represents a race effect. One
scholar demonstrated the indirect effect of race on sentence through
type of attorney and failure to make bail.[17]

Interpreting the Black/White Variation after Controls

Third, one of the most common errors made by researchers who examine racial disparities in outcome involves the interpretation made
after the introduction of control factors. Let us go back to the 1980
Dade County homicide cases and the longer sentences handed down to
blacks. Suppose that one controlled only for type of murder and found
that the average sentence difference between blacks and whites was
reduced from two years to eighteen months. The eighteen months
would represent the difference in sentences for blacks versus whites
that was unaccounted for by type of homicide. But one could not
assume that the eighteen-month difference was due to race, since several other control factors could be introduced that might account
for all or part of the remaining variation in outcome. Thus this remaining difference is *unexplained* variation or variation yet to be accounted
for. It may be due to race, or it may be due to other factors not controlled for.

The error of attributing the remaining variation after controls to a
race effect is quite common in the literature. One study of 600 indictments in twenty Florida counties in 1976–1977 found that when one
controlled for type of homicide ("primary," or domestic, versus "nonprimary," or those involving strangers) there was a tendency for the
killers of whites to receive more severe sentences than the killers of
blacks.[18] The author concludes that the racial differences (the unexplained variance) in the processing of those indicted for homicides
indicates that the system "appears to place a lower value on the lives of
blacks than on the lives of whites."[19] In short, the unexplained variance
is attributed to race, though the racial differences might have been
further reduced with additional controls. Numerous examples of this
error of interpretation can be found in the literature.[20]

Unfortunately, the nature of the research process is such that we cannot attribute the remaining unexplained variation to race unless all the

most important potential control variables have been introduced. There is always the possibility that the introduction of one or more additional (and theoretically important) controls might have reduced the remaining variation to zero. And often the most appropriate controls cannot be utilized since data is not available. For example, few studies of sentencing control for prior record,[21] though this is the most obvious factor one would want to control for in studies of sentencing.

One way to illustrate the dangers of interpreting unexplained variation, after a limited number of controls, as a race effect is to look at a hypothetical study of grades in a college classroom. Suppose that black students made significantly lower grades than white students even after one controlled for the overall grade point average of students in the class. The classroom teacher would certainly not agree that this remaining variation in performance by black and white students was due to a race effect (that is, racial discrimination by the instructor). He or she would maintain that there might be many other variables explaining the gap in grades. The instructor would suggest that such variables as class attendance, type of notes taken, attentiveness, motivation and interest, and writing skills should be controlled before one concluded that there was racial discrimination in the classroom. Those academics who are quick to interpret unexplained variation as a race effect would probably not be as quick to make such an interpretation if their own decisions were the subject of the study. In fact, many academics might suggest that statistical analysis is invalid since it does not accurately model their decision-making process (see the section "Model No. 7: Rejecting Variable Analysis," in Chapter Seven).

Reliance on Statistical Significance

Fourth, many studies of possible discrimination focus on the extent to which the results are statistically significant. However, statistical significance may be confused in the minds of the public (or the researchers) with practical significance. Statistical significance tells us only whether the results found in the sample are likely to have occurred by chance if the relationship in the "population" (from which the sample was drawn) was zero. Statistical significance is a function of two factors, the strength of the relationship and the sample size. If the sample size is great enough, even a very small relationship is statistically significant. Let us look at some examples of the misinterpretation or misuse of statistical significance as a measure of the "causal" importance of an independent variable with a dependent variable.

One often cited book, *The Lunar Effect*,[22] reported a statistically significant relationship between the phases of the moon and the murder rate in two metropolitan areas. And yet only 2 percent of the variation in murder rates could be explained by the phases of the moon (and this was without any controls for differences in visibility, beliefs of the offender about self-control during the full moon, and so on). Thus though the results were statistically significant, the practical results were not significant, in that little aid in predicting homicides could be gained by knowing the phase of the moon. And yet this study is widely reported as having "proven" that the moon affects homicide. One scholar who reviewed the literature purporting to show a relationship between "lunacy" and violence found that advocates of the thesis focused on the reporting of statistical significance while ignoring the fact that less than 1 percent of the variance could be accounted for by the phases of the moon.[23] Numerous studies of race and disposition rely on tests of statistical significance to "prove" a race effect while failing to report any measure of association that would indicate the predictive power of race for disposition.[24]

The Appendix illustrates how the reporting of *both* the test of significance and a measure of association can demonstrate the inadequacy of a reliance only on tests of significance to draw inferences about the importance of race as a predictor of disposition. Table 10 of that study indicates that though race of defendant was statistically significant (at the .0000 level) at five decision points of the California criminal justice system, it did not account for even 1 percent of the variance at any of these decision points (and this was before the introduction of controls). In a similar vein race was statistically significant (at the .0000 level) at seven decision points of the Pennsylvania criminal justice system (Table 11) but accounted for less than 1 percent of the variance at four of those seven points (it did account for 11 percent of the variance in whether the defendent received five or more years in prison). And again the unexplained variance was before the introduction of controls.

The seemingly contradictory measures (statistical significance and measure of association) in the studies of California and Pennsylvania resulted from the large "sample"[25] sizes utilized—over 180,000 cases in California and almost 60,000 in Pennsylvania. Any difference between blacks and whites will be statistically significant in a large sample. For the 100,000 felons convicted in California, for example, there was only a four-percentage-point difference in conviction probabilities between whites (76 percent) and blacks (72 percent), and yet this difference was statistically significant at the .0000 level. At the same time race of defendant accounted for less than 1 percent of the variation in whether defendants were convicted. It would obviously be misleading to report the significance level as a measure of the importance of race in determining conviction probability.

Many studies of discrimination focus on the existence or nonexistence of a statistically significant relationship between race and disposition but do not report on the strength of the relationship. But since large sample sizes produce statistically significant results even when the strength of relationship (the proportion of variance explained) is minimal, the practical significance of the racial difference in outcome is best indicated by the strength of the relationship (that is, a measure of association).

Aside from measure of strength of relationship, another useful measure of "importance" was used by a sentencing study that statistically estimated the length of sentences imposed on black and white defendants after various control variables had been introduced.[26] Thus the authors were able to estimate the practical difference in months that the race of the defendant made once various control variables were made constant.

The Canceling-Out Effect

Fifth, the search for possible discrimination is confounded by the possibility that racial discrimination may be masked by the "canceling-out effect." Most studies examine the decisions of numerous police officers and judges collectively rather than individually. But it may be that some judges are lenient toward poor and black defendants and that other judges discriminate against them on the basis of race. Thus it is possible that the combined effect of the decisions of all judges as a whole would indicate no racial difference in outcome (that is, the average sentence might be identical for black and white defendants). In fact it would be incorrect to assume that no discriminatory decisions had been made by any of the judges in a jurisdiction where no overall difference in sentence length was found for black and white defendants. It may be that some judges were more lenient toward whites, that others were more lenient toward blacks, and that some treated the two races equally. Thus the overall pattern of no discrimination masks considerable variation among individual judges.

The failure to consider variation among judges or police officers may provide a hint as to why large overall racial differences are seldom found, and yet many continue to believe that discrimination (either for or against black defendants) is widespread. It may be that discrimination against or for black defendants is widespread among individual judges but that the different tendencies of judges cancel one another out. Thus even when a study finds no overall difference in outcome by race, one cannot assume that no decisions by individuals were based on racial bias. A study that finds no overall racial difference does not exclude the possibility that some judges discriminated against black defendants. On the other hand, it also does not exclude the possibility that some judges were more lenient toward black defendants.

It is interesting to note that studies of individual decision makers are rare. Four such studies, however, have demonstrated the importance of considering possible variation among decision makers at a particular point. Gibson examined 1,219 felony sentences handed down from 1968 to 1970 by eleven judges in Fulton County (Atlanta), Georgia.[27] Though he found no evidence of racial discrimination by "the court" (with all eleven judges considered as a whole), he did find considerable variation in sentences for blacks and whites among the different judges. For example, the percentages of blacks receiving severe sentences ranged from 11 percent to 56 percent among the judges. He also calculated a "discrimination index" consisting of the difference in percentages of blacks and whites receiving severe sentences. This index ranged from +55.6 for one judge (who gave 66.7 percent of whites a severe sentence but only 11.1 percent of blacks) to -32.1 for another judge (who gave 56.1 percent of blacks a severe sentence but only 24 percent of whites). It would appear that the first judge discriminated against whites and that the second discriminated against blacks. And yet the overall result was that "the court" did not discriminate. But many individuals (both black and white) appear to have suffered from the biases and discrimination of individual judges.

Thus Gibson found that blacks were the "victims of discrimination by some judges but the beneficiaries of discrimination by others."[28] He concludes that "anti-black judges are balanced by pro-black judges,"[29] illustrating the canceling-out effect. It is also important to note that his study illustrates the importance of choice of research methods in determining results. He says:

> The findings also suggest that methodological issues must be a central concern for judicial researchers. Without proper controls we would have concluded that discrimination exists; with controls we would have reached the opposite conclusion had the analysis remained at the aggregate level. The latter conclusion would have been incorrect, and the former correct but for the wrong reasons.[30]

A researcher can often find average differences in outcome for black and white defendants at a particular point in the criminal justice system. When controls are introduced, however, the black/white differences are usually diminished or disappear altogether. And yet if one looks at individual decision makers, one is almost certain to find considerable variation between black and white dispositions. The difficulty in Gibson's method would come in deciding how to interpret the variation that would inevitably be found among individual judges but that did not reach the magnitude he found.

In a second study of individual decision makers, Uhlman focused on the race of judges.[31] (Gibson did not identify the race of his eleven judges.) Uhlman found considerable variation across ninety-one judges, but the "cause" of the variation in sentencing was not race of judge, because sentences by black judges differed little from those of white judges. Eleven of the sixteen black judges convicted black defendants more frequently than white defendants,[32] and all sixteen handed down harsher sentences to blacks than whites.[33] Thus in this study the canceling-out effect was less pronounced, since both black and white judges tended to treat blacks more harshly. Uhlman found this harsher treatment to be largely a function of two factors, a greater likelihood of a prior record by blacks and their socioeconomic status, which precluded private counsel and resulted more often in pretrial detention.[34]

A third study actually looked at decisions of individual judges in cooperation with their "workgroup" (prosecutor, defense attorney, and probation officer). Eisenstein and Jacob examined the bail, conviction, and sentencing decisions of individual court workgroups in Baltimore, Chicago, and Detroit for 1972.[35] They found that the variable *identity of courtroom* (that is, of the workgroup including judge) accounted for 29.8 percent of the variance in prison/probation decisions in Baltimore, 27.4 percent in Chicago, and 21.1 percent in Detroit. Likewise, identity of courtroom accounted for 26.8 percent of the variance in the length of prison term imposed in Baltimore, 13.6 percent in Chicago, and 12.7 percent in Detroit. Eisenstein and Jacob found that race had little effect in all three cities. Unfortunately, they do not indicate the extent to which this overall negative race effect masked considerable positive and negative race effects for individual judicial workgroups.

In a fourth and final study of individual decision making, Zalman and his colleagues examined sentences in Michigan to create a set of sentencing guidelines for that state.[36] Their report indicates that the substantial amount of unexplained variance in sentences at the aggregate level was not the result of an "aggregation bias." Unfortunately, they provide no data on the pattern of sentencing of blacks and whites by individual judges.

Studies of other individual decision makers (the police, prosecutors, probation officers) are almost nonexistent, and thus it is difficult to determine the extent to which "collective" decisions by groups of decision makers mask discrimination by the canceling-out effect. Certainly future research should utilize the methods pioneered by Gibson and Uhlman. It may be that those who maintain that there is no "systematic" discrimination (in the sense that in general blacks are not treated worse than whites "other things being equal") are correct; but it may also be that those who maintain that discrimination often occurs in individual cases are correct, since these cases of discrimination are canceled out by cases where blacks receive more-favorable treatment. Thus those who contend that racial discrimination *against* blacks often occurs but doubt that racial discrimination *for* blacks occurs as frequently will have to explain where the cases come from that cancel out the cases of discrimination against blacks.

The canceling-out effect may also occur when studies include data from several jurisdictions. The studies of felony processing in California and Pennsylvania that are reported in the Appendix, for example, found little variation in the processing of blacks and whites. It may be, however, that racial discrimination is masked by the grouping together of all black defendants from across the state. Harsher treatment of blacks by rural and suburban police and courts may be canceled out in statewide figures by relatively lenient treatment of blacks (and whites) by urban police and courts. Thus state averages may mask racial discrimination from rural and suburban areas. One study, of New York sentences, did not find an overall race effect but did find a race effect for rural and suburban areas that was masked by considering all areas of the state as a whole.[37]

The canceling-out effect may also result when several offenses are examined in the aggregate. Some studies have found a race effect disfavoring blacks for some offenses and favoring blacks for other offenses, with no overall race effect.[38]

Another example of the canceling-out effect involves the time periods studied. It may be that a race effect occurs during some periods but not at others. Thus an overall finding of no race effect may mask one period showing discrimination against a particular group and another period showing discrimination for the same group. One sentencing study found that race had an effect on sentences in Milwaukee in 1967-1968 but not in 1971-1972 or 1976-1977.[39] If the researcher had combined all three periods, he might have found no overall race effect for 1967-1977.

A more complicated example of the canceling-out effect involves studies in which there is considerable interaction among variables, so that race and other variables do not have a consistent impact on decisions. One study, for example, found that race had a different effect on sentences for different types of crimes, so that for some types black defendants received longer sentences and for others they received shorter ones.[40] Studies using methods that do not detect interaction effects may overlook a race effect because of the inconsistent way in which race can influence cases.

Summary of Difficulties of Direct Proof

Given the five difficulties in obtaining direct proof of racial discrimination that are cited above, it should not be surprising to learn that:

1. Social scientists studying aggregate decision making who find a substantial difference in outcome between blacks and whites should not interpret that difference as the race effect, since controls might eliminate the difference.

2. Even if a study of aggregate decision making finds a racial difference in outcome after one or more control variables are introduced, it

is not appropriate to label this remaining variation as the race effect, since other (and more important) variables might reduce this difference to near zero. Thus one can never prove racial discrimination unless one can be reasonably certain that the most important control variables have been isolated, measured, and controlled by a suitable statistical technique.

3. And even if an aggregate study finds no racial discrimination in average outcomes for blacks and whites, it may be that cases of discrimination and reverse discrimination have canceled each other out.

Thus when racial disparity occurs we cannot safely say (even if controls are introduced) that the disparity is due to race, and when there is no disparity we cannot safely say that the result indicates that no discrimination exists (since the absence of disparity in aggregate outcomes may mask disparity in individual cases). It is accurate to say that we cannot "prove" either discrimination or nondiscrimination given the methods used to date. The greatest hope for a more definitive answer would seem to lie in the type of study (like those of Gibson and Uhlman) that examines decision making among individuals. If a substantial disparity in outcomes for blacks and whites occurs across individuals, there is certainly discrimination in decisions regardless of the equality of outcome that may result when aggregate outcomes are examined.

Indirect Proof

Beyond the direct means of looking for differential outcome by race at various decision points, there are other ways to determine if racial discrimination is pervasive in the criminal justice system. If discrimination were widespread, one would expect several patterns to emerge as a result of the correlation between racial prejudice and discrimination and dispositions of blacks. The following list of patterns would be expected if racial discrimination were pervasive in the system and if that discrimination were a direct result of racial prejudice:

1. In studies of the decisions of individuals we would expect to find that those who were the most prejudiced (as determined by objective measures) should be the most likely to treat blacks harshly.

2. In studies of the decisions of individuals we would expect black decision makers to be less harsh toward black offenders and white decision makers to be less harsh toward white offenders, since it would be assumed that each race is less prejudiced toward "its own."

3. If we agree that racial prejudice has declined over time, we would expect the greatest disparity in outcomes to have existed in periods when prejudice was greater.

4. In studies across jurisdictions we would expect greater gaps in outcome probabilities between blacks and whites in those jurisdictions that were presumed to be more prejudiced. For example,
racial disparities should be greater in southern states than in other
states.

5. Racial disparities in outcome at various stages of the criminal justice system should be greatest in jurisdictions (and at the decision
points of a particular jurisdiction) where there is the greatest disparity between the racial makeup of the decision makers and that
of the "clients" of the system. Those cities with a largely white
police force but a largely black offender population, for example,
should have greater racial disparity in outcomes than those cities
with a more racially balanced police force and offender population.

6. Since it is assumed that racial discrimination is pervasive and
cumulative across the decision points of the system, the black/
white disparity in outcome should increase from arrest to sentence
and time served.

All of the above represent hypotheses that would appear to grow
directly out of the DT. If the thesis of pervasive racial discrimination in
criminal justice is true, one would expect the "facts" to be consistent
with these hypotheses. As will be noted in the final chapter, however,
the facts appear to be largely inconsistent with the above hypotheses.

Summary

Several difficulties are encountered in studies that have attempted to
"prove" the existence or nonexistence of racial discrimination at a
particular decision point of the criminal justice system. These difficulties include the failure to control for legal variables that might indicate
a spurious relationship between race and outcome, different interpretations of the black/white variation after controls, the reliance on tests
of statistical significance rather than measures of association, and the
canceling-out effect.

Because of the inadequate methods used, we cannot conclude that
the racial differences found in outcomes stem from racial discrimination or that the failure to find differences indicates an absence of discrimination. In short, the literature available on this issue does not
allow us to draw any firm conclusion. In the absence of direct proof it
is suggested that six factual patterns, if they exist, should provide indirect proof of the DT, since such patterns should be present if racial
discrimination is pervasive in the system.

Notes

1. Matulia, 1982.
2. National Urban League, *Police Use of Deadly Force: A Minority Perspective,* 1983 (draft version).
3. See Swartz, 1975, and Del Olmo, 1975.
4. Kleck, 1985.
5. He cites his own review (Kleck, 1981) and that of Hagan (1974).
6. Kleck, 1985, p. 272.
7. See, for example, the reviews found in Nettler, 1984, pp. 43–47, and Akers, 1985, pp. 17–18. Both authors overselect studies that find no evidence of discrimination in their discussion of the impact of race on dispositions.
8. Wilbanks, 1984c.
9. For example, see "Black on Black Crime," 1979, for a lengthy discussion on the impact of leniency on black-on-black crime for the black community.
10. Swigert and Farrell (1976) argue that blacks are viewed as "normal primitives" and that this stereotype involves a less rational and more impulsive actor. They also argue, however, that this stereotype results in more severe sentences. There is considerable research indicating that juveniles and women are considered less "in control" and thus less responsible for their acts. For a review of the literature on reasons for leniency toward female defendants see Parisi, 1982, pp. 207–208.
11. Kleck, 1981, p. 800.
12. Hepburn, 1978.
13. Hollinger, 1984.
14. Fyfe, 1981.
15. Myers and Hagan, 1979, p. 447.
16. See Austin, 1984, pp. 182–183; Pepinsky and Jesilow, 1984, p. 86; and Reiman, 1984, p. 79.
17. Lizotte, 1978.
18. Radelet, 1981.
19. Radelet, 1981, p. 926.
20. See, for example, Petersilia, 1983, pp. 240–241; Chiricos, Jackson, and Waldo, 1972, p. 557; Bullock, 1961, p. 415; and Rhodes, 1977, p. 350.
21. Kleck (1981) and Hagan (1974) list the various controls used for each of the studies they review. Kleck lists fifty-seven studies and includes studies completed after Hagan's review. For a discussion of the importance of controls for prior record and strength of evidence before equating the remaining variation with a race effect, see Hardy, 1983, p. 193.
22. Lieber, 1978.
23. Rotton and Kelly, 1985.
24. Hagan (1974) lists several studies that fail to report a measure of association and report only a test of significance. Uhlman (1978, p. 888) differentiates between "substantive" and statistical significance and urges the use of measures of association rather than tests of statistical significance.
25. One might even argue that the Offender Based Transaction System data from California and Pennsylvania are populations rather than samples and thus that a test of significance is inappropriate.
26. Tiffany, Avichai, and Peters, 1975.
27. Gibson, 1978.
28. Gibson, 1978, p. 470.
29. Gibson, 1978, p. 475. J. Q. Wilson, in *Thinking About Crime* (1985, p. 168), suggests that the canceling-out effect may occur in studies of the effectiveness

of rehabilitation. Thus some clients may be rehabilitated and some may actually get worse, with the net result being no overall effect.

30. Gibson, 1978, p. 475.
31. Uhlman, 1978, 1979a.
32. Uhlman, 1979a, p. 69.
33. Uhlman, 1979a, pp. 94–95.
34. Uhlman, 1979a, pp. 94–95.
35. Eisenstein and Jacob, 1977, p. 278.
36. Zalman, Ostrom, Guilliams, and Peaslee, 1979, pp. 276, 282–283.
37. Zimmerman and Frederick, 1984. For a discussion of several types of canceling-out effects see Hardy, 1983, p. 195.
38. Blumstein, Cohen, Martin, and Tonry, 1983, p. 92; Zalman et al., 1979, pp. 230–269. Miethe and Moore (1984) suggest that the canceling-out effect with respect to types of offender and offense may be responsible for the frequent finding of no race effect. They maintain that their data show no overall race effect but that various subgroups of offenders (for example, high-risk black offenders) were treated more severely at several points and that other subgroups (for example, low-risk black offenders) were treated more leniently. They suggest that "interactive" models be utilized rather than "additive" models, so that interaction effects can be discovered. They further suggest that both models be used in the same data set, so that the impact on conclusions about an alleged race effect can be examined under different models of analysis. They write that conclusions about the "declining significance of race" are premature. "While it may be true that race no longer operates in a fashion similar to 'caste-like' distinctions (a fundamental statistical and theoretical assumption underlying the additive model), its impact on criminal justice decision-making in this study appears far from being eradicated" (p. 20).
    Several researchers (Zatz, 1984; Farnworth and Horan, 1980; Miethe and Moore, 1984) examined the impact on outcome of different types of offenders. In addition, log-linear analysis is able to detect interactions between race and other variables (see Miethe and Moore, 1984, p. 5).
39. Pruitt and Wilson, 1983.
40. Tiffany et al., 1975.

5

The Police
and Racial Discrimination

There can be no doubt that the charge of racial discrimination is directed at the police more often than at any other segment of the criminal justice system. It would appear that laypersons, especially blacks, are more likely to perceive the police as prejudiced than they are prosecutors, judges, or probation officers. The criminological literature reflects this greater concern for police racial bias. A search of the literature finds that at least five major charges involving racial discrimination are often lodged against the police. Each of these charges, or claims, will be stated in turn in this chapter, along with the rationale or evidence generally given supporting it. I will also list and discuss several criticisms of each claim of racial discrimination so that the myths are exposed. The five charges to be considered are:

Charge No. 1—that police departments are guilty of racial discrimination in deploying their officers, so that crimes committed disproportionately by blacks are the focus of patrol and detection efforts.[1]

Charge No. 2—that the large racial gap in offense levels indicated by police arrest statistics is a product of discrimination by the police rather than an accurate portrayal of the actual level of offending by blacks and whites.[2]

Charge No. 3—that individual officers are guilty of racial discrimination against blacks in making arrests, so that encounters with blacks are more likely to result in an arrest than are encounters with whites.[3]

Charge No. 4—that officers, because of racial discrimination, are more likely to engage in acts of "police brutality" in encounters with blacks and are less likely to be disciplined for brutalizing blacks.[4]

Charge No. 5—that the police, because of racial discrimination, are more likely to use deadly force against blacks.[5]

Charge No. 1:
Deployment Patterns Are Discriminatory

Some suggest that the vast literature addressing the influence of racial discrimination on the arrest decisions of the police is bound to underestimate police bias, since these studies ignore deployment patterns. Because the police choose to deploy more officers against "street crime" than against white collar crime, they are bound to catch a disproportionate number of the poor and blacks.

It is argued that all social classes and races are equally criminal but that the different social classes and races engage in different types of crime. If the police were as concerned with "crime in the suites" as crime in the streets, blacks and whites would be arrested in proportionate numbers according to their representation in the general population. It is sometimes argued that this decision to cast the police net so that it catches only street criminals is a conscious decision made by the white power elite that controls society. This position is illustrated by the following two quotations:

> The rich are as violent and crooked as the poor, so why are they not punished in equal proportion? . . . Suppose that most of the officers of an urban police force were to patrol the suites rather than the streets (leaving sufficient cars on the streets to cover emergency calls). Some officers would go through a city hospital's records looking for patterns that suggest unnecessary surgery, and would pursue the suspicion by interviewing patients, their families, and doctors. Doctors who had operated unnecessarily, without informing patients that surgery was elective, might be charged with aggravated assault, or where patients died, with manslaughter. Other officers could go through city records to find improper expenditures by officials, and make arrests for theft. Others might experiment with buying goods and services, finding owners and managers to arrest for fraud. If a high proportion of officers did this kind of investigation, those of wealth and position might well be arrested more often than the poor, or if practically all officers did so, the wealthy might even be convicted and punished more than the poor.[6]

> The only explanation for this obvious discrepancy is conscious choices of key decision-makers to focus on crimes committed more frequently by blacks and other minorities.[7]

Those who make this charge often point to self-report studies—that is, questionnaires or interviews in which subjects are asked to admit offenses they have committed—indicating that almost everyone in the population commits some type of felony but that only a few get caught. It is pointed out that the racial gap between blacks and whites is almost nonexistent according to self-report studies but is 4.5:1 for the eight "index" crimes reported in the FBI's *Uniform Crime Reports* (*UCR*). Thus it is argued that *offending* rates are equal for blacks and whites but that *arrest* rates reflect a greater extent of black criminality because the police select those to be arrested from the pool of those who offend.[8]

Some critics of police deployment have suggested remedies. The quotation above indicates one suggestion—deploying the police to corporate suites. Bell suggests that racial quotas be applied to prison admissions according to the representation of blacks and whites in the general population.[9] Such quotas would force the police to search out more white and middle- and upper-class criminals. Thus Bell would force the police to redeploy officers to focus on white collar crime.

Arguments against Charge No. 1

1. The deployment pattern of the police is a legitimate response to public desires, from blacks as well as whites, rather than the result of a conspiracy to divert the police from the "real" crime problem.

The black community would be the first to complain about any redeployment of officers from a focus on street criminals to white collar criminals. The black community wants more police protection from street criminals, not less. The average black (as well as white) citizen lives in fear of muggers, robbers, and burglars, not price fixers, bribers, and embezzlers.[10] Those who contend that the "real" crime problem is white collar crime, not street crime, should try to convince those residents of the black community who live in fear of street criminals that they have been brainwashed by the power elite. Surely in our free society they can, if they are right, convince the black community where the real danger lies. Let them go to a Neighborhood Crime Watch meeting in the black community and suggest that the police redeploy away from the ghetto and into corporate offices.

2. The entire character of the police force would have to be changed if deployment of manpower were shifted from street crime to white collar crime. Police forces would have to have large numbers of trained accountants, lawyers, and the like to investigate business activities. Obviously, this would make any kind of affirmative action hiring program difficult, since there are fewer minority group members so trained.

Police street patrols would be replaced by complicated and time consuming investigations of the activities of those in the business world. The police could not rely as much as they now do on complainants, since those who are wronged in white collar crime often do not even recognize their victimization. The police would have to become far more aggressive.

Prosecutors would also face much more difficult and time consuming cases in white collar crime. Witnesses and complainants are fewer, and prosecutors are opposed by privately retained defense attorneys who are generally more experienced and competent. When the Ford Motor Company was accused by a local prosecutor in Indiana of reckless homicide after deaths resulted from an allegedly defective Pinto, the defense spent more than a million dollars on private counsel. Obviously, the state cannot compete with this kind of opposition.

3. The shift of police deployment from street to white collar crime would send a signal to street criminals that they could continue, and even increase, their activities with impunity. Thus the focus on white collar crime would lead to a great increase in street crime.

4. The police focus on street crime is based on a class rather than a race bias (if any bias is involved at all). Such a deployment of officers is only incidentally related to race, since a greater percentage of blacks than whites are lower class. Police departments in Washington, D.C., and Atlanta, both of which have had black mayors or black police chiefs, have not deployed officers differently from other American cities. The black officials do not change their deployment practices because they are responding to community desires and because whatever bias does exist is a class, not a racial bias.

Racial gaps in offense rates occur even in some countries where blacks are the ruling majority. A study of crime in Guyana, for example, found that the black conviction rate for indictable offenses was more than twice that of the East Indian rate and the rate for "others."[11]

5. The claim that all classes and races are equally criminal is based on an incorrect analysis and interpretation of self-report studies. The most exhaustive review of racial differences in self-report studies concludes that there is a racial gap in serious offenses reflected in these studies, though not as great as the 4.5:1 gap found in police arrest figures.[12] Furthermore, black subjects were found to be more reluctant to admit offenses than whites. It is also pointed out that self-reports have been done exclusively with juveniles; thus the comparison of self-report racial gaps with those found for adult arrests is inappropriate. The use of self-report studies to argue that adult criminality is equal for blacks and whites is simply an erroneous interpretation of the results.

6. Finally, those who contend that police deployment patterns are discriminatory should join Bell[13] in demanding quotas to overcome the racial imbalance in arrests. If quotas are suitable for overcoming discrimination in other areas (education, employment), then surely they would be appropriate and effective in overcoming bias by the police. No one can deny that racial quotas for prison would force the police to change their deployment practices, and if that is the case, it would appear that quotas would be effective in overcoming a serious racial imbalance. Those who criticize current police deployment should explain why they would not support the type of remedy suggested by Bell.

Charge No. 2:
Arrest Statistics Reflect Discrimination

The American public learns of the patterns and trends in criminal victimization and arrests from figures published by the FBI and dissemi-
nated via newspapers and television. It is fair to say that the public
perception of the crime problem is largely shaped by the FBI's annual
UCR. The bureau receives and compiles reports of crime victimizations and arrests from over 15,000 police departments, which serve
98 percent of the U.S. population. The *UCR* focuses on victimization
rather than arrests, so that the crime rates reported refer to the number
of victimizations. The *UCR* does not break down its published victimization rates by race, so one cannot determine from national police statistics the difference in victimization levels between blacks and whites.

However, the *UCR* does publish arrest totals that are broken down
by race (and sex and age). Though there are problems with the arrest
figures compiled by the local police and published by the FBI, there is
no evidence that the errors in gathering arrest totals are other than
random with respect to race of defendant.[14] Though the FBI does not
publish arrest rates for blacks and whites, one can easily calculate such
rates by obtaining population estimates for the two races and applying
a simple formula (total arrests divided by the population multiplied
by 100,000). Since arrest totals by race are so readily available on a
national (and local) basis, it is not surprising that the criminological
literature has numerous references to the difference in arrest rates for
specific crimes for blacks and whites.

The arrest rates reported in the literature reflect a significant gap
between arrest probabilities for blacks and whites for almost all crimes.
For use in this chapter I calculated arrest rates by race from arrest
totals found in the *UCR* for 1984 (see Table 5.1). The ratio of the
black arrest rate to the white rate for the eight index crimes (murder,
rape, robbery, aggravated assault, burglary, larceny, auto theft, and
arson) was 4.51:1. The black arrest rate for these crimes was 3,159.84
per 100,000 for people age 18 and above, and the white rate was 700.32
per 100,000.

In terms of actual "odds" of being arrested in 1984 these rates mean
that one black age 18 and over was arrested for every thirty-two blacks
18 and over in the U.S. population. Likewise, the white rate means that
there was one arrest of a white 18 and over for every 143 whites 18 and
over in the U.S. population. The probability of being arrested over a
lifetime is much greater. It has been estimated that 51 percent of black
males living in large cities (compared with 14 percent of white males)
are arrested at least once during their lifetime for an index crime.[15]

The "fact" that blacks are almost five times as likely to be arrested
for the eight index crimes is subject to several interpretations. The

Table 5.1   U.S. arrest rates by race, 1984[a]

Crime	Total	Black	White	Black/white ratio
Index crimes				
Murder	9.44	40.36	5.97	6.76:1
Rape	17.83	75.68	11.37	6.66:1
Robbery	60.26	338.89	28.35	11.95:1
Aggravated assault	149.46	540.05	106.77	5.06:1
Burglary	153.97	473.32	120.74	3.92:1
Larceny-theft	499.89	1,537.85	387.41	3.97:1
Motor vehicle theft	44.32	137.88	34.37	4.01:1
Arson	6.28	15.80	5.34	2.96:1
Violent index crimes	236.99	994.99	152.46	6.53:1
Property index crimes	704.46	2,164.85	547.86	3.95:1
Crime index total	941.45	3,159.84	700.32	4.51:1
Nonindex crimes				
Other assaults	254.49	749.70	202.27	3.71:1
Forgery, counterfeiting	42.56	132.37	33.34	9.97:1
Fraud	138.71	365.24	116.96	3.12:1
Embezzlement	4.35	10.31	3.78	2.73:1
Stolen property	53.97	193.32	39.07	4.95:1
Vandalism	76.33	149.36	69.93	2.14:1
Weapons; carrying, poss.	87.42	293.17	65.60	4.47:1
Prostitution, vice	64.13	261.53	42.11	6.21:1
Sex offenses (not rape)	46.42	74.72	44.59	1.68:1
Drug abuse violations	368.83	1,065.77	299.03	3.56:1
Gambling	19.92	99.09	10.26	9.66:1
Against family, children	23.15	61.09	19.43	3.14:1
Driving under influence	979.15	822.69	1,034.45	0.80:1
Liquor laws	209.26	253.77	207.87	1.22:1
Drunkenness	642.04	1,023.71	612.13	1.67:1
Disorderly conduct	328.36	915.07	266.46	3.43:1
Vagrancy	15.36	52.33	11.05	4.74:1
Others (not traffic)	1,183.39	3,498.53	937.72	3.73:1
Suspicion	10.38	53.62	5.36	10.00:1
Nonindex crimes total	4,548.13	10,075.40	4,021.41	2.51:1
All arrests, index and nonindex	5,489.58	13,235.24	4,721.73	2.80:1

[a] Based on total population age 18 and above.

Source of arrest totals: *Uniform Crime Reports, 1984* (Table 37, p. 182) by the Federal Bureau of Investigation. Washington, D.C.: U.S. Government Printing Office, 1985.

charge that police arrest statistics are discriminatory suggests that this racial gap is just a reflection of police bias in selecting more blacks from the large "pool" of potential offenders rather than a reflection of a corresponding discrepancy in actual levels of offending.

The argument for the DT for individual police officers might be illustrated by thinking of the dilemma facing detectives in a large store who are assigned to stop shoplifting. Those detectives face a difficult problem; some students of shoplifting who randomly watched customers entering a store have found that as many as 10 percent of customers steal. But there are few store detectives, and thus they cannot follow every customer who enters the store. It is common practice for the detectives to watch the customers whom they perceive to be the most likely to steal.

If detectives suspect and thus watch only certain types of customers, for example, blacks and juveniles, they are likely to confirm their suspicions, because it is inevitable that a certain proportion of the type they watch will steal. As a result they have no idea how many customers of other types steal. Thus the greater arrest rate of blacks and juveniles for shoplifting is a self-fulfilling prophecy. Proponents of the DT might suggest that society is like a large store, with the police acting in the role of store detectives. They catch and arrest those whom they watch, and thus arrest rates are a function of police prejudices in deciding whom to watch.

The major argument for Charge No. 2 derives from self-report surveys. When subjects are asked to disclose their own previous criminal involvement, racial differences in offending have been "slight or nonexistent."[16] In other words, it is claimed that black and white juveniles report almost equal levels of offending, or that the racial gap in offending is far below the 4.5:1 ratio found in arrest figures. Since self-report surveys measure the level of criminality in the general population that is uncaught, it is claimed that the racial gap in arrested offenders simply reflects police bias.

A second argument in support of Charge No. 2 involves the results of national crime victimization surveys conducted each year in 60,000 households by the U.S. Census Department for the Department of Justice. The racial gap in victimization is far less than the racial gap for offending (as measured by arrests). For example, the 1981 survey found a per capita racial victimization ratio of only 1.5:1 for blacks to one white for the violent crimes of robbery, assault, and rape. This racial gap is far below the black/white arrest ratio for the same three crimes of 6.5:1 (see Table 5.1). Since it is claimed that violent crime is predominantly intraracial, the racial gap in arrests should approximate that found for victimization if the police are focusing equally on black-on-black and white-on-white crime. The fact that police arrest statistics reflect an overrepresentation of black offenders indicates that the police are focusing on black-on-black crimes in the ghetto more than on white-on-white crimes in suburbia.

Arguments against Charge No. 2

1. One comprehensive review of self-report surveys prior to 1980 found that the failure to find a large racial gap stemmed from the methodological failings of the self-report instruments.[17] This review

found by checking self-reported offenses resulting in arrests with actual arrest records that there was a tendency for black males who had been arrested to substantially underreport the offenses found in the official record. Thus the review concluded that self-report surveys were "differentially valid," meaning that the self reports might be valid for measuring white levels of offending but not black levels.[18]

2. Self-report studies have been limited to juvenile populations, whereas the official arrest figures generally refer to those 18 and up. Furthermore, the types of offenses most frequently asked about in self-report surveys are quite trivial and are certainly not comparable to the index offenses of the *UCR*. Even if self-report surveys of juveniles are valid in indicating that black and white juveniles have equal offense levels, the type of offenses reported in self-reports are so much less serious than the FBI's index offenses that one can draw no conclusions about uncaught black and white index offenders from such self-reports.

3. The argument that the difference in racial gaps between victimization surveys and arrest figures indicates a police focus on black-on-black crime is based on the faulty premise that crime is predominantly intraracial. A recent article contended that the commonly held view that violent crime is intraracial is based on a misrepresentation of data from the national victimization surveys.[19] Though it is true that crime is intraracial from three perspectives—whites are more likely to be victimized by whites, blacks are more likely to be victimized by blacks, and white offenders are more likely to choose white victims—it is interracial from a fourth perspective—black offenders are more likely to choose white victims. Therefore the surprisingly small racial gap in victimization rates is largely due to the tendency of black offenders to choose white victims, thus lowering the "expected" black victimization level and raising the "expected" white level. Blacks can offend at much greater levels than whites and yet the victimization levels can remain approximately equal.[20]

4. Perhaps the most important criticism of Charge No. 2 is derived from data from the national crime victim surveys. One of the questions asked of those who report being victimized concerns the race of the offender. Though it is obvious that the race of the offender is rarely known in such crimes as burglary and auto theft, such information is generally known in cases of robbery, assault, rape, and personal larceny.

Hindelang calculated rates of offending for blacks and whites from victimization survey data.[21] He found that the racial gap in *offending* for robbery, assault, and rape (whether or not an arrest occurred) was almost equal to that found for *arrest* statistics. This result indicates that black and white levels of violent crime are not equal in the pool of offenders from which police select arrestees. On the contrary, these results indicate that the police select black and white arrestees in approximately the same proportion as they are found in the pool of offenders who are thus "eligible" for arrest. In short, Hindelang's calculations argue against police bias in the arrest process, since the racial gap between black and white *offense* levels is approximately the same as the gap between black and white *arrest* rates.

It should be noted that those who support Charge No. 2 question the validity of the data in victimization surveys on race of offender and thus question Hindelang's conclusion that blacks commit violent crimes at a much greater rate than whites.[22] These critics suggest that there is no definitive body of knowledge concerning the accuracy of victims' perception of the offender's race and point out that the white victims' identification of black offenders may be based on racial biases or stereotypes. Though such racial biases may exist in a limited number of cases, it is extremely unlikely that such incorrect attributions of race could be so common as to produce a racial gap on the order of 6.5:1 when no gap actually existed.

Furthermore, it would seem that black victims would be as likely to incorrectly identify their offenders as being white as white victims would be to incorrectly identify their offenders as being black. Also, if blacks are as likely as whites to attribute evil motives and acts to the opposite race (as was argued in Chapter Two), then we can only assume that incorrect racial identification of offenders by whites and blacks would cancel each other out and that the racial gaps in offense levels found by Hindelang are essentially correct.

5. The pattern of gaps between black and white arrest rates for different offenses is not consistent with the view that the gap is greatest when police discretion is greatest. In fact the opposite appears to be the case. In violent crimes the police generally make arrests based on information given to them by victims or those who witnessed the crime. Thus they have less discretion than would be the case in property crimes, when more proactive police work is necessary to find a suspect and make an arrest. Furthermore, the victims of violent crimes are likely to be more insistent on an arrest than those of property crimes. And yet the black/white gap in arrests is greater for the violent offenses (see Table 5.1). The racial gaps at arrest in 1984 were 6.76:1 for murder, 6.66:1 for rape, 11.95:1 for robbery, and 5.06:1 for aggravated assault. By contrast the racial gaps in arrest rates for property crimes were far less: 3.92:1 for burglary, 3.97:1 for larceny–theft, 4.01:1 for auto theft, and 2.96:1 for arson.

Furthermore, an examination of the less serious nonindex crimes in Table 5.1 indicates that some of the crimes in which police have the greatest discretion result in relatively small racial gaps. One offense that is highly discretionary is drunken driving. Since there are estimates that as many as one in ten drivers may be driving drunk on a weekend night, it is obvious that the police have a large pool of "eligible" offenders from which to make arrests. If the police are prone to racial discrimination, it would appear that drunken driving would be the perfect opportunity to exercise that bias. And yet the racial gap in arrests for drunken driving was 0.80:1, indicating that whites were actually more likely than blacks to be arrested on a per capita basis. Likewise, the racial gaps for liquor law violations and for drunkenness were 1.22:1 and 1.67:1, much lower than one would expect if the police routinely discriminated against blacks in arrests for crimes that are highly discretionary. Though large gaps do exist for some highly discretionary offenses— for example, the racial gap for gambling arrests was 9.66:1, and the gap for arrests for suspicion was 10:1—it is clear that there is no consistent pattern of large racial gaps in all (or even most) crimes in which discretion is great.

6. Additional evidence for the thesis that arrest statistics fairly represent the levels of actual offending by blacks and whites comes from a study by Hollinger of arrests for drunken driving in a mid-sized Georgia city.[23] He compared the racial (and other) characteristics of drivers who were randomly stopped and found to be drunk or near drunk with those of drivers who had been arrested for drunken driving over the same period. He found no racial differences between the offending but not arrested drivers and the arrested drivers, once socioeconomic status was taken into account. In his words, the study found that the "slightly greater numbers of non-white drivers found in the DUI arrest populations are a function of their generally lower occupational status, not their race."[24]

One could argue that national arrest statistics for driving under the influence indicate an approximately 1:1 ratio because the police tend to overselect blacks from a population of drunken drivers that actually underrepresents blacks. In other words, blacks may be much less likely on a per capita basis to drive drunk, but those relatively few black drivers may be overselected by the police. Hollinger's study would appear to refute this argument, at least for one Georgia city during one period of time. He found no overselection of blacks for arrest from the drunken driving population.

7. A second study supporting the thesis that police statistics are fairly accurate in representing the actual levels of offending involves another crime for which arrest is highly discretionary—marijuana use.[25] This study compared estimates of marijuana use for various demographic subgroups in three metropolitan areas (Chicago, Omaha, and Washington, D.C.), with the actual arrest rates for these groups based on police figures. In Chicago, blacks were about twice as likely as whites to be "selected" for arrest, controlling for actual offense levels. But in Omaha the reverse was found: whites were about twice as likely as blacks to be selected for arrest. In Washington, the arrest probabilities for the two races were approximately equal (with whites being slightly more likely

to be selected than blacks). Thus overall it would appear that blacks are not overselected for arrest for marijuana use. And if one argues that blacks were discriminated against in Chicago, it would also have to be conceded that whites were discriminated against in Omaha. Thus we have another example of the canceling-out effect, with national statistics masking different kinds of discrimination in individual cities.

Charge No. 3:
Individual Police Officers Discriminate

Charges No. 1 and No. 2 dealt with the possibility that deployment patterns and arrest decisions make it more likely that the police will encounter and arrest black offenders from a pool of "eligible" black and white offenders. Charge No. 3 concerns the decisions of individual police officers once an encounter occurs. Though it is difficult to directly measure the process by which the police select certain people from some unknown population of offenders for an encounter that may lead to an arrest, it is quite common to find studies that attempt to determine the extent to which the police are more likely to arrest blacks than whites once those encounters have occurred. Numerous writers have argued that this type of study has demonstrated racial discrimination by the police. Two studies that are often cited as proof of racial discrimination in arrest encounters will be examined, followed by a number of arguments and studies that tend to refute Charge No. 3.

One study commonly cited to support Charge No. 3 examined the impact of race on 5,688 police/citizen encounters in 24 police departments in the metropolitan areas of St. Louis, Rochester, and Tampa/ St. Petersburg.[26] This study controlled for race, sex, age, and demeanor of offender; seriousness of offense; victim/offender relationship; and presence of bystanders. Blacks were arrested in 21.4 percent of their encounters with the police, compared with 13.1 percent for whites. When the controls were used in a multivariate causal model, there was still a significant relationship between race of offender and arrest (though the authors do not indicate to what extent the original 8.3 percent difference in outcome by race of offender was reduced).

Four points should be made with respect to the above study. First, several variables were better predictors of the officer's decision whether to arrest than race of offender. For example, 37.4 percent of the offenders who were "antagonistic" were arrested, compared with 12.8 percent of those who were "civil"; 42.5 percent of felons were arrested, compared with 13.7 percent of misdemeanants; and 46.6 percent of offenders were arrested when a victim requested a formal disposition, compared with 6.6 percent when a victim requested an informal disposition. Second, though it is true that the relationship between race of offender did not disappear with the addition of the controls, some important potential controls were not used. No data were collected by the trained observers riding with the patrol officers as to age, sex, and race of the police officer. Assuming that race of police officer makes a difference, the rather small difference in outcome for black and white victims could easily have been reduced to zero. It was noted in Chapter Four that it is inappropriate to interpret the variation after controls as a race effect. Unfortunately, this study made that error.[27]

Third, it should be noted that the disparate outcome by race (though not given, it is doubtless less than the 8.3 percent found before controls were used) could not account for a racial gap on the order of the 4.5:1 that is found in official arrest statistics. Finally, the extent of racial discrimination that may have occurred among the encounters observed is really unknown, since the research team chose to examine patrolmen from twenty-four departments as a collective. Considerable variation is likely to have occurred among individual officers (see the discussion on this point in Chapter Four), so that some officers may have made "antiblack" arrest decisions, and others may have made "antiwhite" decisions.

A second study that is often cited in support of Charge No. 3 involved a more indirect test, in that police/citizen encounters were not observed. Hepburn examined the presence or absence of a subsequent warrant by the prosecutor in 28,235 adult arrests in a large midwestern city for 1974.[28] He assumed that arrests by the police that did not result in a warrant by the prosecutor had been based on less evidence or had been made with a different purpose in mind (for example, harassment). Hepburn found no significant difference in the proportion of cases that resulted in warrants for blacks and whites for index offenses, but he did find a significant difference for less serious offenses: arrests of blacks were less likely to result in the issuance of a warrant.

Given this rather inconclusive finding, it is surprising that this study is so often cited as one that supports the DT. As Hepburn points out, several important potential control variables (for example, prior record and demeanor of offenders) were not used, which may have reduced the race effect to below statistical significance.[29] Also, it seems odd that leniency *for* blacks at one stage of the criminal justice system (the decision of the prosecutor) is viewed as racial discrimination *against* blacks at the earlier arrest stage. One can only speculate as to the interpretation that would have been given if blacks had been *more* likely than whites to be issued a warrant by the prosecutor.

A study of police release rates in burglary cases in a California police department found a race effect.[30] When controls such as prior record of the defendant were introduced, however, the race effect disappeared.

Arguments against Charge No. 3

1. When studies of police/citizen encounters are considered as a whole, it is clear that the results at the very least are inconclusive with respect to the DT and at best refute that thesis. One review of studies that have examined the relationship between race and arrest concluded that the previous literature "suggests that the bivariate association between race and arrest is spurious. That is, controlling for levels of antagonism or seriousness of the offense eliminates the race/arrest relationship."[31]

The study most commonly cited as contradicting the DT is that of Black and Reiss.[32] Their study observed police/citizen encounters in areas of Boston, Chicago, and Washington, D.C., in 1966 and noted the great discretion (and thus possible discrimination) in the arrest decision:

> Officers decided not to make arrests of one or more suspects for 43 percent of all felonies and 52 percent of all misdemeanors judged by observers as situations where an arrest could have been made on probable cause. Something other than probable cause is required, then, for the officer to make an arrest.
>
> For the police, that something else is a *moral belief* that the law should be enforced and the violation sanctioned by the criminal justice system. The line officer usually reaches that decision by conducting an investigation to establish probable cause and by conducting a "trial" to determine who is guilty. His decision, therefore, is in an important sense judicial. This judicial determination will be influenced, as it is in the courts, by the deference and demeanor of the suspect, arguments as to mitigating circumstances, complainant preferences for justice, and the willingness of the complainant to participate in seeing that it is done. All in all, an officer not only satisfies probable cause but also concludes after his careful evaluation that *the suspect is guilty and an arrest is therefore just.*[33]

Yet with all this discretion (and in 1966, before the civil rights movement and the influx of black officers onto police forces) the study team found no racial discrimination in the decision to arrest once a police/citizen encounter had occurred. In fact, the study team found that "police officers appear less hostile and brusque toward Negroes and to ridicule them less often than whites."

2. There is little evidence that white police officers make different decisions with respect to arrest than black ones. Certainly if racial discrimination by white police officers against black defendants were the cause of the disproportionate arrest rate of blacks, it should follow that black police officers, who are ostensibly not racially prejudiced toward blacks, would "make a difference." It is often asserted that black officers do make a difference,[34] and yet the only major study attempting to test this thesis found little difference in the behavior of officers of the two races. Smith and Klein observed 5,688 police/citizen contacts in 1977 in St. Louis, Tampa/St. Petersburg, and Rochester,

New York.[35] They found that the black officers, who composed 16 percent of the officers in those metropolitan areas, had an arrest pattern, with respect to arresting blacks and whites, similar to that of white officers. In fact, black officers were more likely than white officers to make arrests in some departments.

3. Much of the "proof" often cited for the DT at the point of arrest relies on anecdotes ("I saw a black guy arrested once just for . . ."); "common-sense" scenarios (a white man in a black neighborhood will be warned to leave for his own protection, whereas a black man in a white neighborhood will be investigated to protect the white community);[36] or statements from authorities such as black judges who assert that racism is pervasive in law enforcement.[37] Notably absent are citations of empirical studies supporting this position. One reviewer of the literature on the existence of racial discrimination at the point of arrest cited eight studies contradicting his thesis (that racism was pervasive) and none supporting it (he cited only "authorities" or persons who believed that racism existed). Yet the reviewer dismissed the empirical studies and concluded that racism was pervasive.[38]

Charge No. 4:
The Police Are Guilty of Brutality

There can be little doubt that the vast majority of blacks in the United States are convinced that police brutality is more likely to occur against blacks and that the police are less likely to discipline officers who brutalize blacks. This "fact" has touched off many riots, because blacks see a particular incident of excessive force as typical of the police and vent their anger against the continuation of this discriminatory pattern of brutality.[39] It appears that the Miami riot of 1980 was caused by outrage at the failure of the criminal justice system to punish white officers who had beaten a black man to death. The verdict of acquittal was seen as another in a long line of acts of police brutality against blacks that had gone unpunished.[40]

There are no empirical studies of the use of excessive force by the police that would allow a thorough examination of the impact of race of victim and race of officer on such acts. Studies observing officers on patrol for a large number of police/citizen encounters have noted incidents of excessive force but have not, with one exception, focused on the importance of the race of those involved. The major reason for this lack of attention to police brutality is that such acts generally occur when the victim is under police control and away from the public eye. Reiss did examine thirty-seven incidents of excessive force out of 3,826 police/citizen encounters in three American cities in 1966,[41] but it is clear that excessive force occurs more often out of the view of such observers.

The evidence for racial discrimination in excessive use of force has consisted of anecdotes and testimonials. Numerous investigations have been made of cases filed by victims reporting excessive force,[42] but these case histories look only at those who complained. The probability of bias in such samples is indicated by the fact that only one of the thirty-seven incidents of excessive force observed by Reiss's study team resulted in a complaint to the police.[43]

In the absence of more empirical data it is common to find in the literature testimonials from "authorities" asserting that police brutality is a fact and that the race of the victim is a primary motivating factor in such beatings. These statements are often given by commissions or investigators of riots,[44] social scientists,[45] black leaders,[46] and black police administrators.[47]

Finally, many assert that the complaint process whereby victims seek redress for the excessive use of force is racially discriminatory. One critic suggested that the police method of handling citizen complaints is "the world's biggest washing machine. Everything that goes in dirty, comes out clean."[48] Thus critics charge that the police are more likely to beat blacks and are then more likely to cover up such beatings.

Arguments against Charge No. 4

1. The fact that a police officer was white and a beating victim was black, or that this racial combination occurs more frequently than any other, does not in itself prove that the primary motive for the beating was racial prejudice. Bias may be the motive in a particular case or in most cases, but it is also possible that other explanations are equally valid. The attribution of cause that one chooses depends largely on one's prejudice for or against the police, blacks, and whites.

Let us take four scenarios of beatings to illustrate the different attributions of cause that might arise depending on the racial characteristics of the officer and the victim. In each case let us assume that the officer has attempted to arrest a young male, who is supported by several companions of the same race, for harassing and threatening passersby on a sidewalk. The attempted arrest leads to the refusal of the young man to submit to the arrest, then to a struggle, and then to a beating. The four racial combinations are white officer beats a black, white officer beats a white, black officer beats a black, and black officer beats a white.

Those who readily accuse the police of racial discrimination would probably attribute the beating in the first scenario (white officer beats black citizen) to racial prejudice by the white officer. It is unlikely, however, that these critics would attribute the beating in the fourth scenario (black officer beats a white citizen) to racial prejudice by the black officer. As discussed in Chapter Two, racial prejudice is viewed by many as a characteristic of whites but not of blacks. Supporters of the police would probably attribute the beating to some act of the victim and might even suggest that the black victim had provoked the beating by racial epithets directed at the police officer (calling the officer a white "mother" or an "Uncle Tom"). Critics and supporters of the police are thus selecting an explanation from the multitude that are available that is favorable with respect to "us" and unfavorable with respect to "them."

In police beatings, numerous factors may be involved in "causing" the use of excessive force:

1. Police officers may be racially prejudiced toward members of the victim's race.
2. Police officers may be emotionally unstable or be psychologically incapable of accepting rejection of authority and verbal abuse.[49]
3. Police officers may feel that once they announce their intent to arrest, they cannot "back down" and thus must meet the resistance of the victims with sufficient force to subdue them. This view may be buttressed by the presence of bystanders, who might see the officers as weak and be encouraged by this weakness to resist authority.[50]
4. There may be a "culture gap" between the officers and the victims, so that the officers do not recognize the "game" that the victims are "running on them" and the victims do not understand "where the officers are coming from" in perceiving the situation as requiring force. This culture gap, or set of mutual misunderstandings, thus leads to a series of steps that culminates in the use of force.[51]
5. The victims may be trying to improve their image with their companions by defying authority, making the officers back down, or provoking the officers to "lose their cool."
6. The officers may beat victims to "get their kicks."[52]

Attribution theory (that is, the new definition of racial prejudice—see Chapter Two) suggests that one's choice of factors from the above list (or similar ones not listed) largely depends not on "the facts" but on whether one of the participants is considered to be part of "us" or "them." Blacks are likely to choose the first factor (racial prejudice) as the primary cause of the beating. The police are likely to choose the third. A black officer may select the first factor if he is a *black* officer or the third if he is a black *officer*.[53]

It is also possible that such beatings are much more complex or multifaceted than critics of the police or the police themselves appear to

believe. It may be that racial prejudice is always a factor in any interaction and that it is characteristic of the victim as well as the officer. In
other words, there may be many causes of, or factors involved in, police
brutality. It seems impossible to determine just what proportion of
blame should be assigned to each factor or even to discern all the factors. Though civil cases often result in a court ruling that one or the
other person is to blame to a certain extent (for example, the com-
plainant was 40 percent at fault, and the defendant was 60 percent at
fault), such determinations are impossible to make in cases involving
excessive force. One cannot just ask the participants why they acted as
they did, since they may not even be aware of the causes of their behavior and, if they are, will probably not report them accurately.

A closer determination of the factors responsible for police beatings
could be made if we had a large sample of cases of beatings and "non-
beatings" (confrontations that did not result in excessive force) and
could control for the numerous factors involved other than race of
officer.[54] Unfortunately such data are not likely to become available.
In their absence we will continue to rely on anecdotes and the attribution of cause from people with vested interests (for example, the police
and black leaders).

2. Since more direct evidence is not likely to be available, we must
rely on indirect evidence. There is considerable literature documenting
the tendency of black officers to be as likely as or more likely than
white officers to use excessive force on blacks. Reiss found that both
black and white officers were more likely to use excessive force against
members of their own race,[55] and thus he concluded that "race is not
an issue in the unnecessary use of force by the police."[56] I would argue
that his conclusion is premature given the nature of the indirect evidence he presents. It should be noted that his figures do not involve
the relative probability that black or white officers will use excessive
force if confronted with similar situations; that is, his figures are biased
by the far greater likelihood that black officers, generally assigned to
black areas, will confront blacks rather than whites in situations that
may require force.

With the above qualification in mind, however, it is interesting to
note that Reiss found the rate of excessive force (based on the thirty-
seven incidents) to be greater for black officers than for white ones (9.8
to 8.7 per 1,000 officers).[57] He also found that white citizens were
more likely than black citizens to be victims of excessive force (5.9 to
2.8 per 1,000 citizens) and that white offenders were more likely than
black offenders (41.9 to 22.6 per 1,000 offenders) to be the victims of
excessive force by the police.[58] Thus in the only empirical study available it appears that black officers are more likely to be offenders and
that blacks are less likely to be victims. Certainly these data do not
support the DT with respect to police brutality.

A black police chief in Pennsylvania has indicated that though black officers make up only 17 percent of his force, they are responsible for 61 percent of all complaints against police officers.[59] Surely this is indirect evidence that race of officer is not the primary cause of excessive use of force. Why would black officers be more likely to use excessive force against blacks than white officers? Surely it would be difficult to maintain that blacks are beating blacks because of racial prejudice. The police chief indicated that the problem was "attitude" (not race) and that "attitude transcends racial or ethnic group identification."[60] If black police officers patrolling the same areas as white officers are at least equally likely to use excessive force, doesn't that indicate that racial prejudice is not the primary cause of police use of excessive force in such neighborhoods?

White female officers are seldom involved in excessive use of force against blacks. But if race of officer is the primary cause of police brutality, why don't white female officers, assuming they are as racially prejudiced as white males, beat blacks? It may be that the primary cause of police brutality is the "macho" personality and that female officers are less likely to have that characteristic. One can only speculate about the extent to which the infusion of women into policing has reduced the level of police brutality against blacks. If for no other reason brutality may have declined because white male officers can no longer count on female and black officers' maintaining the code of silence if such a beating occurs.

It may also be that young black males find little image enhancement in fighting white female officers. They may choose to "test" the female officers sexually rather than physically.[61] The causal process in police beatings is surely more complex than the simplistic charge that the black victim was beaten "just because he was black."

3. It is assumed by many that since white officers are racially prejudiced and often beat blacks, prejudice is the cause of the physical abuse. Reiss did find that the police commonly expressed prejudicial views of blacks, but he maintains that this attitude did not affect their behavior (at least with respect to physical abuse).

> White policemen, even though they are prejudiced toward Negroes, do not discriminate against Negroes in the excessive use of force. The use of force by the police is more readily explained by police culture than it is by the policeman's race. Indeed, in the few cases where we observed a Negro policeman using unnecessary force against white citizens, there was no evidence that he did so because of his race.[62]

On the same point, one study found that sexual slurs or prejudices against women were much more common among the police than racial slurs or prejudices,[63] and yet the police are less likely to beat women than men. But if racism results in racial discrimination against blacks, why doesn't sexism result in sexual discrimination against women? It is clear that women are far less likely than men to be beaten by the police: only two of the thirty-seven brutality events reported by Reiss had women victims.[64] There is considerable evidence that words and attitudes are only loosely linked to deeds, and thus attempts to predict what people will do from what they say have been disappointing.[65] However, the human attribution process makes a much closer tie between words and deeds. It is assumed by laypersons that if someone is prejudiced toward blacks (or women or hippies) and behaves in a negative manner toward them, his or her motive must have been the prejudice. Research does not support this rather simplistic view.

4. Most critics of the police see them as quite rational and calculating in their use of excessive force. (Such critics may charge that beatings occur in private to eliminate witnesses or that the police beat blacks to "keep them in line.") But if that were the case, why would white police officers beat blacks (simply because they were black) when they knew that such a beating would surely result in a complaint, that the charge of racism would be raised, that the police administration was "gun shy" with respect to such charges, and that there were numerous parties (civil rights groups, the news media) likely to pressure the department to discipline officers for such beatings? Surely a rational officer would simply avoid any confrontation that might result in a beating to avoid the "hassle." In fact, if the rational officer were prone to beating someone, why not pick a white victim? Who would complain to the police department other than the victim? There is no organized group looking after the interests of whites in such situations.

I suggest that there is considerable evidence that white officers do shy away from confrontations and the use of force with blacks, especially in times of community tension.[66] A rational officer (even if he disliked blacks and wanted to beat them) would probably avoid situations that might lead to violence. In fact, he would "lean over backward" to avoid the escalation of conflict to the point of physical force.

5. The charge that the police disciplinary process for officers who use excessive force is a big "washing machine" that refuses to hold officers accountable for brutality may be accurate. However, the point is not whether the police department hides or cleans its dirty linen but whether the process is racially discriminatory. It may be that the police are as likely to absolve officers in white-on-black cases as they are in white-on-white or black-on-black cases. If that is the case, it may be accurate to charge the police with failure to punish those who engage in police brutality, but it is inaccurate to charge them with racial discrimination.

There is little evidence with respect to the alleged existence of racial discrimination in the police disciplinary process for brutality. And what evidence does exist appears to contradict the anecdotal evidence and public statements supporting the DT. A *Miami Herald* series in 1980 pointed out numerous examples of police brutality against blacks and charged that the disciplinary process had discriminated against blacks. The authors went so far as to say that there was "one standard for white citizens who complain of police brutality" and "another for blacks," so that there was a "subtle but persistent pattern of racial bias in [the county police agency's] record of investigating incidents of alleged police brutality."[67] The newspaper reported that its computer analysis of records in 1,319 complaints against the agency supported this charge.

At the request of the police chief of the city of Miami, a colleague and I secured the newspaper's data and conducted our own analysis.[68] We found no evidence of racial discrimination in the sustaining of complaints when other variables were controlled. Furthermore, we found that the percentage difference in sustained complaints (the standard used by the newspaper to charge discrimination) actually favored blacks in the city of Miami, though it favored whites in the county. And yet the newspaper did not charge Miami with racial discrimination against whites, though its criterion for racial discrimination seemed to require that.

I know of no empirical study of the complaint process for police brutality that has found evidence of racial discrimination. This is not to say that racial discrimination is not involved in individual cases but to suggest that the "proof" that many assume exists is absent. Belief with regard to the alleged existence of racial discrimination in the processing of complaints will have to continue to rely on anecdotes and testimonials.

Charge No. 5: The Police
Discriminate in the Use of Deadly Force

The vast majority of blacks are convinced that the police are more likely to use deadly force against blacks than whites, other things being equal. This viewpoint is commonly expressed by black leaders.[69] One black judge even suggests that police killings of blacks are similar to the killing of deer for sport or of Indians in South America.[70]

It is well documented that approximately 60 percent of those killed by the police in the United States are black, though only 12 percent of the population is black.[71] This disparity is considered by some to be prima facie evidence of racial discrimination by the police. Goldcamp has found two schools of thought in the literature on the reasons for the racial disparity in police killings.[72] One school (the other school is discussed under "Arguments against Charge No. 5") includes both those who think the entire range of police activities are racist and those who believe that only some individual officers are racist. In either case the major determinant of the disparity is seen as racial prejudice, discrimination, or racism. The most commonly cited article providing evidence of racial discrimination in the use of deadly force is Fyfe's study of shootings in Memphis from 1969 to 1976.[73] Fyfe separated "elective" shootings (those in which the officers had elected to shoot or not to shoot at little or no risk to themselves or others) from "non-elective" shootings (those in which the officers had had little real choice but to shoot lest they risk death or serious injury to themselves or others). The elective shootings generally involved arrests for property crimes. The Memphis study calculated the number of people who had been fired at per 1,000 suspects in property crimes arrested by the police. Fyfe concluded:

> During the years studied, 4.3 black property crime suspects were shot at for each 1,000 black property crime arrestees; the comparable white rate is 1.8. The table also indicates that the black wounded rate (0.6) is six times higher than the white rate (0.1), and that the black non-injured rate (3.2) is nearly three times higher than the white rate (1.2).
>
> This last rate may hide other sources of this variation (e.g., the legal categories used to define "property crimes" include many divergent activities; blacks may run from property crimes, while whites surrender). Even given this possibility, however, the table suggests that Memphis blacks were in far greater risk of being shot or shot at in these circumstances than can be explained by either their presence in the general population or the arrestee population.[74]

Arguments against Charge No. 5

1. Numerous studies have examined the use of deadly force by the police. Many of these have attempted to find explanations for the disproportionate use of deadly force against blacks. The conclusions of the majority of these studies fall under the second school of thought mentioned by Goldcamp—that factors other than race account for the variation.

Two issues are involved in examining this disparity, the variation across cities and the variation within one city. First, it would appear that the probability that a U.S. citizen (whether black or white) will be killed by the police varies sharply across cities. For example, one survey found that the justifiable homicide rate in over 50 cities ranged from .08 for Sacramento to 2.13 for New Orleans, indicating that a citizen in New Orleans was twenty-seven times as likely to be killed by the police as a citizen in Sacramento.[75] Several studies have attempted to learn why these rates vary so dramatically in the United States. Among the factors found to be important predictors of the rate of police killings across cities are the following:[76]

1. income inequality
2. measures of social cohesion (divorce, suicide)
3. gun ownership among the citizen population
4. the "culture of violence" in a community
5. the number of police officers per 1,000 citizens
6. the violent crime rate
7. the arrest rate for violent crimes
8. the rate of police officers killed
9. the police policy on the use of deadly force
10. the rate of justifiable homicides by civilians

None of the studies cited found that the percentage of the population that was black was a good predictor of the city's rate, when controls were used. Thus it would appear that a black's (or white's) chances of being killed by the police vary across the country because of community characteristics other than racial composition.

Second, within a particular community (or for the United States as a whole) it is clear that the relative probability of being killed by the police varies sharply for blacks and whites. The first school of thought attributes this black/white disparity to race, and the second school suggests that factors other than race are better predictors of the different probabilities. Though blacks across the country represent 60 percent of all victims of police killings, it is also true that 73 percent of all justifiable homicides by civilians are by blacks, 66 percent of all homicide arrests are of blacks, 71 percent of all robbery arrests are of blacks, 64 percent of all violent crime arrests are of blacks, and 58 percent of all weapon violation arrests are of blacks.[77] From these figures it would appear that the 60 percent figure for black victims of police killings is in line with what one would expect, given the greater tendency of blacks to be involved in violent confrontations with citizens and the police.

2. The Fyfe study of police shootings in Memphis is an exception, in that the racial disparity in shooting rates appears to hold up even when one controls for the numbers of blacks and whites arrested for property crimes. Though, as Fyfe suggests, it may be that the types of property crimes in which blacks and whites are shot are different and that black property offenders may be more likely to run, it is unlikely that these differences would be great enough to account for the large black/white gap in shooting rates. Fyfe suggests that the Memphis data were different from his data from New York City (where no "unexplained" racial gap was found—see discussion below) because there were no clear shooting guidelines in Memphis as there were in New York.[78] He concluded that the validity of the DT or the NDT with respect to police shootings may be "place dependent";[79] that is, there may be racial discrimination in some cities but not others. Fortunately, most large

cities do have clear shooting guidelines that would reduce the possibility of the "shooting pattern" found in Memphis for 1969–1976.

3. Other studies of the police use of deadly force have found indirect evidence rebutting the DT. The most important is a study by Fyfe, who calculated shooting rates of white, black, and Hispanic police officers for the 2,926 shootings by New York City police officers from 1971 to 1975.[80] He found that black officers had higher rates of killing per 1,000 officers (186.7) than did white officers (98.1) or Hispanic officers (154.8) and that the rate of black officers' shooting black victims (19.6) was greater than the rate of white officers' shooting black victims (8.2) and Hispanic officers' shooting blacks.[81]

Fyfe explains the relatively higher killing rate for black officers by citing two factors: (1) their assignment to black precincts and (2) the greater frequency of off-duty killings involving black officers, who more often resided in high-crime areas. When he examined the (largely) black precincts alone, the killing rate for black and white officers (who were assigned to those precincts) was almost identical (198.6 for blacks, 196.5 for whites, and 210.2 for Hispanics).[82] Thus it would appear that in high-crime areas in New York in 1971–1975, white and Hispanic police officers were no more likely to shoot and kill blacks than were black officers. If this is the case, something other than race of officer must have been responsible for the greater killing rate in black areas (197.4) than in medium-crime areas (112.8) or "country-club" areas (72.7). The approximately equal killing rates of blacks by black, white, and Hispanic officers would support the view that the police are simply confronted with more hostility, resistance, crime, and provocation in black areas.

A study of police killings in Chicago found that black officers were 2.5 times as likely as white officers to shoot black civilians.[83] A survey of fifty-four U.S. cities indicated that 16 percent of all police officers who killed civilians were black, 58 percent were white, and 25 percent were unknown.[84] Though there are no data on the proportion of police officers in those cities who were black, it appears that white officers are no more likely to kill than black officers.

Summary

Five specific charges of racial discrimination are made against the police: (1) that police departments are guilty of racial discrimination in *deploying officers,* so that crimes committed disproportionately by blacks are the focus of police patrol and detection efforts; (2) that *arrest statistics* showing a racial gap in levels of offending reflect discrimination; (3) that individual police officers are guilty of racial discrimination against blacks *in making arrests,* so that encounters between the police and blacks are more likely to result in an arrest than are encounters between the police and whites; (4) that the police, because of racial discrimination, are more likely to engage in acts of *brutality* in encounters with blacks and are *less likely to discipline officers* who brutalize blacks; and (5) that the police, because of racial discrimination, are more likely to *use deadly force* against blacks than whites. For each of these charges the supporting evidence is sparse, inconsistent, and contradictory to the DT.

Notes

1. For examples of Charge No. 1 see Reiman, 1984, pp. 77–90; Peirson, 1977, p. 108; Box, 1981, pp. 167–171; Pepinsky and Jesilow, 1984, p. 81; Harries, 1984, p. 41; and Napper, 1977, p. 14.
2. For examples of Charge No. 2 see L. P. Brown, 1977, p. 87; Napper, 1977, pp. 10, 14; Sample and Philip, 1984, p. 27; Peirson, 1977, p. 108; and Pope, 1979, pp. 347*ff.*
3. For examples of Charge No. 3 see Peirson, 1977, p. 111; S. L. Johnson, 1983, pp. 214, 256; Hollinger, 1984, p. 173; L. P. Brown, 1977, pp. 79–104; and Karmen, 1984, p. 165.
4. For examples of Charge No. 4 see L. P. Brown, 1977, p. 89; Wilbanks and Lewis, 1981; Crockett, 1984, p. 202; and Wright, 1984a, p. 209.
5. For examples of Charge No. 5 see Takagi, 1974; Goldcamp, 1976; Peirson, 1977, p. 115; Wright, 1984a, p. 209; Center for Research on Criminal Justice, 1975; Geller, 1982; and Matulia, 1982.
6. Pepinsky and Jesilow, 1984, p. 81.
7. Mobley, 1982, p. 13.
8. For an analysis of race in self-reports and official crime statistics see Hindelang, Hirschi, and Weiss, 1981, pp. 157–180; and McNeely and Pope, 1981b, pp. 41–43.
9. Bell, 1983.
10. J. Q. Wilson, 1977, p. 52. But some argue that more police are assigned to black communities to protect whites who might stray into those areas. See Ostrom, 1983, p. 109.
11. H. Jones, 1981, pp. 45–55. The offending rates for blacks and East Indians in Guyana did vary sharply by type of offense, with blacks having higher rates for robbery and burglary and East Indians higher rates for violence without theft.
12. Hindelang et al., 1981, pp. 157–182.
13. Bell, 1983.
14. The Police Foundation funded the study evaluating FBI arrest figures. The study is summarized and reported in Sherman and Glick, 1984, and Burnham, 1984.
15. Blumstein and Graddy, 1982.
16. McNeely and Pope, 1981b, p. 42.
17. Hindelang et al., 1981, pp. 157–180.
18. Hindelang et al., 1981, p. 179.
19. Wilbanks, 1985a.
20. For the 1981 national victimization survey I calculated offense and victimization rates for the three crimes of robbery, rape, and assault for both blacks and whites. The black/white victimization rate ratio (gap) for the three combined

crimes was 1.3:1, and the black/white offending rate ratio was 3.1:1. The difference between the victimization and offense gaps was even more pronounced for robbery (2.4:1 to 10.2:1).

21. Hindelang, 1978, 1981. Hindelang examined those aged 12-17, 18-20, and 21 and over. A similar study, but only of juveniles, is Laub and McDermott, 1985. Though they focused on juveniles, they found racial gaps in offending (with perception of offender data in the NCS) that were similar to those found by Hindelang.

22. McNeely and Pope, 1981b. See also Georges-Abeyie, 1984c, p. 12.

23. Hollinger, 1984.

24. Hollinger, 1984, p. 180.

25. W. T. Johnson, Petersen, and Wells, 1977.

26. Smith and Visher, 1981.

27. See Smith and Visher, 1981, p. 172, for conclusion; see p. 176 for admission that additional and important controls were omitted.

28. Hepburn, 1978.

29. Hepburn, 1978, pp. 67-68.

30. Pope, 1978.

31. Smith and Visher, 1981, p. 172. It should be noted that this quotation refers to the authors' review of the literature. Their own study did find a race effect (see Note 26 above and corresponding text).

32. Reiss, 1971. Trained observers provided detailed descriptions of the behavior of patrol officers and citizens in more than 5,000 encounters. A separate analysis of juvenile encounters from this study is found in Black and Reiss, 1970.

33. Reiss, 1971, p. 135.

34. Claims that black police officers make a difference are made in Beard, 1977; Bannon and Wilt, 1973; Jacobs and Cohen, 1978; Campbell, 1980; Teahan, 1975a; "Black Police Officers," 1985; and "Blacks in Blue," 1985.

35. Smith and Klein, 1983.

36. L. P. Brown, 1977, p. 87. Also see the story told in S. L. Johnson (1983, pp. 256-258) of a black man stopped (and subsequently arrested) in a white neighborhood for pushing a wheelbarrow containing a television set. His lawyer, a white woman, did the same thing in the same neighborhood and was not stopped, though a police officer saw her.

37. Georges-Abeyie, 1984b, pp. 129-132, 142; Wright, 1984a, 1984b; Crockett, 1984.

38. Georges-Abeyie, 1984b, pp. 129-132, 142.

39. See National Advisory Commission on Civil Disorders, 1968; Porter and Dunn, 1984; and Justice, 1969.

40. Porter and Dunn, 1984, pp. 1-44, 181-200.

41. Reiss, 1980. See also Trojanowicz and Banas, 1985, p. 1.

42. See, for example, Chevigny, 1969. Cray (1972, p. 8) lists several sources of anthologies or anecdotes on brutality.

43. Reiss, 1980.

44. For example, see National Advisory Commission on Civil Disorders, 1968, pp. 299ff., and Porter and Dunn, 1984, pp. 21-46, 181-186.

45. See Stark, 1972, pp. 98-106, and Wesley, 1970, pp. 109-148.

46. See Webster's account (1982) of an NAACP project to curb police brutality. Also see Hinds, 1979, and Conyers, 1981.

47. L. P. Brown, 1977, p. 80. For a dissenting view from a black police chief see Dean, 1984.

48. L. P. Brown, 1977, p. 89.

49. This type of explanation is given in Toch, 1969.

50. This type of explanation is given in Wesley, 1970, pp. 124-133.
51. This type of explanation is given in Toch, 1969; Foster, 1974; and Kochman, 1981.
52. An example of this type of explanation is given in Remmington, 1981, pp. 43, 46.
53. Martin (1980, pp. 185-199) makes a distinction between *police*women and police*women*, with the former being more officer than woman and the latter being more woman than officer. Blacks who join the police force may choose to become either more officer than black or more black than officer. Some black police officers seem to identify more with the department than the black community (critics say they have been co-opted), and others seem to identify more with the black community than the department. Several writers see considerable role conflict and ambivalence among black officers as they try to decide whether they are officers first or blacks first. On this issue see Sealy, 1977; Alex, 1969; Beard, 1977; Campbell, 1980; Jacobs and Cohen, 1978; Dean, 1984; Sherman, 1980; Teahan, 1975b; and Martin, 1980, p. 67.
54. This approach was suggested by Geller, 1982.
55. Reiss, 1971, p. 147, and Reiss, 1980, p. 289.
56. Reiss, 1971, p. 147.
57. Reiss, 1980, p. 289.
58. Reiss, 1980, p. 288.
59. Dean, 1984.
60. Dean, 1984, p. 161.
61. See Foster, 1974, pp. 283*ff.*, and Martin, 1980, p. 158.
62. Reiss, 1980, p. 289. For other references to prejudicial beliefs of white officers see Wesley, 1970, pp. 99-109, and Martin, 1980, p. 146.
63. Martin, 1980, p. 146.
64. Reiss, 1980, p. 290.
65. See the discussion of the link between words and deeds in Nettler, 1984, p. 260.
66. Porter and Dunn, 1984, pp. 77, 84.
67. The quotation is from the *Miami Herald* series in December 1980 and is given in Wilbanks and Lewis (1981, p. 2).
68. Wilbanks and Lewis, 1981.
69. For sample statements from black leaders see those cited in Matulia, 1982, p. 58, and Fyfe, 1981, p. 367. Fyfe quotes one leader as having suggested that there is a "conspiracy of genocide against minority citizens." See also Hinds, 1979.
70. Quotation by Judge B. M. Wright of New York City in Wright, 1984a, p. 209.
71. The 60 percent figure is based on justifiable homicides by the police forwarded to the FBI. Unfortunately, Sherman and Langworthy (1979) maintain, the FBI figures are a 50 percent undercount of the actual number of police killings in the United States (based on a comparison of FBI figures with figures found by independent studies). Matulia (1982, p. 64) gives the percent figure from 1975 to 1979.
72. Goldcamp, 1976.
73. Fyfe, 1982a.
74. Fyfe, 1982a, p. 720.
75. Matulia, 1982, p. 81. See also Geller, 1982, pp. 162-163, for a review of the literature on internal and external "causes" of police shooting rates.
76. The list of community characteristics from various studies is taken from Geller, 1982, pp. 161-163, and Matulia, 1982, pp. 39-72. Matulia (1982, p. 56) found the following correlation coefficients for justifiable homicides by the police (across fifty-four cities): .88 with homicide in general, .68 with justifiable

homicides by civilians, .55 with police officers killed, .76 with robbery, .77
with violent crime, .83 with population, and .83 with number of police officers.

77. Matulia, 1982, p. 63.
78. Fyfe, 1982a, p. 720.
79. Fyfe, 1982a, pp. 709, 720–721.
80. Fyfe, 1981.
81. Fyfe, 1981, p. 371.
82. Fyfe, 1981, p. 376.
83. A study by Geller and Karales cited in Matulia, 1982, p. 71.
84. Matulia, 1982, p. 70.

6

Prosecution
and Racial Discrimination

Much has been written about the discretionary powers of police officers and judges, but there is little doubt that the criminal justice official with the greatest uncontrolled discretionary power is the prosecutor. This country's foremost authority on the abuse and control of discretion says:

> Viewed in broad perspective, the American legal system seems to be shot through with many excessive and uncontrolled discretionary powers but the one that stands out above all others is the power to prosecute or not to prosecute. The affirmative power to prosecute is enormous, but the negative power to withhold prosecution may be even greater, because it is less protected against abuse.[1]

The concern for possible abuse of discretion through racial discrimination at the point of prosecution is heightened by two additional factors. First, the exercise of discretion by the prosecutor is less visible than at other points in the system. Decisions to prosecute or not to prosecute, to charge one offense or another, to offer a plea bargain, and so on are made in private offices with almost no opportunity for review. Second, few blacks or other minority group members serve as assistant district attorneys, since this position is not considered attractive by aspiring black lawyers. Young black attorneys more often opt to serve as a public defender. Thus an almost totally white district attorney's staff in many large U.S. cities is making prosecutorial decisions about a largely black group of defendants. These two factors combine to create a suspicion in the black community about the fairness of prosecutorial decisions.

Decisions of prosecutors have been explained from at least three perspectives.[2] *Conflict theorists* maintain that prosecutors are guided by group and class interests and "throw the book" at less powerful segments of society while ignoring the crimes of the powerful. This perspective views blacks as being subjected to the "crime control" model of criminal justice and asserts that the "due process" model is reserved for whites.[3] The *interactionist perspective* sees the prosecutor as being guided by perceptions and stereotypes, with character assessment of the defendant largely determining decisions. The *organizational perspective* views the prosecutor as largely reacting to occupational pressures such as the need to pursue only "winnable" cases and the need to take into account the views of the police, the victim, the judge, and others. This view sees any personal bias of the prosecutor as being largely muted by organizational constraints and interactions with the defense attorney and others in the courtroom "workgroup."[4] Each of these perspectives considers race to be a possible influencing factor on the decisions of prosecutors.

At least six charges of racial discrimination have been made against those involved in the prosecution of criminal cases against black defendants. Each of these charges will be examined in turn, along with the rationale or evidence generally given to support it. I will then discuss criticisms of each claim that tend to refute it. The six charges are:

Charge No. 1—that the criminal prosecution process discriminates against blacks at the point of bail, so that they are more likely to be detained in jail awaiting trial, and that this detention results in a greater likelihood of conviction.[5]

Charge No. 2—that racial discrimination occurs at the point of charging, in that blacks are less likely to receive the benefit of deferred prosecution and are more likely to be charged with more serious offenses.[6]

Charge No. 3—that racial discrimination occurs because blacks are less likely to receive attractive plea-bargain offers from the prosecutor.[7]

Charge No. 4—that racial discrimination occurs in that blacks are less likely to have effective counsel, since they must rely largely on the public defender rather than a privately retained attorney.[8]

Charge No. 5—that racial discrimination occurs in the systematic exclusion of blacks from juries and the frequent conviction of blacks by all-white juries that are racially biased.[9]

Charge No. 6—that racial discrimination at the point of prosecution results in blacks' being more likely to be convicted than whites.[10]

Charge No. 1:
The Bail Decision Is Discriminatory

Many defendants have to await the disposition of their case, whether by plea bargain or trial, in jail. Some of those detained in jail are held for nonbailable offenses (such as capital crimes), but most are detained for failure to raise bail money. Since U.S. jails are disproportionately black—the black/white ratio, or gap, was 5.4:1 in 1978 for pretrial detention (see the Appendix)—it has been argued that the bail system discriminates against blacks, who are less likely to be able to raise the required amount. Furthermore, several studies have found that the simple fact of pretrial detention increases the likelihood of subsequent conviction, and thus the failure to raise bail has a cumulative impact on later decisions.[11]

One study maintained, for example, that "not making bail is a form of sentence"[12] and that race and occupation had an "indirect effect" on length of prison sentence through the inability to make bail.[13] A black judge, nicknamed by critics "Turn 'em Loose Bruce" for his tendency to release black defendants on their own recognizance or on low bail, suggests that there is a "subtle interaction between judgments reached on the basis of poverty and those reached on the basis of racial bias. . . . It is difficult to know when there is a basic discrimination against one because of his poverty or because of his race or because of both."[14]

Arguments against Charge No. 1

1. It would appear that the racial disparity found in pretrial detention is more a function of class than of racial discrimination. Blacks are detained more often than whites because they do not have the bail money, not because they are black. There is no evidence that poor blacks are detained more frequently than poor whites. The point is that black defendants are more likely to be poor and thus less likely to be able to post bail. To call this racial discrimination is to confuse class with race.

Some would argue that since blacks are poor because they are black (that is, because of racial discrimination in schooling, employment, and elsewhere), it is silly to think one can separate class from race. But it seems unfair to accuse the prosecutor and the courts of racial discrimination because of racial and economic discrimination that occurred before the detention hearing. Some authors argue that racial discrimination at this point is "indirect," in that it occurs through the class factor. But such reasoning opens up a Pandora's box, because any type of discrimination can be "proven" through "indirect" factors. There is some evidence, for example, that black defendants are less likely to be convicted, partly because of greater difficulties with witnesses in black-on-black cases.[15] If this is the case, whites are clearly discriminated against at the point of conviction, though indirectly, through the witness problem. But does it make any sense to call this *racial* discrimination?

2. Studies examining black and white pretrial detention rates have not found a direct correlation between race and whether bail was

made or the amount of bail. Three studies found no significant relationship between pretrial release (either on recognizance or by making bail) and race.[16] A fourth study found that black defendants were 13 percent less likely to be released than nonblacks after the introduction of control variables.[17] It should be noted, however, that unexplained variation after the introduction of controls is not equivalent to a race effect (see Chapter Four).

There is certainly no clear pattern of blacks' being released less often than whites for similar offenses. The best argument that can be made is that blacks are discriminated against indirectly, through socioeconomic status, in all jurisdictions and directly in some. Also, the expected indirect effect does not always materialize. One study found that a respectful demeanor increased the probability of receiving release on recognizance by 35 percent and a conventional appearance raised it by 23 percent.[18] And yet race was not strongly related to either conventional appearance or demeanor.

3. If one is convinced that the greater pretrial detention rates for black defendants constitute racial discrimination and thus that this result is evil, why not endorse Bell's proposal, which would place racial quotas at each point in the system?[19] In other words, the courts could be required to detain one white defendant for every black defendant detained (or at least to maintain equal release rates for blacks and whites). This would certainly remove the pretrial detention disparity by race. But obviously such "justice" would result in the release of some black defendants who were charged with serious crimes and in the detention of some white defendants who were charged with white collar offenses, which present less concern to the community. Unfortunately class is also related to type of crime; the poor (and thus blacks) are more likely to be charged with "street" crime, and the middle and upper classes are more likely to be charged with white collar crimes. Thus the elimination of racial discrimination would result in a new kind of discrimination, against white collar offenders.

Charge No. 2:
Racial Discrimination Occurs at Charging

It is sometimes claimed that blacks are charged with more serious offenses than whites in similar circumstances. Though little empirical evidence is generally cited, many blacks would agree with the black judge who said that "the charge most often leveled against a white male in a stolen car case is 'unauthorized use of a vehicle.' But, virtually all black males [are] charged with 'grand larceny, auto.'"[20]

It is important to note at this point that the literature is almost unanimous in reporting that charges against blacks are more likely to be dismissed before indictment.[21] The fact that blacks are actually more likely to have their cases dismissed before indictment is even interpreted by some as proof that blacks are often arrested on flimsy evidence.[22]

An empirical study by Radelet of murder indictments in twenty Florida counties did find evidence of racial discrimination in charging in that prosecutors were more likely to file first-degree murder charges against suspects in the killing of white victims than against suspects in the killing of black victims.[23] This study argued that racial discrimination in sentencing had been overlooked by many researchers because they had failed to test for the possibility that discrimination took place at an earlier stage—at the indictment. Thus this study found some confirmation of an old southern maxim: "When a white man kills a black man, that is justifiable homicide. When a black man kills a white man, that's murder. And when a black man kills another black man, that's just another dead nigger."[24]

Some have pointed to another prosecutorial decision—whether the defendant will be placed on a deferred prosecution program—as being a likely source of racial discrimination.[25] Such "diversion" programs are viewed by some critics as being an "out" for white defendants, who are considered more responsive to treatment.

Arguments against Charge No. 2

1. Much of the evidence cited to prove racial discrimination at the point when a charge is lodged by the prosecutor is anecdotal. Many who are predisposed to believe that such differential charging based on race exists, remember selectively and point out individual cases that illustrate this view. Likewise, those who think that racial discrimination at charging does not exist point out cases that demonstrate equality of charging. Unfortunately most of those who hold either view are ignorant of the little empirical evidence that does exist, and thus their views are based on ideology instead of facts.

2. There is little empirical research on the possibility of racial discrimination in charging except for studies of murder charges for which the death penalty was a possibility. Perhaps the best known such study is that by Radelet, who found that those who were accused of having killed whites in twenty Florida counties in 1976 and 1977 in nonprimary homicides (felony-related killings, as opposed to domestic killings) were more likely to be indicted for first-degree murder and thus placed at risk of ultimately receiving the death penalty.[26]

Unfortunately, Radelet did not control for any variable other than primary/nonprimary homicide and then attributed the remaining variance (see Chapter Four) to the effect of race. It is likely that further controls would have reduced the variation to near zero, since those studies that have controlled for the most variables have found little or no race effect. Kleck critiqued several studies that had examined the impact of the race of the victim and the offender on the sentence.[27] He found that only four studies had introduced controls for such variables as whether the homicide was victim precipitated, the prior record of the defendant, the type of counsel, and so on. These studies found no difference in sentence corresponding to the race of the victim or offender. Also, those reporting racial discrimination by race of victim seldom mentioned that, by their criteria, white defendants were discriminated against, since white defendants were more likely to be charged with first-degree murder.

3. There is some indication in the literature that whites are more likely to be charged with first-degree murder than are blacks. A study of all homicide cases in North Carolina in 1977 and 1978 found that whites were slightly more likely than blacks to be indicted for first-degree murder.[28] This study concluded that there was no consistent race effect at the point of indictment even after jurisdiction, strength of evidence, and so forth were controlled. The study discounted the influence of race of victim as an explanation for differences in indictment, since 90 percent of the homicides were intraracial and only 6 percent involved murders of whites by blacks. There is also evidence that the execution risk for whites outside of the South is actually greater than that for blacks.[29] And yet no one has suggested that this disparity is evidence of racial discrimination against whites.

4. There is also little evidence that more serious charges are lodged against black defendants than whites in non-death penalty felony cases. The Appendix indicates that there was little racial difference in Pennsylvania in 1980 in whether a case initially prosecuted as a felony was reduced to a misdemeanor. Table 9 indicates that 96.7 percent of black defendants did not have their charges reduced to a misdemeanor, compared with 95.5 percent of white defendants. It does appear, however, that blacks are more likely than whites (57.1 percent to 36.6 percent) to be convicted of two or more offenses. But in the absence of controls it would be inappropriate to conclude that such a difference had occurred in spite of "other things being equal." Likewise, Table 8 shows that in 1980 blacks in California were more likely than whites (73.2 percent to 62.8 percent) to be convicted as a felon (rather than as a misdemeanant after being prosecuted as a felon). But again no conclusions with respect to racial discrimination can be drawn in the absence of controls.

5. Though little research has been done on deferred prosecution, the two studies found in the literature failed to find a significant relationship between race and referral to a prosecutorial diversion program

when control variables (for example, prior record, whether defendant used violence, whether defendant was charged with more than one offense) were introduced.[30]

Charge No. 3:
Plea Bargaining Is Discriminatory

You may be surprised to learn that plea bargaining is a rather recent development, having been virtually unknown in the United States until the late 1800s.[31] Criminal trials up to the twentieth century rarely lasted more than one day (in fact, several cases were generally tried in one day), and there was usually no defense attorney or professional prosecutor to engage in lengthy adversarial proceedings. The plea bargain developed when the trial process became longer and more "professionalized," necessitating some means to avoid trials in all cases.

It has been suggested that blacks may be offered less attractive plea bargains than whites, because

> blacks are less able than whites to make bail and are more likely to have court-appointed lawyers. Research has shown that under those circumstances defendants are more likely to be convicted and to get harsher sentences. Apparently, both circumstances result in weaker cases for the defendant. In this situation, prosecutors may simply not be interested in plea bargaining. ... It is also possible that unless a minority defendant is represented by a sophisticated attorney, the prosecutor will not regard him as a candidate for plea bargaining.[32]

Another writer suggests that prosecutors may see the black defendant as more dangerous and likely to recidivate and thus less qualified for the lesser term inherent in a plea bargain.[33]

Arguments against Charge No. 3

1. Unfortunately, research on race of defendant and plea bargaining has been almost nonexistent. The only study in the literature dealing directly with the attractiveness issue found no significant difference between blacks and whites with respect to whether a plea bargain had been offered or to the value or attractiveness of the plea bargain offered.[34] Another study is in progress in California.[35] Both of these were observational and interview studies of cases proceeding through a prosecutor's office. Those involved in research at this decision point seem to agree with those critics who argue that "variable analysis" (calculating the numerical relationship of numerous independent variables with a dependent variable) is inappropriate for the analysis of such a complex decision.[36] Plea bargaining decisions depend largely on

the prosecutor's evaluation of the "real self or character" and whether that perceived attribute is consistent with the criminal act charged.[37]

The most extensive observational study of the plea bargaining process was done by Maynard, who found that race of defendant was "used" as information both as an aggravating and mitigating factor in the plea negotiation process, depending on the "context" of the case.[38] Maynard argues that race is considered in the "character assessment" process when the prosecutor decides if the crime charged is consistent with "this kind of person" (that is, consistent with the prosecutor's character assessment). Thus a black defendant may be offered a better plea if he or she is perceived as being less responsible (a type of racial discrimination via leniency based on a racial stereotype).

2. Several factors would seem to increase the probability of blacks' pleading guilty, and others would seem to decrease the probability. There may be little difference in the offering and accepting of plea bargains because these factors cancel out. Among those factors that would appear to increase the probability of blacks' pleading guilty are (1) being held in jail in pretrial detention and thus under pressure to plead to get out; (2) having a public defender, who might be more likely to suggest a plea of guilty rather than demanding a trial; and (3) knowing from others who have gone through the system that punishment is certain to be more severe, especially for blacks, who refuse to admit guilt.

Factors that would appear to decrease the probability of blacks' accepting a plea would be (1) greater distrust for the system, especially any "good" deal suggested by a public defender paid for by the state; (2) knowledge that black witnesses may be less likely to cooperate with the prosecutor; and (3) knowing others who "beat the system" by going to trial. Since many of the factors that determine whether a plea bargain is "attractive" from the perspective of the prosecutor and defendant are highly subjective and difficult to measure, it appears that this issue will remain unresolved. Opinions about whether blacks are given "equal deals" will continue to be based on bias rather than empirical research. This stems partly from the fact that "neutral" researchers would tend to rate the attractiveness of "deals" offered to defendants without respect to the (perhaps contrasting) perceptions of attractiveness on the part of black and white defendants. Or the attractiveness of bargains would be inferred from whether the offer was accepted.

3. The focus on the role of racial discrimination in getting a good "bargain" or "deal" from the prosecutor in exchange for a plea assumes that the benefits from such bargains are very important in determining the sentence. There is some evidence, however, suggesting that the benefits of the plea bargain may be an illusion or part of a "con game" in which the prosecutor gives up little (in terms of severity of sentence)

in exchange for the plea of guilty. One article that reached this conclusion was entitled "A Plea Is No Bargain."[39]

Charge No. 4:
Discrimination Occurs in Providing Legal Counsel

Several authors have suggested that racial discrimination may occur indirectly through the less effective legal counsel (public defenders) that blacks and other poor people are forced to accept.[40] The reasoning seems to be that blacks are more likely to use public defenders, who in turn are less effective in winning acquittal or a lenient sentence. Thus blacks are viewed as likely to be convicted more often and sentenced more severely.

Arguments against Charge No. 4

1. Though one might expect a strong relationship between type of counsel and race of defendant, this is not necessarily the case. In an unpublished study I found that for all 1980 felony cases in Pennsylvania, blacks and whites were equally likely to be represented by a public defender (48 percent for both races).[41] Thus it is likely that the percentages of black defendants and white defendants being represented by the public defender are much more similar than most people in and out of the criminal justice system believe.

2. Perceptions of the relative effectiveness of public defenders and private lawyers may also be inaccurate. My study of the outcome of cases involving public counsel and private counsel found very small differences at the various decision points examined.[42] In some cases the differences did not bear out the view that private attorneys are more effective. Defendants represented by private attorneys were less likely to be convicted than those represented by public attorneys (48 percent to 59 percent), for example, but they were more likely to be sentenced to prison (14 percent to 13 percent). There was certainly no indication of a systematic positive effect for private lawyers across the Pennsylvania criminal justice system. Some studies have found that court-appointed attorneys are less effective than private attorneys.[43] But the precise relationship between race of defendant and type of attorney has generally not been examined in these studies, and thus the syllogism commonly heard (race leads to a public defender, which leads to more negative outcomes) has not been tested.

3. Even if the assignment of a public defender proves to be an assignment to the "prison track" of assembly line justice,[44] a race effect has not necessarily been established. Class discrimination is very different from racial discrimination. It may well be that poor black and poor

white defendants are more likely to receive negative outcomes through ineffective public counsel, but this does not constitute racial discrimination.

Charge No. 5:
Jury Selection Is Discriminatory

The most commonly lodged charge of racial discrimination against prosecutors involves the exclusion of blacks from juries in cases involving black defendants and the subsequent verdicts of these all-white juries.[45] Historically there is no question that blacks have been underrepresented as jurors in American criminal courts. In fact blacks were excluded by law in many states in earlier periods and by practice in many southern states until the 1960s. All those who have seen a movie such as *To Kill a Mockingbird* have seen the pernicious effect of the exclusion of blacks from a jury that decides a case of a black defendant accused of a crime against a white. It is argued that the exclusion process is more subtle today but just as effective.

Thus the argument is that by the peremptory challenge and the challenge for cause prosecutors exclude blacks from juries and that the resulting all-white juries are more prone to convict black defendants, especially if a white person is the victim. The evidence for the racial exclusion of blacks from juries and for the impact of this exclusion on the dispositions of black defendants is rather scant with respect to data on "real" juries. However, there are numerous studies of mock juries and the extent to which race affects their decision making. In one simulation, "jurors" who were told that a black defendant had raped a white, rather than a black, woman were more likely to convict.[46]

Those who accuse the criminal justice system of racial discrimination in jury selection and jury decisions often point out specific cases in which all-white juries failed to convict whites accused of having killed blacks or convicted blacks accused of having killed whites. One of the most commonly cited cases is the McDuffie trial in Florida, in which several white policemen were tried and acquitted by an all-white jury of the killing of a black motorcyclist. This acquittal set off the 1980 riot in Miami.[47]

Arguments against Charge No. 5

1. Those who criticize the exclusion of blacks from juries assert that blacks are excluded because they are black (that is, because of racial prejudice) and because they are more likely to sympathize with a black defendant. Prosecutors are likely to counter that they attempt to exclude anyone whom they deem to be "prodefense" and that blacks are

more likely to be biased for the defense and to be skeptical of "the system," which includes state prosecutors.[48] They argue that they see most blacks as being likely to be biased against the prosecution whatever the race of the defendant or the victim may be.

The implicit suggestion behind this argument is that blacks are often excluded because they are racially prejudiced (for a black defendant and against a white victim). Since blacks generally believe the criminal justice system to be racist, if chosen to serve on a jury they may take the attitude "Show me that this is not another case of the white system picking on and discriminating against a black defendant." In summary, prosecutors are suggesting that they often attempt to exclude blacks from the jury because of prejudice *by* blacks and not because of their own prejudice.

2. Perhaps an example will illustrate the complexities involved in the exclusion of certain subgroups of the general population as jurors. Suppose that a white police officer were on trial for beating a white citizen. The prosecution would doubtless attempt to exclude any former police officers, or even relatives of current officers, as jurors, since it would be assumed that they would be biased for the police officer on trial. It would be assumed that such jurors would share the perspective of the officer on trial in that they would tend to see that officer as part of the "in-group" and thus excuse or explain away any apparent misbehavior as noncharacteristic of the officer or at least "understandable under the circumstances." It might also be pointed out that such jurors could come under considerable pressure from the police subculture to decide the case the "right way."

Most blacks would agree with the above assessment about the bias of former police officers or their relatives and agree that they would be prodefense in this case. But why is such a view not "blue racism," in that it is being suggested that a particular subgroup of the population be excluded as potential jurors precisely because they are likely to identify with and empathize with the defendant, a police officer? Doesn't such an exclusion deny the police officer a jury of his peers? Doesn't it attempt to exclude precisely those people who are most likely to understand the considerable pressures of police work and how apparent misbehavior might be "reasonable" from this perspective? And how is the exclusion of police officers in such a case any different from the exclusion of blacks as jurors in "racially sensitive" cases?

I would agree with prosecutors who try to exclude any *individual* for bias against the state. I would not agree that *all* people in a particular subgroup (whether blacks or former police officers) should be excluded because of the assumption that bias exists. There are former officers who would be quite tough on a defendant who had "shamed the department" by an act of brutality; after all, the former officer knows that the police can resist such pressures to retaliate against citizens.

Likewise, some blacks are likely to be tough on blacks and whites alike who commit crimes, since they have been victimized themselves and see no excuse for such behavior; that is, they have faced the same discriminatory environment but have not turned to crime. In fact blacks may be even tougher in cases involving black-on-black crime, since they may view such crimes as being particularly inexcusable and may view past leniency by the system as having encouraged such intraracial crime.[49]

In reality neither the prosecution nor the defense wants a "fair" jury. Each wants a jury that is biased toward "its side." Unfortunately this is the essence of the adversary model of criminal justice.

3. In some cases the defense strikes all or most black jurors. In the 1980 case in Florida the defense successfully struck all blacks from the jury pool. Defense attorneys in such cases, some with a strong liberal reputation, routinely attempt to exclude blacks from the jury, since black jurors are presumed to be prejudiced against white officers and prejudiced for the dead black victim. In fact, most attorneys would agree that failure to attempt to exclude blacks as jurors in such cases would represent a dereliction of duty. If such a practice does not represent racial discrimination when practiced by the defense, why does the same reasoning not apply when it is practiced by the prosecution? Why is the defense perceived as "just doing its job" and the prosecution as exercising racial discrimination? It would appear that when the defense attempts such exclusions, its actions are viewed by many as a "recognition of reality" (that blacks are likely to be biased against their white client), whereas similar efforts on the part of the prosecution are seen as simple racial prejudice.

4. Another way to determine if racial prejudice is the basis for the more frequent exclusion of blacks as potential jurors in interracial cases is to examine the practice of black attorneys. Suppose that a black attorney were hired by a white police officer to defend against the charge of having beaten a black man. Certainly this choice would be strategic, in that it would be similar to an accused rapist's choosing a female defense attorney to suggest to the jury that "she wouldn't represent him if she thought he were guilty." Would the black attorney attempt to exclude most or all blacks from the jury? No doubt he or she would, as the best way of representing the defendant. Would this attempt at exclusion be motivated by racial prejudice? If not, why would a similar attempt by a white attorney?

By the same token, would a black prosecutor attempt to exclude most or all blacks from a case involving a black man accused of having killed a white victim? An effective prosecutor would attempt to get the "best" (biased in his or her favor) jury possible, and this would be a jury with no blacks unless those blacks were seen as proprosecution (for example, a middle-aged, conservative, black woman who had been a victim herself and who saw crime as the greatest problem in the black community). Would this attempt to exclude most blacks from the jury pool be based on racial prejudice? I doubt if anyone would make such a charge. Then why is not the same benefit of the doubt given to white prosecutors?

5. When all-white juries return a verdict that is viewed as going against blacks, either when the victim is black, such as in the McDuffie case, or when the defendant is black, it is often assumed that the decision is based on racial prejudice. After all, what else can one expect from an all-white jury but racial prejudice and discrimination? But it may be that the "fact" of a racially biased verdict is actually a "perception" based on prejudice. For example, the McDuffie verdict is often pointed to as an example of a prejudiced verdict by an all-white jury, and in fact that perception touched off a riot in Miami. And yet a black co-author of a book analyzing that verdict and the subsequent riot has said that the verdict was correct given the contradictory evidence presented to the jury.[50] In fact he has argued that if the members of the jury had all been black and "card-carrying members of the NAACP," they would have returned the same verdict (acquittal) *if* they had decided the case on the evidence presented.[51] Of course such jurors would have been excluded by the defense precisely because of the belief that the decision would not have been based on "just the facts" or the evidence presented.

In other words it is common for racial prejudice to be assumed if the verdict is handed down by an all-white jury in a "racially sensitive" case. And yet such an assumption might be viewed as an example of racial prejudice in that the all-white jury is assumed to be biased and prejudiced, whereas blacks on the jury would attempt to be fair and would be free from racial bias.

In line with the "two-sided" definition of racism given in Chapter Two, it is not surprising to find examples of racial discrimination in jury verdicts handed down by predominantly black juries. In some jurisdictions, such as Washington, D.C., it is quite common to have all-black or predominantly black juries trying cases involving white defendants or white victims. As discussed in Chapter Two, for example, a recent book asserts that a predominantly black jury acquitted a black man who was accused of having raped a white woman because the members felt some sense of (racial) loyalty to the black defendant.[52] Prosecutors in Washington have found it difficult to convict blacks charged with crimes against whites when the jury is largely black. Does this reluctance to convict in such cases by black juries constitute racism?

The appearance of racism by all-white juries is a serious problem and should be remedied by the type of reform recently mandated by the Florida Supreme Court. The court ruled in 1984 that the burden of proof is on the party, whether prosecution or defense, that excludes all members of any race to show why such does not constitute racial discrimination.[53] The judge, if not satisfied with the response, can begin the jury selection process again. This rule applies even if the defendant and victim are both white or Hispanic.[54]

6. There is some empirical evidence that the racial composition of juries is correlated with jury verdicts. For example, a study of racial composition and jury verdicts in Dade County, Florida, in 1984 found that biracial juries (those with at least one black) were more likely than all-white juries to find white defendants guilty (73 percent to 56 percent) and less likely to find black defendants guilty (51 percent to 79 percent).[55] Thus one might argue that biracial juries are biased for black and against white defendants and that all-white juries are biased for white and against black defendants. In other terms, biracial juries were more likely to convict white than black defendants (73 percent to 51 percent), and all-white juries were more likely to convict black than white defendants (79 percent to 56 percent). It should be added that the bivariate relationship between racial composition of jury and outcome does not necessarily mean that race of jurors "causes" the outcome.

The kinds of cases heard by biracial juries may be different from those heard by all-white juries. All that can be said is that race appears (without controls) to be a factor in verdicts. Thus there is some substance to the commonly held view that all-white juries decide cases differently from biracial juries. But since we do not know what verdict is "correct," one could just as easily argue that biracial verdicts rather than all-white jury verdicts are the result of racial discrimination. And if one argues that all-white jury verdicts discriminate against blacks, one could also argue that biracial jury verdicts discriminate against whites.

7. If one agrees that racial discrimination is so pervasive that all-white juries are inherently discriminatory, then one should agree with Bell[56] and Banks[57] that there should be a mandatory inclusion of blacks on all juries. It is unlikely, however, that much public support could be generated for any type of quota system in juries. And if quotas were used, would the fair representation refer to the race (and sex, age, social class) of the defendant or the victim? Or perhaps the jury should represent the community regardless of the characteristics of the defendant and victim.

Charge No. 6:
Conviction Rates Show Discrimination

Some critics of the criminal justice system believe that racism is so pervasive in the system that blacks receive more severe dispositions at every decision point, including conviction. Some authors contend that conviction rates are higher for blacks than whites; they either cite a study that "proves" their point or cite no studies in support of the claim.[58] Most critics, however, concede that conviction rates are lower for blacks but assert that this apparent leniency actually represents discrimination at arrest; that is, blacks are more often arrested on flimsy evidence.[59]

Arguments against Charge No. 6

1. The overwhelming consensus of recent studies (obviously, conviction rates may have been higher for blacks in earlier periods) has been that blacks are less likely to be convicted than whites. The fact that critics would suggest otherwise is indicative of an ignorance of the available data and a bias that suggests that this "fact" must be true, since racial discrimination exists and must influence convictions. When one critic says that there is a "strong suspicion" that conviction rates for blacks are much higher than for whites, he manifests that bias in the absence of empirical data.[60] It is likely that black laypersons would maintain that blacks are more likely to be convicted, given discrimination throughout the trial process. Yet the empirical evidence indicates otherwise.

2. You are referred at this point to the Appendix, which presents figures indicating the likelihood of conviction for blacks and whites in California and Pennsylvania for 1980. In California (Table 8) whites were more likely than blacks (76 percent to 72 percent) to be convicted, but in Pennsylvania (Table 9) the opposite result was obtained (50 percent of blacks were convicted, compared with 46.1 percent of whites). If the California results indicate that blacks were convicted less often than whites because they were more prone to arrest on flimsy charges, what do the opposite results in Pennsylvania indicate? Why don't critics suggest that these latter results indicate that whites must be arrested more often on flimsy charges? Furthermore, if these results indicate racial discrimination against blacks, consistency would demand that it also be argued that sex discrimination is greater at the point of prosecution than racial discrimination, since the disparity with respect to conviction is greater for sex (46.7 percent for males to 33 percent for females) than race (50 percent to 46.1 percent).

Others have reported on the greater likelihood of conviction for whites than blacks.[61] One study of three states found that blacks were favored at the "front end of the system" (charge, conviction), though the opposite resulted at the "back end" of the system (sentencing, time served).[62] Another study went beyond the mere reporting of greater white conviction rates and found that this disparity was largely due to a different mix of offenses for the two races (that is, the difference disappeared when type of offense was controlled).[63] The conclusions of two studies on the adjudication process indicate the failure to find a race effect:

Race appears to have little detectable effect upon disposition; and even that effect tends to be the reverse of what might be expected under the presumption of discriminatory treatment of nonwhites. When type of offense is not controlled, it appears that nonwhites are more likely than whites to have their cases dismissed, etc., and somewhat less likely to have judgment withheld. But even these effects disappear when type of offense is controlled, leaving us with the finding that race has no independent effect upon case dispositions. . . . Nevertheless, even this limited exploration demonstrates that assertions of such bias in the legal system require better evidence than has so far been offered in their support.[64]

The emphasis that interactionists place on the role of the deviants' social attributes in explaining variation in societal reactions seems very much overstated. Our finding that age, education, employment stability, marital status and race have no effects on the first two societal reaction decisions (whether prosecutor drops the case and whether convicted) and only small effects on the third societal reaction decision (severity of sentence), suggests that the theoretical focus requires considerable shifting.[65]

Summary

Six charges of racial discrimination involving the prosecutor are made: (1) that the criminal prosecution process discriminates against blacks at the point of bail, so that blacks are more likely to be detained in jail awaiting trial, and that this detention results in a greater likelihood of conviction; (2) that racial discrimination occurs at the point of *charging*; (3) that racial discrimination occurs in that blacks are less likely to receive *attractive plea bargain offers*; (4) that racial discrimination occurs in that blacks are less likely to have *effective counsel*, since they must rely largely on the public defender rather than privately retained counsel; (5) that racial discrimination occurs in the trial process in that blacks are often *systematically excluded from juries* and that black defendants are often *convicted by all-white juries* that are racially biased; and (6) that racial discrimination results in blacks' being more likely to be *convicted* than whites. The evidence for each of these six claims is sparse, inconsistent, or even contradictory.

Notes

1. K. C. Davis, 1977, p. 188.
2. For a full explanation of the three models and literature supporting each, see Hagan, 1975b, pp. 620–623, and Maynard, 1984, pp. 140–141.
3. Hepburn, 1978, p. 55.
4. For an elaboration of this viewpoint see Eisenstein and Jacob, 1977, pp. 9–11.
5. For a review of the prior literature on racial discrimination at the bail decision see Lizotte, 1978, p. 565; Frazier, Bock, and Henretta, 1980, pp. 162–166; and Bynum, 1982, pp. 67–68. For specific charges of racial discrimination at this point see Bell, 1983, p. 20, and Wright, 1984a, p. 213.

6. For a review of the prior literature on racial discrimination at the point of charge see Center for the Study of Race, Crime and Social Policy, 1983, and Bernstein, Kelly, and Doyle, 1977, pp. 743-745. For specific examples of racial discrimination at this point see Wright, 1984a, p. 209.

7. For a review of the literature on racial discrimination at the point where it is decided whether a plea is to be offered see Horney, 1980; Center for the Study of Race, 1983; Petersilia, 1983, pp. 27-32; and Maynard, 1982, pp. 347-350.

8. For a review of the literature on racial discrimination and type of attorney see Lizotte, 1978, and Wheeler and Wheeler, 1980, pp. 319-323. For specific charges of racial discrimination at this point see Bell, 1983, p. 20.

9. For a review of the literature on racial discrimination and the racial composition of juries see Benokraitis, 1982; Benokraitis and Griffin-Keene, 1982; Denno, 1981; Jorgenson, 1984; and Mar, 1981. For specific charges of racial discrimination in jury selection see Denno, 1981; Porter and Dunn, 1984, p. 198; and Potash, 1973.

10. For a review of the literature on racial discrimination and conviction see Petersilia, 1983; Burke and Turk, 1975; and Bernstein et al., 1977. For specific charges of racial discrimination in conviction rates see Hepburn, 1978; Bell, 1983; and Peirson, 1977, p. 110.

11. For a review of the literature indicating that pretrial detention status subsequently affects disposition and sentence see Wheeler and Wheeler, 1980, and Lizotte, 1978.

12. Lizotte, 1978, p. 565.

13. Lizotte, 1978, p. 573. This study used path analysis to discern indirect race effects.

14. Quotation is from Judge Bruce McM. Wright in Wright, 1984a, p. 214.

15. Petersilia, 1983, p. ix.

16. Frazier et al., 1980, p. 172; Lizotte, 1978, p. 570; F. P. Williams, 1981b.

17. Bynum, 1982, p. 77.

18. Frazier et al., 1980, pp. 171-172.

19. Bell, 1983. See the discussion in Chapter Two on Bell's proposal for quotas.

20. Wright, 1984a, p. 209.

21. For a review of these studies see Hardy, 1983, p. 187. The lone exception is a study by Eisenstein and Jacob, 1977.

22. Hepburn, 1978.

23. Radelet, 1981.

24. Quotation by L. P. Brown, 1977, p. 86.

25. See Hagan, Hewitt, and Alwin, 1979.

26. Radelet, 1981. Paternoster (1983, p. 767) makes a similar charge. Though controlling for no other variables he concludes that racial discrimination is present in "death requests" of prosecutors. But he does not explain why his data also show that whites who kill blacks are more likely to be subjected to a death request by the prosecutor than whites who kill other whites.

27. Kleck, 1981.

28. Hardy, 1983, p. 197.

29. Kleck, 1981, p. 794.

30. Friday, Malzahn-Bass, and Harrington, 1981, p. 169; Hagan et al., 1979.

31. On the history of plea bargaining see Langbein, 1979. An entire issue of *Law and Society Review* (1979, *13*[2]) is devoted to plea bargaining; it contains two other articles on the history of this practice.

32. Petersilia, 1983, p. 95. See also p. 101.

33. Horney (1980, p. 8) did find that prosecutors in eighty-nine cases in one midwestern county did see black defendants as being more likely to recidivate. She found that on a 100-point scale of "likelihood of future felony" nonwhites

received an average rating of 60, compared with 46 for whites. Petersilia (1983, pp. 98–101) and Blumstein and Graddy (1982) have found, however, that recidivism rates for blacks and whites are approximately equal. Though blacks as a group have a higher prevalence rate than whites, there is no evidence that those who do offend are more likely than whites to recidivate.

34. Horney, 1980, p. 6. See note above.
35. Center for the Study of Race, 1983.
36. Maynard, 1982.
37. For a discussion of this process see Maynard, 1982, p. 356.
38. Maynard, 1984.
39. Uhlman, 1979b. See also Hagan, 1975a, and Rhodes, 1977.
40. For reviews of the literature on the impact of race on sentence through type of counsel see Wheeler and Wheeler, 1980; Spohn, Gruhl, and Welch, 1981–1982; Unnever, 1982; Clarke and Koch, 1976; Chiricos and Waldo, 1975; and Bowers, 1983, p. 1072.
41. Wilbanks, 1985d.
42. Wilbanks, 1985d.
43. See, for example, Wheeler and Wheeler, 1980, and Lizotte, 1978. Swigert and Farrell (1980) suggest that blacks are not able to secure trial delays as readily as whites as a result of their reliance on public defenders and their detention in jail.
44. Terms utilized by Wheeler and Wheeler, 1980, p. 331.
45. See McNeely and Pope, 1981b, and Wasserman and Robinson, 1980.
46. For a review of such jury simulations see McNeely and Pope, 1981b, pp. 37–38. See also Feild, 1979, and Ugwuegbu, 1979. The simulation study mentioned as an example in the text is from Miller and Hewitt, 1978.
47. See Porter and Dunn, 1984, pp. 198–199.
48. McGonigle and Timms (1986) give several examples of the view of prosecutors that blacks are biased in favor of defendants or blacks and against the police and the criminal justice system. " 'I think that hurts the judicial system because then they're not concentrating on the fact that Johnny is a no-good scum-bag who beat up this old lady, stole her purse, put her in the hospital and nearly killed her. . . . They're concentrating on the fact that, 'well, it's racist.' " (March 9, p. 28A). These authors also quote prosecutors as saying that they don't want blacks as jurors because " 'they don't want that racial sympathy' " (March 9, p. 29A). They add: "Many minorities in the state, because of past oppression, might look at a police officer's testimony 'with a great deal of chagrin' because either they know someone or have themselves seen 'some officer bending the truth.' Those minorities would not be good jurors . . . because of the possibility of residual hostility toward law enforcement figures— not because of their race. . . . Blacks seem to have had . . . more than their share of run-ins with the law and as a result they view the legal system with a little more jaundiced eye" (March 9, p. 29A). Finally, these authors say that prosecutors want " 'someone that's going to give the facts and the law a fair shake,' and memories of past negative experiences with law enforcement could affect a potential juror's objectivity" (March 10, p. 10A).

   McGonigle and Timms also write that the stereotype of defense-prone blacks is often incorrect. They present a poll showing that two-thirds of blacks actually identify with the system and may be likely to be harsh on black defendants whom they see as bringing shame to their race and causing the high crime rate where they live (March 9, p. 29A).
49. Foley and Chamblin, 1982. See also Rossi, Simpson, and Miller, 1985, pp. 76, 80.
50. Marvin Dunn of Porter and Dunn, 1984.

51. Quotation from Marvin Dunn in my class at Florida International University (where Dunn and I are on the faculty) in March 1985.
52. Pekkanen, 1977. See the complete discussion of this case, with accompanying page citations, in Chapter Two. One jury simulation study (Ugwuegbu, 1979) found that black jurors were as biased as white jurors. Both black and white jurors were more likely to give the benefit of the doubt to defendants of their own race when the evidence was marginal. However, black jurors, but not white jurors, were more likely to favor a defendant of their own race even in the "strong evidence condition" (pp. 143-144).
53. *Neil* v. *Florida,* 1983.
54. Hampton, 1985.
55. Study by the Dade County Circuit Court research division, headed by Dr. David McGriff. The study is unpublished but is summarized in Freedberg, 1984b.
56. Bell, 1983.
57. Banks, 1975.
58. Bell, 1983, p. 20; Peirson, 1977, p. 110; Karmen, 1984, p. 165.
59. Hepburn, 1978; Dehais, 1983; Petersilia, 1983, pp. 19, 26. Chiricos, Jackson, and Waldo (1972) found racial discrimination in the withholding of adjudication.
60. Quotation from Peirson, 1977, p. 110.
61. See the literature review and data from Los Angeles County in 1980 in Petersilia, 1983, pp. 27, 32. Petersilia (p. 19) adds that no study has found a relationship between race and conviction.
62. Petersilia, 1983.
63. Burke and Turk, 1975. This was a study of 1,213 felony cases in New York State. Also see the variation in conviction probabilities for blacks and whites for different offenses in California and Pennsylvania in Tables 5 and 6 of the Appendix of this book.
64. Burke and Turk, 1975, pp. 328-329. It should be noted that Turk is a conflict theorist, and thus this "admission" takes on additional significance.
65. Bernstein et al., 1977, p. 754.

7

Sentencing and Racial Discrimination

There are more empirical studies on discrimination at sentencing than at any other decision point in the criminal justice system. The reason does not appear to be that researchers view judges as those in the system who are most likely to discriminate (most would make that charge against the police); rather, data are more readily available at this point for statistical analysis. Furthermore, sentencing is a popular subject because the judge makes decisions that can result in lengthy prison terms or even death.

About seventy studies examining the impact of race of defendant or race of victim on sentencing had been published by 1985. In addition there had been numerous reviews of the sentencing literature by textbook writers and others seeking to summarize this large body of research. The Bibliography of this book lists over eighty citations with the designation "S" (indicating that sentencing is a topic of research or comment). Many of the empirical studies are on a rather small scale, such as the 474 burglary and robbery sentences for El Paso, Texas, and Tucson, Arizona, in 1976–1977.[1] Others are on a much wider scale; the Appendix of this book examines more than 65,000 felony sentences handed down in California criminal courts in 1980. The research methods vary widely, as do the conclusions reached by the researchers.

Three Major Reviews of the Literature

Three major reviews of the literature in recent years have summarized and critiqued "what we know" about the impact of race on criminal sentencing. The first was in 1974 by Hagan, who reviewed twenty published studies.[2] In 1981 Kleck reviewed fifty-seven studies.[3] And the National Research Council reviewed more than sixty studies in 1983.[4]

Hagan computed a measure of association for seventeen of the studies that he had reviewed and found that (before controls) knowledge of race of offender improved accuracy in predicting the sentence by a maximum of only 8 percent. (Several of them improved predictive ability by less than 1 percent, though the results were statistically significant.) Hagan concluded that the researchers' failure to calculate measures of association and reliance only on tests of statistical significance had left the incorrect impression that race was an important predictor of sentence. Furthermore, those studies that had controlled for type of offense and prior record found that the small relationship between race and sentence was reduced to statistical insignificance.

Hagan found similarly low measures of association in studies of capital sentencing. Even before controlling for type of offense the median measure of association was only .015, indicating that knowing the race of the offender in capital cases increased the accuracy of predicting sentence by only 1.5 percent. Hagan also compared intraracial with interracial cases but found that knowing the race of defendants and victims was important only in capital rape cases in the South (increasing prediction of outcome by 22.6 percent, before controls). He summarized his review with respect to race in the following words:

> Evidence of differential sentencing was found in inter-racial *capital cases* in the southern United States. In samples of *noncapital cases*, however, when offense type was held constant among offenders with no prior record, the relationship between race and disposition was diminished below statistical significance. Holding offense type constant, among offenders with "some" previous convictions, a modest, statistically significant relationship between race and disposition was sustained in two of three studies. The need for stricter control over the *number* of previous convictions was indicated.[5]

Kleck reviewed seventeen studies of the imposition of the death penalty and forty studies of noncapital sentencing. He summarizes his conclusions as follows:

1. The death penalty has not generally been imposed for murder in a fashion discriminatory toward blacks, except in the South. Elsewhere, black homicide offenders have been less likely to receive a death sentence or be executed than whites.
2. For the 11 percent of executions which have been imposed for rape, discrimination against black defendants who had raped white victims was substantial. Such discrimination was limited to the South and has disappeared because death sentences are no longer imposed for rape.
3. Regarding noncapital sentencing, the evidence is largely contrary to a hypothesis of general or widespread overt discrimination against black defendants, although there is evidence of discrimination for a minority of specific jurisdictions, judges, crime types, etc.
4. Although black offender–white victim crimes are generally punished more severely than crimes involving other racial combinations, the evidence indicates that this is due to legally relevant factors related to such offenses, not the racial combination itself.
5. There appears to be a general pattern of less severe punishment of crimes with black victims than those with white victims, especially

in connection with imposition of the death penalty. In connection with noncapital sentencing, the evidence is too sparse to draw any firm conclusions.[6]

The third major review of the empirical literature on impact of race on sentencing is by the Panel on Sentencing Research, which was established by the National Academy of Sciences on request of the U.S. Department of Justice. The panel itself drew some conclusions and also reported the conclusions of consultants.[7] After reviewing over seventy sentencing studies it concluded:

> Our overall assessment of the available research suggests that factors other than racial discrimination in the sentencing process account for most of the disproportionate representation of black males in U.S. prisons, although discrimination in sentencing may play a more important role in some regions, jurisdictions, crime types, or the decisions of individual participants
>
> We also note, however, that even a small amount of racial discrimination is a matter that needs to be taken very seriously, both on general normative grounds and because small effects in the aggregate can imply unacceptable deprivations for large numbers of people. Thus even though the effect of race in sentencing may be small compared to that of other factors, such differences are important.[8]

> Some studies find statistical evidence of racial discrimination; others find none. While there is no evidence of a widespread systematic pattern of discrimination in sentencing, some pockets of discrimination are found for particular crime types, and in particular settings. The studies, however, are vulnerable in varying degrees to a variety of statistical problems that temper the strength of these conclusions.[9]

The panel also addressed the combined impact of the race of the victim and offender. Though it found that ten of the fourteen studies examining the offender's and victim's race did find a race effect, it also pointed out that

> the 10 studies finding an effect for offender and victim race either fail to include or only partially control for these dimensions of offense seriousness. Four other studies that do control for factors associated with interracial offenses do not find any effect on sentence for offender and victim race. . . . The suppression of the estimated discrimination effect when controls for these other elements of offense seriousness are included suggests that the biases in the offender/victim race effect are likely to be dominated by overestimates.[10]

The conclusions of the panel's consultants are similar to those above. Two of these articles, however, attempt to explain why some sentencing studies find a race effect and others do not. An article by Hagan and Bumiller points out that the increased tendency in recent (post-1969) studies to control for more legal variables has not resulted in fewer findings of racial discrimination but in more such findings:

The challenge is to explain why some studies find discrimination while others
do not, and why among those studies including controls for legitimized variables the proportion finding discrimination has shown signs of increasing. Our
explanation is that with increasing sensitivity, those researchers who find
evidence of discrimination have specified for study structural contexts in
which discrimination by race is most likely to occur.[11]

Hagan and Bumiller suggest that those "structural contexts" that increase the likelihood of finding a race effect include the death penalty
in the South, rural rather than urban courts, politically sensitive crimes
like rape, and jurisdictions where probation officers make sentencing
recommendations. In contrast, studies in the last decade that did not
find discrimination had focused on areas such as large urban courts,
which are so highly bureaucratized that they may be too constrained by
a lack of time and resources to allow direct discrimination by race.[12]

The second review article that attempts to explain why some sentencing studies find a race effect but others do not is by Klepper, Nagin,
and Tierney.[13] The authors argue that "sample selection bias is likely to
cause all the studies to underestimate the magnitude of discrimination
in sentencing decisions."[14] Sample selection bias refers to the possibility that studies examining only the sentencing stage may underestimate the race effect in sentencing, since the race effect does not occur
at the point of sentencing but at earlier decision points (arrest, charging, conviction). They point out, however, that sample selection bias
can mask a race effect at sentencing only if there is a demonstrable race
effect at one or more earlier points in the system. Their analysis appears
to have led the panel to recommend that future research compare
black/white ratios by type of crime at each of the intermediate stages
of the criminal justice system between arrest and prison.[15] (This suggested method was used in the study reported in the Appendix.)

Differences in Method and Interpretation

The conclusions of the three reviews described above have not gone un-
challenged. Austin maintains that Kleck's evidence "shows discrimination to be more widespread than he allows."[16] According to Austin,
some studies that Kleck claims showed no discrimination had been
improperly interpreted. Also, Kleck is sometimes misread as having concluded that there was *no* evidence of racial discrimination, when he had
actually concluded that the evidence was *largely* contrary to the discrimination thesis and that discrimination was not *general or widespread* (not that it did not exist).[17]

Going further, one can find numerous assertions in the literature that
"the evidence" clearly indicates widespread racial discrimination at the

point of sentencing (a view opposite to that expressed by the three major reviews). Note the following:

> The nature and extent of racial discrimination in criminal sentencing is seldom addressed by legal authorities or discussed in judicial circles. Yet such discrimination is widely perceived in our communities and clearly supported by statistics.[18]

> Numerous studies have shown that African-Americans are more likely to be arrested, indicted, convicted, and committed to an institution than are whites who commit the same offenses, and many others have shown that blacks have a poorer chance than whites to receive probation, a suspended sentence, parole, commutation of a death sentence, or pardon.[19]

Why do the more exhaustive reviews of the literature find little evidence of racial discrimination, whereas individual studies often find evidence of a race effect at the point of sentencing? Kleck maintains that commentators selectively choose studies (from among those with contradictory conclusions) to support their position.[20] But the problem is more than simple bias in the selection of studies. Different models of method and interpretation contribute to the disagreement found in the literature. The sections to follow focus on seven models of analysis and interpretation that characterize sentencing studies found in the literature:

Model No. 1—interpreting black/white variation in outcome without controls as evidence of racial discrimination.

Model No. 2—interpreting black/white variation in outcome with one or more controls from multivariate analysis as evidence of racial discrimination.

Model No. 3—interpreting black/white variation in outcome with one or more controls from multivariate analysis as unexplained variation.

Model No. 4—interpreting the failure to find black/white variation in outcome with one or more controls from multivariate analysis as evidence of the absence of racial discrimination.

Model No. 5—suggesting that multivariate analysis that does not examine the variation among decision makers (judges) is invalid, in that aggregate decisions may mask racial discrimination by individual judges.

Model No. 6—suggesting that multivariate techniques that attempt to statistically control for variables related to race and outcome mask the impact of race-related factors on outcome and thus are misleading if not invalid.

Model No. 7—suggesting that multivariate analysis, whether individual judges are examined or not, is invalid and should be abandoned in favor of a process-oriented analysis that examines factors crucial to the judge for each individual case.

Model No. 1:
Interpreting Variation without Controls

Many laypersons and even some academics believe that any variation in sentences between blacks and whites is evidence of racial discrimination even if no control variables have been introduced to determine if the black/white differences can be accounted for by some factor that the judge should consider in passing sentence.

Some articles in the literature, for example, point out that blacks are incarcerated in state prisons at a rate eight times that of whites.[21] This fact alone is seen as evidence of racial discrimination, though others suggest that this gap might be accounted for by more black offenses and convictions. The fact of a racial gap in incarceration is seen as evidence of institutional racism, in that the institutions of society and the criminal justice system produce sharply different rates of offending and imprisonment.

Thus it is argued that black/white differences in outcome (for example, incarceration) are evidence of (institutional) racial discrimination regardless of what others might term explanations for those differences.[22] One author suggests that though there may be differences in levels of offending between blacks and whites, these differences are due to differential socialization and unequal opportunities for the two races (that is, institutional racism).[23] This type of interpretation is analogous to the suggestion (see Chapter Two) that differences on high school literacy tests or police entrance exams are evidence of institutional racism, in that blacks have been subjected to inferior schools.

One author has suggested that the racial gap in prison be corrected by a quota system that would force the police to arrest blacks and whites in proportion to their numbers in the population (approximately 8:1, white to black).[24] In other words racial discrimination in outcome would be overcome by forcing the police (and consequently prosecutors and judges) to find and arrest eight whites for every black arrested.

Though few published empirical studies make inferences about racial discrimination on the basis of black/white variation in outcome without controls, it is not uncommon for laypersons to support the claim of racial discrimination by the criminal justice system by the citing of racial gaps at a particular decision point.

There are several problems in equating black/white variation in outcome without controls with racial discrimination. First, in many cases the variation is opposite to what one would predict by the DT. For example, Table 9 in the Appendix indicates that a greater percentage of whites than blacks (12.8 percent to 10.8 percent) who were convicted in felony cases in Pennsylvania in 1980 were sentenced to prison rather than given probation (the "in/out" decision). Those who claim that racial disparity in outcome is equivalent to racial discrimination would have to argue that whites were discriminated against in Pennsylvania in 1980. Certainly it would be inconsistent to claim that such a racial disparity in prison sentences in California in 1980 (17.8 percent for blacks and 14 percent for whites—see Table 8 in the Appendix) is indicative of racial discrimination, ignoring data that "prove" just the opposite in Pennsylvania for the same year.

Second, those who argue that black/white variation in outcome without controls is indicative of (institutional) racial discrimination would have to agree that institutional *sexism* is far more pervasive in society and the criminal justice system than *racism*. Males are incarcerated in state prisons at a ratio of 25:1 to females and are far more likely if convicted to be sent to prison (see Tables 8 and 9 in the Appendix). Yet those who draw the inference of institutional racial discrimination from black/white variation in outcome without controls would not infer a greater degree of institutional sexism (than racism), since similar figures indicate greater male/female variation in outcome without controls.

Third, this interpretive approach simply assumes what should be proven—that racial discrimination is the cause of the black/white variation in outcome without controls. In other terms, this approach begs the question.

Model No. 2: Interpreting
Variation after Controls as Race Effect

The most commonly cited evidence for racial discrimination at the point of sentencing involves empirical studies that examine the black/white variation in sentences for particular crimes in a particular jurisdiction after the introduction of one or more important control variables. Since it is assumed that "other things are equal" after the introduction of such controls, the remaining black/white variation is interpreted as the race effect. Several examples of this approach and interpretation will be given.

Statisticians disagree with the assumption that all things are equal after the introduction of one or more important control variables. They point out that the black/white variation remaining after the introduction of controls is more properly called unexplained variation, since it is the variance between black and white cases that cannot be accounted for by the control variables used. The unexplained variation may be the result of a race effect, but it may also stem from numerous other factors that were not controlled or simply from unsystematic variation. The exact proportion of the unexplained variation that can be attributed to race is always unknown. In short, it is statistically improper to equate unexplained variation with the race effect.

One of the better known examples of this interpretive approach involves the research by Bowers into possible racial discrimination in the imposition of the death penalty.[25] His book attempts to document a pervasive race effect in death sentences. It examines the probability of the death sentence given four offender/victim racial combinations of homicide (white offender on white victim, white on black, black on black, and black on white). The analysis involves data from several states and examines the death sentence probabilities for the four subgroups controlling for type of homicide (that is, felony versus nonfelony).

Bowers found the following results in felony murders in Florida, Georgia, and Texas from 1974 to 1977: Blacks who had killed whites had a 32 percent probability of receiving the death penalty (46 of 143 cases). Whites who had killed whites had a 22 percent probability. Blacks who had killed blacks had a 4 percent probability. And whites who had killed blacks had a 0 percent probability (0 of 11 cases).[26] Since he had controlled for type of homicide, he concluded that the remaining black/white variation was due to race: "Race of victim is the chief basis of differential treatment."[27] But it is quite possible that other control variables would reduce this black/white variation to near zero. What Bowers calls the race effect is actually unexplained variation, and the extent of the variation (that is, the difference in outcome for different offender/victim racial combinations after one control variable) that is due to the race effect is simply unknown.

Several critics have pointed out this methodological and interpretive fallacy.[28] Kleck found that in studies examining the race of offender and victim that had introduced numerous controls the remaining variation was reduced to near zero. You will realize that several factors might account for part or all of the variation in sentences: the degree of premeditation, strength of evidence, willingness to plead guilty, willingness to testify against others, type of counsel, and prior record. Yet Bowers's research is commonly cited as proof of racial discrimination in the imposition of the death penalty with respect to race of victim and offender.

A second example of this approach (equating unexplained variation with the race effect) is a study by Clayton of the sentences of over 21,000 felons incarcerated in Georgia from 1973 to 1980.[29] He found that blacks had received sentences averaging 2.5 years longer than those for whites for violent crimes even after controls were introduced for age, educational level, IQ, and prior record (including juvenile record). Clayton interpreted the remaining variation as a race effect. What he actually found was a statistically significant difference in outcome for blacks and whites after *some* control variables were introduced. Because his regression model accounted for only 13 percent of the variance in sentences, it is quite likely that the race effect would diminish or disappear altogether if additional controls were introduced. The black and white cases were "equal" only with respect to the few variables utilized as controls; thus the resulting race effect identified by Clayton through his regression equation would more properly be termed variation in outcome by race of defendant given some controls. In other words, the racial difference in outcome could not be explained by the control variables utilized but might be explained by other control variables not utilized. In this sense the racial variation is unexplained and should not be considered a race effect.

A third study that equates the remaining variation with a race effect is one by Petersen and Friday.[30] They studied incarcerated felons in Ohio who either did or did not receive early release in 1970 via "shock probation." Even when type of offense was controlled, the authors found that whites were significantly more likely to receive shock probation than blacks. The authors interpreted this result as support for "differential racial treatment," though other controls might have reduced the black/white difference to near zero.

A fourth study equating the remaining variation with a race effect involved 3,644 inmates in the Huntsville prison in Texas in 1958. Bullock controlled for type of plea and area of commitment, and he suggested that these two controls had ensured that the prisoners were "alike in all effective characteristics except race."[31] Since black/white variation remained after the two controls were introduced, the study concluded that racial discrimination had existed.

It is unusual for researchers claiming to have found evidence for the DT to carefully explore alternative explanations to interpreting unexplained variation after controls as a race effect. Perhaps the most elaborate discussion and critique of competing explanations is by Gross and Mauro in a comprehensive review of the literature and presentation of new data on the impact of race of victim in capital cases.[32] The authors found that even when they used several controls, those who had killed whites were much more likely to have received the death penalty than those who had killed blacks. They then examined the possibility that omitted variables (such as strength of evidence) might greatly reduce the racial disparities they had found, but they rejected that possibility after considerable discussion. Though this study fits Model 2, the interpretation of the remaining variation as a race effect was not made in a cavalier manner but after a careful examination of alternative explanations.

Though numerous other examples could be given of studies equating a race effect with the unexplained variation,[33] the four given above should be sufficient to indicate that it is quite common for studies to make this incorrect inference. Thus the disagreement over whether discrimination has been "proven" is partly due to disagreement on what constitutes discrimination. Many researchers seem to assume that unexplained variation (after controls) is really not unexplained but can be explained by race.

Model No. 3: Interpreting Variation after Controls as Unexplained Variation

Some sentencing studies find considerable black/white variation in sentences after the introduction of controls but are reluctant to interpret this remaining variation as a race effect. Rather, they clearly state that such an interpretation is improper and label the remaining variation as unexplained. Though the methods may be similar to those used in the studies described above (those that equated the remaining variation with the race effect), the interpretations are quite different. Three examples of this interpretive approach will be given.

The first example is a study by Tiffany, Avichai, and Peters of 1,248 criminal cases involving convictions for four crime categories in the eighty-nine U.S. district courts in 1967 and 1968.[34] The study found differences in sentences given to blacks and whites even after controlling for type of crime, prior record, age, and type of counsel, and yet the authors did not attribute this remaining black/white variation to racial discrimination. They were careful to point out that "it may be that race per se is not the cause of the sentencing difference but that race is associated with some other aspect of the case not accounted for in our data."[35]

A second example of this approach involves a study by Kulig of sentencing practices in a federal district court in Nebraska in 1970-1972.[36] Kulig found no racial variation in length of sentence after the introduction of controls but did find that black/white differences remained for the decision between probation and prison. He concluded, however, that this disparity was at least reduced when past criminal record and type of plea were considered and that the remaining disparity was not of great significance and could probably be accounted for by other control variables (if introduced).

A third example of interpreting remaining black/white variation after controls as unexplained variation (rather than as a race effect) is found in a report that examined sentencing practices in Michigan as a first step in creating sentencing guidelines.[37] This study found large differences in mean sentences for blacks and whites after controls had been introduced but suggested that these differences were unexplained variance that might include a race effect. It should be noted that although blacks received longer terms than whites for some offenses, they received shorter terms than whites for other offenses.

Model No. 4:
Interpreting No Variation after Controls

A large number of studies have examined sentencing practices in a particular jurisdiction and found little or no black/white variation in sentences after one or more controls were introduced. These studies have then concluded that no evidence of racial discrimination can be found. Though this conclusion of no race effect may be accurate given the method used, it is quite possible that the design of a study can mask considerable racial differences or discrimination.

Clarke and Koch examined the dispositions of 798 burglary and larceny defendants in Mecklenburg County, North Carolina, in 1971.[38] Though there was, before controls, a black/white difference in whether the defendant received a prison sentence or not (23 percent of blacks received prison, compared with 13 percent of whites), the introduction of controls (age, income, employment, type of offense, prior arrests, and strength of evidence) reduced the racial disparity to near zero. The authors' conclusion of no race effect may be misleading, since many would argue that the effect of race was indirect through income, employment, type of counsel, and prior arrests. Perhaps black defendants were poor, were unemployed, had a public defender, and had a prior record because they were black (that is, because of racial discrimination). It may also be that some individual judges discriminated against blacks and others discriminated for them (because of leniency toward black-on-black crime or a desire to compensate for those thought to be subject to more temptations and fewer opportunities), producing an overall effect of no discrimination. The research design does not allow for the testing of these possibilities. All that can be said of this study is that *given the research design,* no support was found for the DT.

A second study well known for having found no race effect is Eisenstein and Jacob's examination of the processing of felony cases (including sentences of those convicted) in Baltimore, Chicago, and Detroit in 1972.[39] The authors concluded that "sentencing in these three cities was apparently both colorblind and free of class bias."[40] This study utilized stepwise multiple regression and found that several variables (particularly the type of offense and the identity of the judge) were predictive of the sentence but that race was not a good predictor. Unfortunately this study did not test for the possibility that race had influenced sentence by using such control variables as offense, strength of evidence, and type of counsel. The authors' methodology did not allow for the detection of indirect influence (as path analysis does) or for interactions between race and other independent variables. Furthermore, this study analyzed each stage of court processing separately and thus was not able to determine the cumulative impact of race across all stages (a fact the authors acknowledge).[41]

Other studies have suggested reasons why a result of no race effect may be an artifact of the research design. First, if a period of several years is used for the sample of sentences, an overall finding of no race effect may mask a race effect for a shorter period. One study found no race effect for sentencing for the periods 1971–1972 and 1976–1977 but did find a race effect for 1967–1968.[42] Second, a study of the sentencing stage alone may overlook a race effect in the selection of the cases reaching this stage.[43] In other words, studies that examine only one stage of processing are incapable of determining the extent to which their sample of cases was biased through selection by race at earlier points. This point is illustrated by Radelet, who found no race effect at sentencing but did find a race effect at the indictment stage for capital felonies in Florida.[44] Several authors have called for studies that examine the cumulative impact of race across several decision points.[45] (The study reported in the Appendix does so.)

Third, some studies have found a race effect at sentencing for some crimes but not for others. Thus a study that examines sentences for all crimes together will not detect the interaction effect of race with specific crimes. It may be that blacks receive more lenient sentences for some crimes and more severe sentences for others, with the overall result being no race effect because of the canceling-out effect.[46] Finally, it is possible that the introduction of additional controls may increase the black/white variation in sentences rather than reducing it.[47] Certainly one cannot assume that the introduction of controls always reduces the black/white variation. For example, it is relatively rare for studies of noncapital sentencing to examine the impact of race of victim, and yet many studies that find little or no race effect (for race of offender) might find that the introduction of this control would produce a race effect.

Model No. 5:
Rejecting Aggregate Sentencing Studies

Most studies of sentencing examine the sentences of all judges as a whole in a particular jurisdiction and thus assume that there is no variation among judges in that jurisdiction. If there is no overall race effect for the court (with all judges considered together), the inference is made that there is no racial discrimination in that jurisdiction. But it is quite possible that judges vary greatly in a particular jurisdiction, with some being lenient and some being harsh toward blacks, so that the overall effect is that blacks as a whole are treated equally. Certainly it would be incorrect to suggest that no racial discrimination existed *for individual cases* in such a jurisdiction. Gibson's study of sentencing in Atlanta courts, for example, found no overall race effect (with all judges considered as a whole) but considerable black/white variation in sentences when individual judges were considered (the problack and antiblack judges canceled each other out).[48]

Other studies examining the decisions of individual judges have also found wide variation in sentencing practices, thus confirming the commonly held view that the sentence for a particular defendant can be predicted to some extent by knowing the identity of the judge.[49] Eisenstein and Jacob found, for example, that the identity of the courtroom (the judge and his "workgroup") was a better predictor of the length of the sentence than the characteristics of the defendant or the strength of the evidence in two (Baltimore and Chicago) of the three cities they studied.[50] Uhlman found that over 50 percent of the judges in "Metro City" imposed sentences more than 10 percent above or below the mean, with large disparities being quite common.[51] Sixteen of the forty-nine judges were at least 30 percent harsher than the overall average, with Metro City's "hanging judge" handing out sentences 95.6 percent above the mean. Only one study found no significant variation across judges.[52]

Thus one should be skeptical of sentencing studies that report no race effect unless the decisions of individual judges were examined. Disregard for the "judge factor" is a fatal methodological omission for anyone purporting to study the major determinants of sentence. There is evidence to suggest that this factor is at least as important as the characteristics of the defendant and almost as important as the characteristics of the crime.[53] Certainly it is improper to infer the lack of a race effect in decisions of individual judges from examinations of decisions by judges in the aggregate.

The failure of the majority of sentencing studies to find a race effect in light of the widespread belief, especially among blacks, that such racial disparity exists may be due in part to the research designs of studies that have ignored variation by individual judges. The consensus of no *overall* race effect can only occur, however, if harsh and lenient sentences for blacks cancel each other out (that is, if the number of cases in which blacks get more lenient sentences is matched by those in which they get harsher sentences).

Model No. 6:
Rejecting the Control Process

Most sentencing studies do find a black/white difference in average sentences before the introduction of controls, but that difference generally diminishes to near zero when control variables are considered. The study by Clarke and Koch mentioned earlier found that blacks were more likely than whites (23 percent to 13 percent) to receive a prison sentence but that this difference diminished to near zero after the introduction of controls.[54] Several critics of the traditional control process suggest that it is misleading to suggest that the race effect has been diminished by the introduction of control variables, since the variables themselves are related to race.[55] Such variables as income, employment, type of counsel, prior record, and demeanor, for example, may be strongly linked to race, so that the race effect could be seen as operating indirectly through them. The multivariate statistical technique of path analysis is designed to detect these indirect "paths" and has been used to study sentencing. Three studies found that race indirectly affected sentence outcome through such variables as social class, type of attorney, pretrial detention status, charge, and prior record.[56]

But if blacks are poor and unemployed and have a hostile demeanor because they are black and have been subjected to racial discrimination, it is ludicrous to suggest that one can statistically control or separate being black from being poor, unemployed, angry, and so on. Thus it is argued that the control process is a statistical manipulation that only artificially separates race from its effects (poverty, unemployment, demeanor) and thus leads to the incorrect conclusion that there is no race effect in sentencing. In short, this point of view sees little meaningful distinction between "direct" (after controls) and "indirect" (through control variables) racial effects.

Model No. 7:
Rejecting Variable Analysis

Statistical analyses of sentencing are valid only to the extent to which they "model" the actual sentencing process as it takes place in the courts. It is noteworthy that many studies of sentencing can, with the variables and techniques used, account for only a small proportion of the variance in sentencing decisions.[57] Few studies account for more than one-third of the variance in sentences, leaving the remaining two-thirds as unexplained variance.[58] This finding of a minimal explained variance suggests that the model used does not "fit" the actual sentencing process, since the decisions are largely left unexplained.

The lack of fit between the models used and the sentencing process may stem from a failure to include the most important predictor variables or from a failure of the statistical technique to fit the actual decision-making process. First, it is clear that many sentencing studies do not include variables that have been found to be strongly related to the sentence. Many sentencing studies seem to assume that the judge decides on a sentence in a social vacuum rather than as part of a workgroup also including the prosecutor, defense attorney, and probation officer (who makes a sentence recommendation after an investigation). Yet few studies have included the sentencing recommendation of the prosecutor[59] and the probation officer.[60] Moreover, though prior record and strength of evidence are thought to be important factors in determining the judicial sentence, few studies have included these predictor variables.[61]

A potentially more damning criticism of sentencing studies is the suggestion that the multivariate statistical techniques traditionally used do not model the decision-making process of judges. Maynard has conducted perhaps the most intensive observational/interview study of the sentencing (and plea bargaining) process.[62] He concludes that the traditional statistical techniques do not fit the decision-making process in that they impose a structure that is invalid:

> Most models hypothesize an abstract set of attributes, demographic factors, or pre-established categories as affecting the results of plea bargaining. Presumably, lawyers and judges determine the values of these categories in a checklist fashion; the researcher's task is to find out which categories are regularly used when outcomes (charges, sentences) are decided.[63]

Maynard suggests that the participants in the sentencing workgroup make a judgment about what the particular defendant "deserves" in light of the "going rate" for a particular crime and then marshal offender and offense factors to support that judgment. Various demographic and other attributes of a defendant are used to "construct the person as a good or bad character"[64] and decide whether that character is consistent with the nature of the crime committed. The judge's decision represents, to some extent, a compromise between the judgments and recommendations of the other participants in the workgroup.

Race may be a mitigating or an aggravating factor in the judgment process of workgroup participants. Blacks may be seen as having been subjected to greater criminal temptations and opportunities than whites and thus as being less responsible, or they may be seen as "normal primitives"[65] who are in need of severe punishment. In sum, race and other defendant and offense factors must be viewed in the context of their use by the decision maker, and thus the "meaning" or importance of race varies with each decision maker and case according to the unique combinations of factors. This view comes close to the traditional argument by judges that they view each case individually and thus that any attempt to explain sentences by "variable analysis" (analyzing the impact of each variable in a mechanical, checklist fashion) or to structure sentences through sentencing guidelines is doomed to failure.

Likewise, Petersen and Hagan have argued that "theories based on static and simplistic conceptions of the social significance of race fail

to account for anomalous research findings and confuse our understanding of race-related outcomes."[66] They argue for a "contextual
analysis" suggesting that race may contribute to differential leniency
or severity depending on its social significance in a given context. Contextual analysis must examine the meaning of each variable and case
to the judge, and thus it relies heavily on observation and interviews. By
contrast, traditional sentencing studies have assumed a uniform meaning for race and other variables and have simply used the variables that
are available in the written record in a checklist fashion.

Applying the Seven Models
of Interpretation to Class Grades

These seven models of interpretation can be further illustrated by
applying them to a separate but related issue. It is sometimes alleged
that blacks are subjected to racial discrimination in grading in university
classes. Assessing the validity of this charge requires us to decide what
factors are important in assigning grades, how to measure those factors,
and how to determine the impact of each factor on the term grade.

Model No. 1 would suggest that the fact that blacks receive lower
grades, on the average, constitutes racial discrimination and requires a
remedy, perhaps in the form of racial quotas for "A"s, "B"s, and so on.
Model No. 2 would attempt to control for the students' prior grade-
point average and equate any remaining variation after that control
variable is introduced with a race effect. Model No. 3 would control for
the prior grade-point average and suggest that any remaining variation is
unexplained variation, including a possible race effect. Model No. 4
would control for grade-point average and other variables (perhaps
attendance, participation in class, and so forth) and interpret the resulting "equality" (after controls) of blacks' and whites' grades as indicative of no race effect.

Model No. 5 would suggest that any study of grading by professors
in the aggregate is invalid, since it ignores the great potential for variation among professors. (Some might be tougher on black students;
others might be easier on them; and white professors might grade differently from black professors.) Model No. 6 would suggest that it is
invalid to ignore the fact that black university students may receive
lower grades because of prior racial discrimination in primary and
secondary schools. One cannot "control for" (that is, statistically
separate the effects of) the tendency of blacks to score lower on tests,
since such tests are culturally biased. And one cannot "control for"
(that is, separate from race) prior grade-point average, since it is the
result of prior racial discrimination. Thus this model suggests that
blacks may make lower grades in college classes because of indirect

racial discrimination in their prior schooling and testing experience. Model No. 7 would suggest that any checklist analysis of student characteristics and grades is invalid, since the race of the student is meaningful only in the context of a particular class, student, and professor. The presence of racial discrimination can be determined only by a thorough observation and interview study to determine the meaning of race in this context.

It should be obvious that the conclusions we might reach about the existence of a race effect with respect to the assigning of grades is largely a function of the type of statistical technique and variables used and the model of interpretation chosen. Though literature on a race effect in the assigning of grades is sparse, it is likely that empirical research addressing this question would face the same pitfalls as the research on criminal sentences. Disagreement over (interpreted) results would be largely a function of the model of analysis and interpretation chosen.

What Is Known about
Race and Sentencing: A Summary

This chapter has attempted to point out the difficulties in proving or disproving the existence of racial discrimination at the point of sentencing by illustrating how different research methods and interpretations lead to different conclusions about a race effect. You should not be left with the impression, however, that these difficulties prevent us from really knowing anything about race and sentencing. Several findings appear to be generally valid across the literature.

1. *Racial discrimination in sentencing has declined over time.* Two reviews of the literature suggest that a race effect was more likely to have been found (and if found more likely to have been greater in magnitude) in studies from the 1960s and earlier.[67] One study that examined burglary and robbery cases in Milwaukee courts for an eleven-year period found that a race effect found for 1967–1968 had disappeared by 1971–1972 and 1976–1977.[68] The authors of that study attributed the "racial neutrality" in later years to changes in the composition of the judiciary, a greater bureaucratization of the prosecutorial and defense bar, and the rise of decision rules that reduced the effect of judicial ideology on outcomes.

2. *Race of defendant does not have a consistent impact across crimes and jurisdictions.* In other words, some studies have found that in some jurisdictions blacks receive harsher sentences for some crimes but more lenient sentences for others.[69] Likewise, although blacks may be more likely than whites to be sent to prison in one state, they may be less

likely in another. California and Pennsylvania illustrate this change in the "direction" of the relationship between race and sentence (see the Appendix, Tables 8 and 9). Also even within a state the extent of a race effect may vary sharply between rural and urban courts.[70]

3. *Race of victim may be a better predictor of sentence than race of defendant.* This is certainly true for death penalty cases, but the research in noncapital cases has seldom included race of victim as a variable, and thus the pattern is less clear.[71] However, studies finding that cases involving white victims received harsher treatment than cases involving black victims also find that white defendants were treated more harshly than black defendants (since much crime is intraracial). Thus if one argues that racial discrimination exists because of favoritism to white victims (that is, by harsher sentences to offenders against white victims), one should also argue that reverse racial discrimination exists against white defendants because of their tendency to victimize other whites. It is curious that harsher treatment of white defendants is seen as racial discrimination against blacks.[72]

4. *Extralegal variables (for example, race, sex, age, socioeconomic status of defendant) are not as predictive of sentence as legal variables (for example, type of crime, strength of evidence).*[73]

5. *The black/white variation in sentences is generally reduced to near zero when several legal variables are introduced as controls.*[74]

6. *The race effect, even before controls, is not "substantially" significant, in that the predictive power of race is quite low.*[75] Given this result it is difficult to maintain the position that race has a "pervasive" effect on sentences. In other terms, it is difficult to argue from the available evidence that black defendants "always" or even "often" receive harsher sentences (either with respect to the in/out decision or in length of prison term) than whites.

7. *There is no evidence that black judges are less likely than white judges to send blacks to prison or to give them lengthy terms.* The only study comparing sentencing by black and white judges found that all sixteen black judges gave harsher sentences to black defendants than to whites and that the black judges sentenced black defendants more harshly than white judges did.[76] If one argues that racial disparity in sentencing is indicative of racial discrimination, it is clear that black judges are more racist than white judges. The most likely interpretation is that blacks were sentenced more harshly by both white and black judges because of factors other than race that were deemed appropriate to consider. The fact that there is no evidence that black judges "make a difference" suggests that racial discrimination is not an important factor in criminal sentencing.

8. *Most sentencing studies have a large residual variation, suggesting that the models used did not fit the actual decision-making process of*

judges.[77] The large residuals suggest that we know very little about sentencing as a result of the statistical studies that have been conducted.

9. *Since most sentencing studies have not examined the sentences of individual judges, the possibility remains that racial discrimination (both for and against blacks) exists on a rather large scale for individual cases but that the harsher and more lenient sentences by individual judges cancel each other out, thus producing no overall race effect for the court as a whole.*

Summary

It is common to assert that blacks are discriminated against at sentencing, being more likely to receive a prison term if convicted and more likely, if incarcerated, to be given a longer term. Three major reviews of the literature on race and sentencing found little evidence of a *direct* and *substantial* race effect at the point of sentencing. Nevertheless, there is a lack of consensus in the sentencing literature.

This disagreement among social scientists can be traced in part to the existence of seven different models of method and interpretation: (1) interpreting black/white variation in outcome without controls as evidence of racial discrimination; (2) interpreting black/white variation in outcome with one or more controls as racial discrimination; (3) interpreting black/white variation in outcome with one or more controls as unexplained variation; (4) interpreting the failure to find black/white variation in outcome with one or more controls as evidence of the absence of racial discrimination; (5) suggesting that multivariate analysis with aggregate data is invalid; (6) suggesting that multivariate analysis is invalid if the control process masks the impact of race-related factors on outcome; and (7) suggesting that multivariate analysis is invalid in that it fails to model sentencing decisions.

Nine findings were, nevertheless, found to emerge from the literature:

1. Racial discrimination in sentencing has declined over time.
2. Race of defendant does not have a consistent impact across crimes and jurisdictions.
3. Race of victim may be a better predictor of sentence than race of defendant.
4. Extralegal variables are not as predictive of sentence as legal variables.
5. The black/white variation in sentences is generally reduced to near zero when several legal variables are introduced as controls.
6. The race effect, even before controls, is not substantially significant, in that the predictive power of race is quite low.

7. There is no evidence that black judges are less likely than white judges to send blacks to prison or to give blacks lengthy sentences.
8. Most sentencing studies have a large residual variation, suggesting that the models used did not fit the actual decision making of judges.
9. The possibility remains that racial discrimination both for and against blacks may exist on a large scale when individual judges are considered, since most studies have examined judges in the aggregate.

Notes

1. Holmes and Daudistel, 1984.
2. Hagan, 1974. See also two unpublished reviews (Berk, 1984; Miethe and Moore, 1984) that were presented at the 1984 meeting of the American Society of Criminology.
3. Kleck, 1981.
4. Blumstein, Cohen, Martin, and Tonry, 1983.
5. Hagan, 1974, p. 378.
6. Kleck, 1981, pp. 798-799. For criticisms of the Kleck review see Austin 1981, 1984.
7. Blumstein et al., 1983.
8. Blumstein et al., 1983, Vol. 1, p. 92.
9. Blumstein et al., 1983, Vol. 1, p. 93.
10. Blumstein et al., 1983, Vol. 1, pp. 101-102.
11. Hagan and Bumiller, 1983, p. 31.
12. Hagan and Bumiller, 1983, pp. 31-32.
13. Klepper, Nagin, and Tierney, 1983.
14. Klepper et al., 1983, pp. 91, 101, 147-149.
15. Klepper et al., 1983, p. 92.
16. Austin, 1984, p. 184. See also Austin, 1981, and Dehais, 1983.
17. Austin, 1984, pp. 184-186.
18. J. C. Howard, 1975, p. 121. See also Bramwell, 1983.
19. Sutherland and Cressey, 1974, p. 133. See also Karmen, 1984, p. 165.
20. Kleck, 1985.
21. See Christianson, 1980a, 1980b, 1982. Langan and Greenfeld (1985, p. 3) give figures suggesting that 2.044 percent of all U.S. black males were in state prison in 1982, compared with 0.266 percent of white males (a ratio of 7.7:1). This model of interpretation is also at times applied to sex disparities. See, for example, Ducassi, 1985, for an article about disparity in income between female and male attorneys in Florida. The implication is that this disparity, even without controls, indicates discrimination against women. For an argument against the view that income disparity between males and females indicates sex discrimination see Sowell, 1984, pp. 91-108. See also Weisheit, 1985, for a study of how the sex differences in a jail population disappeared when controls were introduced.
22. See Bell, 1983.
23. Bell, 1983.
24. Bell, 1983.
25. Bowers, 1984. For a similar approach see Zeisel, 1981, and Paternoster, 1983.

26. Bowers, 1984, p. 230.
27. Bowers, 1984, p. 23. It should be noted that Bowers in a less frequently cited journal article (1983) did utilize several control variables through a regression equation and still found a race effect (p. 1075). And yet 73 percent of the variance was not accounted for by his model (p. 1073); thus his "race effect" might more properly be termed racial variation after *some* controls.
28. J. Q. Wilson, 1985, p. 191; Kleck, 1981; Arkin, 1980; Hagan, 1974; Farrell and Swigert, 1978a, p. 571. Zalman, Ostrom, and Guilliams (1979, pp. 270-271) separate unexplained variation into discrimination and inconsistency.
29. Clayton, 1983.
30. Petersen and Friday, 1975.
31. Bullock, 1961, p. 417.
32. Gross and Mauro, 1984.
33. Spohn, Gruhl, and Welch, 1981-1982; Foley and Rasche, 1979, p. 105; Rhodes, 1977; Chiricos, Jackson, and Waldo, 1972, pp. 557-560; Holmes and Daudistel, 1984; Zeisel, 1981; Paternoster, 1983; Dehais, 1983.
34. Tiffany, Avichai, and Peters, 1975; Petersilia, 1983, pp. 30-32.
35. Tiffany et al., 1975, p. 388.
36. Kulig, 1975.
37. Zalman et al., 1979, pp. 233-234, 270, 272.
38. Clarke and Koch, 1976.
39. Eisenstein and Jacob, 1977.
40. Eisenstein and Jacob, 1977, p. 282.
41. Eisenstein and Jacob, 1977, p. 284.
42. Pruitt and Wilson, 1983.
43. Zatz and Hagan, 1985.
44. Radelet, 1981.
45. See Dannefer and Schull, 1982; Burke and Turk, 1975; Zatz and Hagan, 1985; Hardy, 1983; and Williams, 1981a.
46. See Gibson, 1978; Kelly, 1976; and Zalman et al., 1979, p. 231. Zalman et al. found that blacks in Michigan received, before controls, longer sentences for six of ten offenses. Whites received longer sentences for assault, fraud, and weapon offenses. And "property" sentences were equal. For the in/out decision blacks were more likely, before controls, to be given prison if convicted for seven of ten offenses (the exceptions being fraud, weapon, and property violations).
47. See the discussion on this point in Hagan, 1974, pp. 363-364.
48. Gibson, 1978.
49. Hogarth, 1971, p. 350. He says "one can explain more about sentencing by knowing a few things about the judge than by knowing a great deal about the facts of the case."
50. Eisenstein and Jacob, 1977, p. 283.
51. Uhlman, 1979a, p. 70; and 1978.
52. Zalman et al., 1979.
53. Hogarth, 1971, p. 350, and Eisenstein and Jacob, 1977, p. 283.
54. Clarke and Koch, 1976.
55. See Austin, 1984, pp. 182-184. Unnever (1982) speaks of indirect discrimination as "organizational discrimination," because race affects sentence through bail status and type of attorney.
56. Swigert and Farrell, 1976; Hagan, 1975a; and Spohn et al., 1981-1982.
57. See Hagan, Hewitt, and Alwin, 1979; and Maynard, 1984. Berk (1984) reports that Baldus, Pulaski, and Woodworth (1983), with data much better than those generally available, were able to account for only 50 percent of the variance,

though they used quite sophisticated techniques and even tested for interaction effects.

58. See, for example, Chiricos and Waldo, 1975, who found R-squared figures ranging from .04 to .19; Clayton (1983) had an R squared of .13.
59. See Hagan et al., 1979.
60. Myers, 1979.
61. See discussion in Hagan, 1974; and Kleck, 1981.
62. Maynard, 1982, 1984; and Hogarth, 1971, pp. 229*ff.* Comer (1985, p. 66) also rejects variable analysis in attempting to determine the cause of criminal behavior by blacks.
63. Maynard, 1984, pp. 151–152.
64. Maynard, 1984, p. 160.
65. Swigert and Farrell, 1976.
66. Peterson and Hagan, 1984, p. 56. They argue that "American drug prohibition began with the portrayal of minorities as the villains behind a growing drug menace" but that over time "big dealers became villains, while middle-class youth and non-whites were reconceived as victims" (p. 67).

    Miethe and Moore (1984) argue that the interactive model is a more appropriate specification of the nature of racial differences in outcome than the additive model. They argue that additive models have a serious flaw in that they fail to take into account that social or case attributes may have different effects *within* racial groups and can suppress the magnitude of racial differences in criminal processing. In other words, the additive model appears to mask racial differences through a type of interaction effect (pp. 4, 17). They further argue that the additive model assumes that race operates in a conceptually analogous fashion to *caste* distinctions. "Race, in and of itself, is presumed to be the major, if not the sole, determinant of dispositional decisions involving individuals of different racial backgrounds. Other status characteristics of the individual (whether ascribed or achieved) are assumed to be inconsequential. In contrast, an interactive or race-specific specification allows one to evaluate whether, and to what extent, race covaries with other configurations of social and case attributes. It is this configuration of individual characteristics, not necessarily race *per se*, that is assumed to contribute to differential treatment in criminal processing under this specification" (p. 18). They argue that "high-risk" black felons are treated more severely by the criminal justice system and that "low-risk" blacks are treated more leniently, with the overall effect being no aggregate discrimination. They urge the use of interactive models to detect the differential treatment of types of black offenders.
67. Hindelang, 1969; Kleck, 1981, p. 794.
68. Pruitt and Wilson, 1983. Perry (1977a, 1977b) found no race effect in military courts and attributed this lack to the greater restriction on discretion placed on judges and sentencing in that setting. See also Petersilia and Turner (1985), who claim that the move toward guidelines has resulted in less direct racial discrimination. However, it should be noted again (see Note 11 above) that Hagan and Bumiller (1983) found that more-recent studies of racial discrimination have been more likely to find a race effect.
69. See, for example, Bullock, 1961, and Foley and Rasche, 1979, p. 101.
70. Pope, 1976; Zimmerman and Frederick, 1984; Hagan and Bumiller, 1983, p. 31.
71. Kleck, 1981, and Berk, 1984. Berk (1984) also critiques and reanalyzes the data of Baldus, Pulaski, and Woodworth (1983). Berk concludes that the case for discrimination by race of victim (in death penalty research) is strong and that it "is difficult to think of other social science findings that have such consistent support." Berk also says that the effects of race of victim were compar-

able to the impact of a number of legitimate variables such as whether the murder was committed to avoid arrest.

72. Gross and Mauro, 1984. A similar study (of race of victim in capital cases)—that by Baldus, Pulaski, and Woodworth (1983)—is discussed by Gross and Mauro. The latter also provide a lengthy discussion of the possible reasons for juries' (and prosecutors') favoring cases with white victims.
73. Kleck, 1981; Burke and Turk, 1975; Hagan et al., 1979.
74. Hagan, 1974; Kleck, 1981.
75. Hagan, 1974.
76. Uhlman, 1979a, pp. 70, 71.
77. Hagan, 1974; Kleck, 1981; Maynard, 1982, 1984.

8

Prisons, Parole,
and Racial Discrimination

There is no doubt that racial discrimination has historically been pervasive in U.S. prisons. Segregation was the rule in northern as well as southern prisons until the late 1960s.[1] Segregation in southern prisons was part of a sociopolitical system that attempted to achieve separation of the races in prisons and was generally mandated by state law. Segregation in northern prisons was not generally sanctioned by state law but was based on policy allegedly designed to curtail violence. Neither southern nor northern prisons desegregated voluntarily after the school integration decision in *Brown* v. *Board of Education* in 1954.[2]

But racial segregation was only the most obvious historical manifestation of racial discrimination by the American prison system. The most blatant form of racial discrimination historically was the post–Civil War practice in the South of leasing adult male felons to private parties.[3] Numerous writers have documented the attempt of southern states to reinstitute a form of slavery by convicting blacks and then leasing them to private enterprise.[4] This practice not only helped to achieve the racial subordination of blacks but was highly profitable in a time when southern states were hard pressed for revenue. One historian suggests that the average proceeds for the leasing program of southern states was 372 percent of costs.[5]

Over 90 percent of those leased were blacks who were placed in the hands of taskmasters. These overseers worked (and disciplined) them with little regard for their health, since the state would replace those who died;[6] at least under slavery the taskmasters had had an incentive to keep the slaves healthy, since they constituted private property. "Violence was not grafted onto a particular system of penal management; rather, a particular system of convict labor was maintained, at least in part, as an institutional outlet for violence."[7]

The reliance on the leasing of inmates was so complete that Florida, which became a state in 1845, did not have to build a major institution (Raiford) until 1913 and that only to house those who could not be leased (women, the elderly, the sick).[8] The profitability of leasing and its virtual limitation to blacks led to a dramatic increase in "prison" populations in the South. For example, there was a tenfold increase in Georgia's prison population during the last four decades of the century.[9] The practice of leasing was not abandoned because of public pressure for reform but because it became unprofitable.

> In sum, then, the economic value of the convict lease system to private businessmen plummeted at precisely the time that other forces converged to deprive it of its social usefulness. Its demise occurred when both its economic and social utility were undermined. Black Georgians were being reminded of their place in society by such alternative, more systematic and official means as Jim Crow and disfranchisement. In addition, the state began to realize the value of chain gangs at the same time that businessmen wished to abandon leasing. The convict lease system, which had been hurriedly instituted to help fill the vacuum left by the destruction of slavery, was itself overthrown by the chain gang.[10]

Even most southerners would agree that racial discrimination was pervasive in prisons historically. Disagreement arises only when the charge of racial discrimination is made against current U.S. prisons. Racial discrimination is seen as being evident in six ways:

> *Charge No. 1*—that the simple fact that blacks are incarcerated at a rate eight times that of whites is evidence of racial discrimination.[11]
> *Charge No. 2*—that the segregation of the races practiced even today in the assignment of inmates to particular prisons and to particular cell blocks or cells within the prison constitutes racial discrimination.[12]
> *Charge No. 3*—that the treatment programs and working assignments in prisons are assigned in a racially discriminatory manner.[13]
> *Charge No. 4*—that the disciplinary process within prisons is enforced in a racially discriminatory manner.[14]
> *Charge No. 5*—that racial hostility between white and black inmates is encouraged by staff members to divert inmate hostility away from them and that white inmates discriminate against black inmates.[15]
> *Charge No. 6*—that the parole process discriminates against black inmates so that the time served for blacks is greater than that for whites with comparable sentences.[16]

Charge No. 1:
Imprisonment Rates Show Discrimination

Blacks are incarcerated in state prisons in the United States on a per capita basis eight times as frequently as whites (see the Appendix). To some the gap between black and white imprisonment rates is evidence enough of racial discrimination. To some critics of the current system the gross overrepresentation of blacks in American prisons establishes a stronger prima facie case for racial discrimination than figures indicating black overrepresentation on death row.

> The data on incarceration rates resemble those for death row, insofar as both reveal greatly disproportionate representation of blacks. These prisoner statistics are sufficiently reliable and up to date to be used for challenge of the constitutionality of imprisonment as presently administered. Unlike death sentence statistics, the statistics for incarceration depict a pattern of racial discrimination which is nationwide, and apparently not as concentrated in the South. Moreover, this pattern of discrimination appears to be growing more pronounced.[17]

Arguments against Charge No. 1

1. The Appendix is an examination of all felony cases processed in California and Pennsylvania courts in 1980. The major point made by this analysis is that the black/white gap (of 8:1) at incarceration is not a product of the criminal justice system, in that it does not increase significantly from arrest to sentence. Though the black/white gap in California did increase 19 percent (from 5.21:1 to 6.18:1—Table 3) from arrest to incarceration, the gap in Pennsylvania actually decreased by 9 percent (8.1:1 to 7.4:1—Table 4). Thus the racial gap remains relatively stable from arrest to sentencing and does not cumulatively increase from point to point across the system. Furthermore, Chapter Five presents arguments that the racial gap at arrest is a product of a gap in offending rather than of racial discrimination by the police.

2. If the argument is made that black overrepresentation in prison is, even when taken alone, indicative of racial discrimination, consistency demands that one also argue that (a) racial discrimination is greatest in such states as South Dakota (where the gap is greatest) and least in the southern states (where the gap is smallest); (b) racial discrimination is greater in American prisons than in South African prisons, since the black/white gap in South Africa is 5:1, compared with 8:1 in the United States;[18] (c) sex discrimination is greater than race discrimination, since the male/female gap is approximately 25:1; and (d) racial discrimination is greater today than at any time in the twentieth century, since the black/white gap is increasing (even though all other indications are that discrimination is decreasing).

Charge No. 2:
Racial Segregation in Prisons Is Discriminatory

Until the late 1960s de jure segregation in southern prisons and de facto segregation in northern prisons was seldom questioned by the judiciary or commented on by academics. Though racial segregation in American prisons is not as pervasive as it was twenty years ago, it is still common practice in most prisons to segregate by such racial surrogates as "gang affiliation," "dangerousness," or county of conviction.[19] Such policy has resulted in some states' (for example, Pennsylvania and Illinois) having one or more prisons that are almost totally black and others that are more racially balanced. Furthermore, most states allow inmates to opt for "protective custody" (a choice made disproportionately by white inmates) and for some degree of choice in cell mates. Consequently, American prisons are highly segregated by cells, by individual cell blocks, and to a lesser extent by entire institutions. This would appear to constitute strong evidence for racial discrimination in the housing of prison inmates.

Arguments against Charge No. 2

1. Prison officials are charged with the safety of both black and white inmates. Unfortunately some American prisons are characterized by what can only be called "racial warfare" between black and white (and in some states Hispanic) inmates. Thus prison officials generally seek the racial and ethnic segregation of inmates at some level to ensure the safety of those in their charge. One of this country's foremost authorities on prisons, James Jacobs,[20] questions the

> unreflective application of school desegregation law to prisons in light of the racial warfare that engulfs prisons and jails, the differing purposes of schools and penal facilities, and the differences in the rights and interests that are at stake. With our racially polarized, conflict-ridden prisons, the time has come to assay the rights and values that are affected by various prison policies that require or condone racial segregation.[21]

> I fear that if we recognize the necessity of separating races in prison it will be argued by some that such policies are just as beneficial in other contexts.
>   Yet, actions appropriate in one context may be wrong in another. It hardly needs pointing out that sexual segregation of prisoners is assumed to be normal and reasonable even though in almost any other context it would be extraordinary and probably impermissible. Thousands of prisoners, black, white, and Hispanic, live in greater danger and insecurity because of what the symbol of an integrated society means to people whose own lives and institutions are far less integrated than those of prisoners.[22]

2. Those who criticize segregation in prisons must be willing to ignore the wishes of the vast majority of both black and white inmates, who want to be in a prison near their home to facilitate visitation and who prefer to share a cell and cell block with a member of their own ethnic group. Of course this argument can be taken too far, in that it is probable that prison administrators, staff members, and inmates would vote for racially segregated institutions if given the opportunity though few outside the prison, especially the judiciary, would endorse such blatant segregation.[23] Yet it is unlikely that many would endorse the "busing"

of inmates throughout the institutions of a state in order to achieve a racial balance in every prison.

3. Prison officials are also civilly liable if their actions needlessly endanger inmates. If a white inmate went to prison officials with a complaint that he or she had been threatened by a group of black inmates and the officials chose not to grant the inmate's request for protective custody since protective custody units were already largely white, they would be in danger of civil action if that inmate were subsequently raped or killed. Certainly few would suggest that the segregation of overt homosexuals constitutes "sexual preference" discrimination, since such segregation is intended to reduce exploitation and violence.

Charge No. 3: Treatment Programs and Work Assignments Are Discriminatory

It is commonly pointed out that blacks are less likely to be placed in "good" jobs in prison and are instead concentrated in working assignments that are viewed negatively by inmates. For example, a commission found that racial discrimination had been present in the Attica prison in New York State before the outbreak of the 1971 riot.[24] This conclusion was based on an examination of work assignments and on interviews with those who made such assignments. In many prisons the largely white staff is more likely to choose white inmates for the more prestigious jobs. Also, in many prisons there is a overrepresentation of white inmates in the educational programs and treatment programs (alcoholism and drug therapy), though black inmates would appear to be in greater need of such programs, based on drug histories and educational level as determined at admission.

Arguments against Charge No. 3

1. Prior literature has simply examined participation rates by black and white inmates in treatment programs without taking into account the possible differential need for treatment by ethnic groups as well as the possibility that inmates may differentially reject treatment opportunities.[25] Petersilia examined the need for and participation in educational, vocational, and drug programs and work assignments for selected inmates in California, Texas, and Michigan.[26] She concluded:

> We found few racial differences in program participation or work assignments among prison inmates in our sample. Where we found differences, they seemed to result from inmates' priorities and attitudes instead of from prison staff decisions. . . . Across states and races, we found that many prisoners with high need for alcohol and drug rehabilitation who did not participate generally claimed that they did not need help with their problems.

This was especially true of blacks and alcohol programs. Even though they had a much lower need for alcohol rehabilitation than whites or Hispanics, a much lower proportion of blacks with need participated in alcohol programs. However, our examination of motives for failure to participate indicates that, if there was discrimination here, the black inmates were discriminating against the program, not vice versa. For drug rehabilitation programs, there was evidence that, in some prisons, programs were not available where prisoners with high need would have participated, but there was no suggestion of racial differences.

The picture for jobs was similar. Although a lower proportion of blacks had jobs in Michigan and Texas, inmates without jobs generally said that they were too busy, did not want jobs, or could not have jobs for other reasons. . . .

We found no statistically significant racial differences in participation—in proportion of participants who had need or in job assignments—that necessarily indicate discrimination.[27]

2. One review of the literature on a possible race effect in treatment programs is ambiguous; it is able to suggest only that "perhaps" discrimination against training and work programs (as was found to be the case at Attica in 1971) occurs but that "unfortunately, these questions cannot be resolved satisfactorily with existing data."[28] Data from a national inmate survey did show disparities in type of work assignments, but the data did not allow for an examination of the reasons for these disparities.[29] The review concludes that the prior studies "are not inconsistent" with Petersilia's conclusion that there was no evidence of racial discrimination in allocating treatment services to inmates.[30]

Charge No. 4:
Prison Discipline Is Discriminatory

The disciplinary process has received considerable attention by researchers with respect to possible racial discrimination. Several studies have concluded that race was a factor in rule enforcement. The 1971 Attica report said, for example, that "the rules at Attica were poorly communicated, often petty, senseless, or repressive and they were selectively enforced."[31] A recent review of fifteen studies of the prison disciplinary process found that seven had reported higher rates of disciplinary write-ups for black inmates than for whites.[32] Seven other studies, however, found no significant difference in disciplinary reports by race.

The prior literature on race and rule enforcement in prison has been dominated by studies that examined only the black/white rates of disciplinary reports, and thus the possibility of differential *behavior* (rule infraction) has been left unexamined. However, one recent study, by Poole and Regoli, examined rule breaking by 182 inmates in a southern prison (via self-report questionnaires) and also official disciplinary

reports against these inmates.[33] After controlling for several variables
(age, time served, prior record of infractions, and self-reported infractions) with a regression equation, blacks were cited for more infractions
than were whites.[34]

Though Poole and Regoli found the direct effect of race to be minimal, they found a more substantial indirect race effect through prior
record.

> Whereas for blacks, prior record was the most important determinant of disci-
> plinary reports, with rule violations having a relatively minor impact, for
> whites, infractions emerged as the most dominant influence, with prior record
> exerting no measurable effect. The inmates' race apparently conditioned the
> guards' understanding and interpretation of the criteria on which decision
> making is based. As a result, patterns of rule enforcement were systematically
> biased against black inmates.[35]

In other words, racial stereotypes depicting blacks as more dangerous
led to greater surveillance of blacks and to the interpretation of their
rule-breaking behavior as more serious and meriting a disciplinary report. Thus black inmates were caught in a self-fulfilling prophecy of
prison guards' expecting, seeing, and reporting more misbehavior. The
prior record then served as confirmation of the stereotypic view of
blacks as rule breakers and justified differential response in succeeding
disciplinary actions.

Another study, by Held, Levine, and Swartz, found that though
black inmates do not rate themselves as more aggressive than white
inmates, guards generally rate them as more aggressive and write them
up more frequently.[36] Furthermore, black inmates are more likely to be
disproportionately written up for rule infractions that leave the officer
with a greater degree of discretion. The study found support for an
"interpersonal theory of dangerousness," that is, the view that dangerousness is more a function of the observer's bias than any trait or
behavior on the part of the observed. It concluded that guards may
differentially write up black inmates because of "their own personally
biased perceptions based on fear and racist attitudes"[37] rather than the
actual behavior of the black inmate.

Arguments against Charge No. 4

1. The Poole and Regoli study relied on self-reports to determine
rule breaking by inmates. The extent to which self-reports are differentially valid for black and white adult prisoners is unknown, but
one study found that self-reports seriously underestimated offenses by
black (but not white) juveniles.[38] Thus Poole and Regoli's finding that
blacks and whites "offend" at equal levels in prison is at least open to
dispute. It would certainly be difficult to explain why the gap between

offense rates of blacks and whites is so great in U.S. society (see Chapter Five) but equal in the prison setting. However, it should be noted that black and white homicide rates are about equal in prison as opposed to a gap of 8:1 outside.[39]

2. If black inmates were written up for rule infractions more frequently because of racial discrimination, we would expect black guards to refrain from exhibiting such discriminatory behavior. But a study of guards in Illinois prisons found that black guards "were more active disciplinarians" than white guards in that they wrote more "tickets" for rule infractions.[40] Though the study did not report if black and white inmates were reported at different rates by black guards, that result is unlikely, given that the thesis of the study was that the occupation of guard (rather than race) was a "master status," so that black guards were more accurately described as being "black *guards*" than "*black* guards." As has been the case at so many points in the criminal justice system, research into differential behavior by black and white staff members has not been undertaken. Certainly there is no evidence that black guards are less likely than white guards to write up blacks.

3. The study by Held et al.[41] described as supporting Charge No. 4 assumes that the view of black inmates that they were not more aggressive than white inmates was valid and that the view of guards that black inmates were more aggressive was invalid. This rather blatant bias on the part of the researchers was maintained in spite of the fact that there was additional empirical evidence, through more guard-reported rule infractions against black inmates, of the guards' perception but not of the black inmates' perception. It would appear that the labeling theory bias of the researchers led them to reject one set of perceptions (that of the guards) and endorse another set of perceptions (that of the black inmates). The obvious bias of this study does not appear to be recognized by others who cite it.[42] The research indicating the prevalence of aggressive acts by black inmates against white inmates (to be described under arguments against Charge No. 5) would certainly provide additional support for greater aggressiveness by black inmates and suggest that, if anything, the perception of the black inmates should be viewed as invalid and the perception of the guards as valid.[43]

4. Though the literature indicates that black inmates generally believe that the dispositional process after a disciplinary report is filed is racially discriminatory, there is little evidence to substantiate this claim. The only study found in the literature addressing this issue found no race effect in dispositions by unit committees for rule infractions by black and white inmates.[44] Yet this finding of no race effect is mentioned only in passing by the researcher, since the focus of the article is on differential rule-infraction reporting by guards to unit committees. The study maintains that the differential reporting was not a product of differential behavior but of bias on the part of the guards

stemming from their wide discretion and lack of accountability for abuse of that discretion. The study does not explain why these two factors did not lead to racial discrimination in the disposition process, since a comparable degree of discretion and lack of accountability exists for the unit disciplinary committees.

5. One study found that white inmates classified as career criminals were more often reported by staff members for rule infractions than were black career criminals.[45] And yet no one has suggested that this fact proves that guards were discriminating against white inmates. Those who support the DT would doubtless point out that it may be that white career criminals are reported by guards more frequently because they are actually more likely to be engaging in rule violations than black career criminals. But why is this possibility not discussed when black inmates are reported more frequently? Could there be an ideological and theoretical (labeling theory) bias present in those studies that see support for racial discrimination in data that indicate greater staff reporting of rule violations by black inmates?

Charge No. 5: Racial Hostility Is Encouraged by Prison Guards

It is often alleged that prison guards ignore or actively condone racial hostility in prison in order to "divide and conquer" the inmate population for management purposes.[46] Furthermore, there is some evidence that black inmates see themselves as targets of racism by white prisoners.[47] To what extent does racial or ethnic discrimination exist among inmates, and to what extent is this discrimination endorsed by the staff? The DT suggests that racial discrimination in prison is largely by white staff members against black inmates and, to a lesser extent, by white inmates against black inmates. The evidence for racial discrimination by guards (for example, in work and training assignments or in the reporting and disposition of rule infractions) has already been examined; it is, to say the least, weak. The evidence of racial discrimination by white inmates against blacks is largely anecdotal, as no empirical study exists on this issue.

Arguments against Charge No. 5

1. The traditional DT completely ignores the evidence of racial hostility by black inmates against white inmates, mistakenly believing that racism involves only actions by whites against blacks (see Chapter Two). Prison critics often state that prison breeds racism, and this is certainly the case, but it would appear that the balance of power has

shifted in American prisons from control of prisons by largely white staff members to control by minority (black and Hispanic) inmates.

Carroll, perhaps the most published and articulate expert on inmate interaction, maintains that humanitarian reforms have led to the virtual takeover of prisons by cohesive groups of inmates (largely black), which have filled the power vacuum created by the elimination of authoritarian, and largely white, staffs.[48]

> My basic contention is that humanitarian reforms of prison social structure have eroded custodial authority and altered convict social organizations in such a way as to transform the prison into an arena within which is acted out racial conflict rooted in the wider community of which the prison is but a part.[49]

> While humanitarian reforms have eroded convict solidarity and fragmented the white prisoners, they have facilitated the development of racial solidarity among the black prisoners.[50]

> All agreed that 75 percent or more of the assaults involve black aggressors and white victims, and that rarely, if ever, is a black prisoner sexually assaulted. . . .

> The prison, according to this interpretation, is an arena within which the rage of black males at their social and psychological oppression is vented against white males, thereby reversing the traditional scale of sexual dominance. I have attempted to show how humanitarian reforms of the prison social structure facilitate this pattern of assault by undermining custodial authority, fragmenting white prisoner social organization, and strengthening black prisoner solidarity.[51]

There are a number of studies documenting the predominance of black-on-white assaults within prisons. Most of this literature is confined to an examination of sexual assaults within adult and juvenile correctional institutions.[52] These studies indicate that sexual assaults by white inmates on black inmates are rare and that such assaults by blacks on whites are common. The interracial victimization of white inmates is not limited to sexual attacks. A study in a North Carolina prison found that 56 percent of the assaults of white inmates were by black inmates but that only 16 percent of the assaults of black inmates were by white inmates. From the choice of victim perspective, black assaulters chose white victims in 47 percent of the cases, and white assaulters chose black victims in only 22 percent of the cases. The higher black rate of offending in assaults (4.4 to 3.3) and the tendency of blacks to choose white victims almost as often as black victims led to a higher white victimization rate for assault (2.2 to 1.2).[53]

Keeping in mind the commonly used concept of institutional racism (that an institution is racist if there is a racial disparity in "outcome" regardless of intent), one might argue that recent prison reforms are part of a "reverse institutional racism." White inmates in a Florida

prison have sued the state for "allowing" black-on-white rape to be pervasive in the institution, as if to say that this is racism that could and
should be avoided.[54]

Furthermore, the interracial victimization of white inmates increases
racial hostility by confirming their negative stereotypes of blacks. "In
prison, most aggressors are black; most targets are white. Prison sexual
aggression, thus, is a case study of interracial crime. White racism follows from or is reinforced by the predatory actions of blacks. Fear of
attack becomes fear of blacks."[55]

Two explanations have been offered for the apparent pattern of
interracial victimization of white inmates by black inmates.[56] Each view
has implications for the importance of racial discrimination in the
prison setting. First, Lockwood blames the prevalence of a subculture
of violence among young black males, which stems in turn from a discriminatory economic and social structure that forces young black
males to prove their masculinity by sexual assaults.[57] White inmates are
chosen, in this view, because they are seen as weak (that is, unorganized)
and sexually attractive. Thus there is little suggestion in this view that
race is directly involved in the motivations of offenders.

A second explanation of prison assaults sees race as the primary motivating factor in interracial prison rapes. Several researchers have suggested that black-on-white rapes are an act of revenge or retaliation for
racial discrimination perpetrated historically and currently in the community by whites.[58] Since the motive is to "get even," this explanation
sees interracial prison rape as being motivated by black racism to compensate for white racism.

2. The view that the largely white prison staff condones or encour-
ages racial hostility to maintain control (by the divide-and-conquer
strategy) ignores the fact that racial hostility increases control problems
rather than alleviating them. The argument seems to be that inmates
will not attack guards if they are busy attacking one another. Most
prison observers would probably respond that guards are in greater danger when the level of aggression among groups of inmates is high. Certainly prison guards who work in states where the level of ethnic group
conflict is high (for example, California, Illinois, New York) would
argue that they are far less safe than guards who work in other states
without gang conflicts. This view is faulty, because it presupposes a
fact (that guards believe they are safer when inmates are fighting among
themselves) that is simply not true. Such a view is part of a "conspiracy
thesis" that sees a largely white staff as somehow responsible even when
racial hostility within the prison is largely directed at white inmates.

3. The view of black inmates that they are subjected to racial discrimination by white inmates is based on self-reports given by black
inmates.[59] Such evidence ignores the perception of white inmates that
they are subjected to racial discrimination by black inmates. A more

accurate view would see both types of racial discrimination as prevalent in the prison setting, though expressed differently. Discrimination by black inmates against white inmates is likely to be more direct, in the form of physical intimidation or actual assault, whereas discrimination by white inmates against blacks is likely to be more indirect or subtle (for example, avoidance of blacks) because of the fear of physical retaliation by the more numerous and organized black inmates.

4. One study of a juvenile correctional system found that black guards (making up half of the total staff) generally intervened in interracial conflicts to help the white inmate victims. "Black staff—very much the victims of racism of southern society—perceived the victim status of whites, recognized the dynamics of victimization, and actively worked to assist whites."[60] It appears that black staff members perceived the racism involved in the victimization of white inmates by black inmates.

Charge No. 6: Parole Is Discriminatory

It is often suggested that black inmates are discriminated against by white parole boards, so that blacks serve longer terms in prison than whites with comparable sentences.[61] It is argued that blacks are labeled more dangerous and untreatable and thus become less suitable candidates for the "privilege" of parole.[62] Parole boards thus force blacks to serve longer terms than whites or use different criteria for their release.[63] One study found that "black prisoners had an additional criterion to meet in order to be paroled—participation in institutional treatment programs."[64]

Perhaps the most extensive examination of possible racial disparity in time served and the decision to parole involves the study by Petersilia of racial differences at various points of the criminal justice systems in California, Texas, and Michigan. This study is sometimes cited as "proving" racial discrimination in time served and parole. It did conclude that "race made a difference."

> It was evident that although minorities received equal treatment in prison, they did not when it came time for release. Controlling for factors that could affect the release decision (including participation in prison programs and prison violence), we found consistent evidence that race made a difference. In Texas, all other things held equal, blacks and Hispanics consistently served longer sentences than whites for the same crimes. In California, minority inmates also served longer sentences, but that was largely determined by the length of sentence imposed. Michigan manifested an interesting reversal. Although blacks received longer court-imposed sentences than whites, they wound up serving about the same time. In Michigan, then, parole decisions seemed to "favor" blacks—that is, blacks evidently served less of their original sentences than whites did.[65]

Arguments against Charge No. 6

1. The Petersilia study does not "prove" racial discrimination in time served and parole. The above quotation and other results from this study can be used to argue against a pervasive racial discrimination against blacks. First, as noted, blacks were actually favored by the parole process in Michigan in that they served less of their original sentences than whites.[66] Thus if one argues that racial disparities (that disfavor blacks) in California and Texas prove racial discrimination against blacks, the disparities in Michigan prove racial discrimination against whites. Second, Hispanics in California and Texas actually served longer terms after controls (age, offense type, race, prison behavior, prior record) were introduced than did Anglos or blacks.[67] Thus if ethnic disparities after controls are indicative of discrimination, Hispanics were subjected to greater discrimination than were blacks. In short, though the study did find that race "made a difference," that difference was not consistently against blacks and for whites (and Hispanics).

Third, in California the racial disparities in time served (for example, blacks served 7.7 months longer than whites, and Hispanics served 8.1 months longer) were largely due not to the parole process but to the disparity in sentences originally imposed by the courts.[68] Fourth, one must not conclude that any black/white variation after (some) controls is equivalent to a race effect (see the discussion in Chapter Seven on interpreting the remaining variation), since this remaining variation is better described as unexplained than as a race effect. Finally, of the three states studied the one with the most "objective" parole guidelines (Michigan) actually favored blacks at the parole stage, and the state with the greatest discretion by the parole board (Texas) showed the greatest disparity against blacks. Since most states now use objective guidelines, it may be that whatever racial disparity did exist against blacks at one time no longer exists.[69]

2. Two studies often cited as suggesting or proving racial discrimination at the parole stage actually provide substantial evidence of the lack of a race effect. One study found that black and white inmates were equally likely to receive parole (though the criteria were different for the parole decision),[70] and the other found that blacks and whites were equal in time served but that blacks were less likely to be granted parole.[71] It is difficult to read these two studies (and Petersilia's) and conclude that there is substantial evidence of pervasive racial discrimination in the parole process.

3. The argument of one study—that racial discrimination was present even when blacks and whites were equally likely to be paroled, because the decision to parole used different criteria for blacks and whites—[72] is problematic. At times those who maintain the DT argue that if there

is a difference in outcome that disfavors blacks at a particular decision point, that fact alone is sufficient to prove institutional racism. And if there is no difference in outcome, it can still be maintained that racial discrimination exists if the criteria for decision making are different. Even if blacks are apparently favored at the parole stage (as they seem to have been in Michigan in the Petersilia study) it can be argued (as it was by Hepburn in proving discrimination in arrests by "leniency" at prosecution) that the parole disparity *for* blacks only proves that later decision makers (the parole board) felt that blacks had been unfairly treated in terms of length of sentence and thus that these results are proof of unjust sentencing. In short, one can interpret any result at the point of parole as being "suggestive of" or "proving" discrimination.

4. One older study of 359 randomly selected inmates from a midwestern prison system in 1968 found that though blacks served an average of seventeen months longer than whites, the positive relationship between being black and serving more time was reversed after control variables (prior record, seriousness of offense, institutional behavior, and so on) were introduced.[73] Thus white inmates, "other things being equal," served an average of one-half month more than black inmates. By contrast, age and marital status were predictive of time served even after controls were introduced. Ten years more in age translated into a sentence that was seventeen months longer, after controls, and single inmates served fourteen months longer than married inmates.[74]

Summary

Six charges of racial discrimination after sentencing are made: (1) that the simple fact of *gross disproportionality of black and white representation in U.S. prisons* is evidence of racial discrimination; (2) that the *segregation* of the races in the assignment of inmates to particular prisons and to particular cell blocks or cells constitutes racial discrimination; (3) that the *treatment programs and working assignments* in prisons are assigned in a racially discriminatory manner; (4) that the rules within the prison are enforced in a racially discriminatory manner so that the entire *disciplinary process* is characterized by racial discrimination; (5) that racial hostility between white and black inmates is encouraged by staff members to divert inmate hostility away from them and that *white inmates discriminate against black inmates*; and (6) that the *parole process* discriminates against black inmates, so that the time served for blacks is greater than that for whites with comparable sentences. The evidence for each of these six claims is sparse, inconsistent, or contradictory.

Notes

1. Jacobs, 1982.
2. Jacobs, 1982, p. 118.
3. For a history of correctional treatment of juveniles and women see Pisciotta, 1983.
4. See Mancini, 1978; Brown and Steiner, 1969; Adamson, 1983; Powell, 1891; Bacchus, 1973; Dobbins and Bass, 1958; and Carper, 1964.
5. Mancini, 1978, p. 339.
6. See Adamson, 1983; Carper, 1964; Bacchus, 1973; and Mancini, 1978.
7. Mancini, 1978, p. 343.
8. Bacchus, 1973; Carper, 1964.
9. Mancini, 1978, p. 343.
10. Mancini, 1978, p. 349.
11. Christianson, 1980a, 1980b, 1982; Christianson and Dehais, 1980; Blumstein, 1982; Dehais, 1983. Weisheit (1985) examined the sex disparity in the national jail survey and found that it was largely explained by legal control factors.
12. Jacobs, 1982. This article reviews the legal cases before 1982 that sought to desegregate prisons.
13. New York State Special Commission on Attica, 1972, pp. 33–45; Petersilia, 1983, pp. 49-72; Goetting and Howsen, 1983; Goetting, 1984.
14. Goetting, 1984; Poole and Regoli, 1980; Ramirez, 1983; New York Commission, 1972, pp. 74-82.
15. Carroll, 1977, p. 426.
16. Few empirical studies of parole decision making are found in the literature. For a list of nonempirical studies see Scott, 1974. For suggestions that race plays a role see Bailey, 1973; Korn and McCorkle, 1959, p. 239; National Minority Advisory Council on Criminal Justice, 1982, p. 308; Carroll and Mondrick, 1976; Elion and Megargee, 1979; and Petersilia, 1983.
17. Christianson, 1980a, p. 63. Likewise, Mobley (1982, p. 13) said: "For years the NAACP has insisted that the presence of such a disproportionately high number of blacks in prison was the result of a carefully calculated, methodical, and systematic racism." See also Karmen, 1984, p. 165.
18. "Racism and Imprisonment Internationally," 1984.
19. Jacobs, 1982, p. 122.
20. James B. Jacobs has written the definitive book on the American prison, *Stateville: The Penitentiary in Mass Society* (Chicago: University of Chicago Press, 1977), and numerous articles on the inmate subculture, guards, and other issues.
21. Jacobs, 1982, p. 118.
22. Jacobs, 1982, p. 143.
23. Jacobs, 1982, p. 123.
24. New York Commission, 1972, p. 39.
25. See Goetting, 1985 and Elion and Megargee, 1979.
26. Petersilia, 1983; Petersilia and Turner, 1985.
27. Petersilia, 1983, pp. 62-63.
28. Goetting, 1985, p. 12.
29. Goetting and Howsen, 1983.
30. Goetting, 1985.
31. New York Commission, 1972, p. 74.
32. Goetting, 1985.
33. Poole and Regoli, 1980.
34. Poole and Regoli, 1980, p. 940.
35. Poole and Regoli, 1980, p. 942.

36. Held, Levine, and Swartz, 1979.
37. Held et al., 1979, p. 57.
38. Hindelang, Hirschi, and Weiss, 1981, pp. 171-180. Also see the discussion on this point in Chapter Five.
39. Sylvester, Reed, and Nelson, 1977.
40. Jacobs and Kraft, 1978, p. 311.
41. Held et al., 1979.
42. See Goodstein and MacKenzie, 1984, p. 276.
43. Also on the greater level of aggression by black inmates see Petersilia, 1983, pp. 84-85.
44. Ramirez, 1983, p. 424.
45. Petersilia, 1980.
46. Carroll, 1977, p. 426. Carroll also argues that white prisoners, like black prisoners, require a class of prisoners to satisfy both sexual and psychological needs and thus participate in the conspiracy of silence so that there will be a supply of "punks" for the white prisoners (p. 432).
47. Goodstein and MacKenzie, 1984, p. 276.
48. Carroll, 1977. A similar argument is made by Engel and Rothman, 1983.
49. Carroll, 1977, p. 418.
50. Carroll, 1977, p. 429.
51. Carroll, 1977, pp. 420, 433.
52. See Bartollas and Sieverdes, 1981, p. 534 (for a complete listing of such studies). Also see A. J. Davis, 1968; Carroll, 1974; Scacco, 1975; Jacobs, 1979; and Lockwood, 1980.
53. Fuller and Orsagh, 1977, p. 42.
54. Duffy, 1985.
55. Lockwood, 1980, p. 2.
56. Goodstein and MacKenzie, 1984, pp. 277ff.
57. Lockwood, 1980, pp. 36-37.
58. Carroll, 1974, p. 185; Scacco, 1975; A. J. Davis, 1968; Jacobs, 1979.
59. Goodstein and MacKenzie, 1984.
60. Bartollas and Sieverdes, 1981, pp. 542-543.
61. Bailey, 1973; National Minority Council, 1982, p. 308; Korn and McCorkle, 1959, p. 239.
62. Owens, 1980, pp. 71-73.
63. Elion and Megargee, 1979; Carroll and Mondrick, 1976; Hussey, 1974.
64. Carroll and Mondrick, 1976.
65. Petersilia, 1983, pp. 49-50.
66. Petersilia, 1983, p. 50.
67. Petersilia, 1983, p. 67.
68. Petersilia, 1983, pp. 67, 70-71.
69. See the literature on efforts to eliminate the race effect in decisions by using objective guidelines: Blumstein, Cohen, Martin, and Tonry, 1983; Stecher and Sparks, 1982; and Petersilia and Turner, 1985.
70. Carroll and Mondrick, 1976.
71. Elion and Megargee, 1979.
72. Carroll and Mondrick, 1976.
73. Scott, 1974.
74. Scott, 1974, p. 220.

9

Conclusions
and Recommendations

This final chapter will state four overall conclusions about the myth of a racist criminal justice system, present a list of questions that are problematic for those who continue to maintain a belief in the DT, and recommend a direction for future research.

Overall Conclusions

First, the debate over the allegedly "racist" character of the American criminal justice system has been plagued by a failure to agree on a definition of racism (Chapter Two). It would appear that much of the disagreement between blacks and whites on the extent of racism in the system stems from the two sides' talking about different phenomena. Blacks (and liberals) are more prone to use the term *racist* in referring to "institutional racism" (disparity in outcome regardless of cause), to indirect racism (through unequal access to attorneys or bail), or even to acts that may be motivated by (unconscious) racial stereotypes. Also, blacks see racism as being typical of whites but commonly deny the possibility of black racism against whites. By contrast, whites (and conservatives) are more prone to see the term *racist* as applicable only to direct, conscious acts by individuals who are atypical of most whites and who represent the caricature of the bigot (for example, Archie Bunker). Also, most whites are convinced that racism is a two-way street and that blacks are as racist as or more racist than whites.

I have argued that the extent of racism in the criminal justice system cannot be intelligently discussed, and certainly cannot be resolved, before some attempt is made to reach a consensus on the definition of racism. At the very least, those who argue either side in this debate should be forced to state explicitly the definition they use and why they reject competing definitions. Furthermore, if a race effect is postulated, the "size" of that alleged race effect should be made explicit. Perhaps the best example of such an attempt at defining racism and defending that definition against competing definitions is the article by Kleck discussed in Chapter Seven.[1] Unfortunately, this issue is seldom addressed in oral debate or in the literature. The failure of laypersons to address the problem of definition is not surprising, but the failure of most scholarly works to do so is surprising and inexcusable.

Second, scholars have failed to address adequately the determinants of black and white beliefs about the validity of the DT (Chapter Three), even though the importance of these perceptions is incontrovertible. (Such perceptions may lead to increased criminality and riots by blacks and to a backlash by whites that forestalls efforts to reduce racial discrimination.) Furthermore, the research literature on a possible race effect at most decision points in the criminal justice system is quite sparse, and most of the studies that have been done are subject to methodological criticisms (Chapter Four). The evidence is inconclusive because of inconsistent results and deficient methods.

Third, the inconclusive nature of the evidence would certainly seem to preclude any claim that the DT has been "proven" for any particular decision point. This is especially true in light of the fact that many who support the DT believe that all or most blacks (the pervasiveness factor) are subjected to harsher treatment by the system and that the extent of that extra harshness (the magnitude factor) is substantial. In other words many blacks (and liberals) believe that the proportion of blacks subjected to a race effect and the size of the race effect in individual cases are both great. But this finds no support in the literature. The possibility remains that *many* blacks are victims of a race effect and that the magnitude of that race effect in individual cases is, at least, statistically significant. It would appear, however, that the size of the race effect *against* blacks is largely balanced by a comparable race effect *for* blacks. The presence of a canceling-out effect is important because there would appear to be no room in the DT for such a result.

Fourth, there is considerable indirect evidence against the DT. Research has failed to show, for example, that black decision makers (police officers, judges) "make a difference" with respect to the treatment of blacks who are processed by the system. There would appear to be two competing explanations for studies that find equal treatment of blacks by black and white police officers or judges. It could be that black and white decision makers make similar decisions because both act on the basis of "legal" factors rather than race, or it could be that the black decision makers are co-opted by the "system." In either case the impact of an infusion of blacks into the system is subject to dispute. The lack of research on any disparity in treatment of black (and white) offenders by black and white decision makers is surprising in light of the assumption that providing more black police officers and judges would ensure equal treatment of black defendants. The evidence thus far indicates that black decision makers make little difference, and thus the claim that black/white variation in outcome (with or without controls) is due to racial discrimination by whites is called into dispute.

The little research that does exist on decisions by blacks and whites who work in the criminal justice system does not indicate that black decision makers are less likely to deal harshly with black offenders. The research by Uhlman[2] on black and white judges and the research by Fyfe[3] on black and white police officers does not suggest that black judges or officers make a difference in formal decisions on processing cases. This is not to say that they do not make a difference in other ways. For example, Uhlman suggests:

> For the disadvantaged defendant, the black judge may symbolize hope and encouragement. Within both the black and white communities he may challenge negative stereotypes, while within the courtroom itself he may act as an educator, reformer, and advocate for social change. . . . On the other hand, atypically successful pre-judicial careers, . . . a rigorous process of legal socialization, and special scrutiny for highly visible black jurists . . . may attenuate the uniqueness of his role.[4]

The quotation above suggests that black judges may be socialized into accepting the discriminatory values of the white, elite middle class. In fact, the quotation is taken from an article entitled "Black Elite Decision Making: The Case of Trial Judges."

Another researcher[5] found that female and male probation officers made similar sentencing recommendations for female offenders that were more lenient than those made for men. The author speculated that this leniency might have been the result of females' in the criminal justice system sharing with males a (paternalistic) tradition of protecting women against the harsher aspects of the system.

Challenges to the Discrimination Thesis

The example above—the fact that black police officers and judges have not been found to make a difference with respect to decisions at various points of the criminal justice system—is one of a number of pieces of indirect evidence against the DT. The eleven questions posed below are also problematic for those who maintain a faith in the DT.

1. *If the DT is valid, why has research failed to demonstrate a sizable race effect at any particular decision point, before or after controls are introduced?* Chapters Four and Seven point out the inadequacy of tests of statistical significance to determine the existence of a "substantial" race effect. The Appendix provides data indicating that race seldom accounted for more than 1 percent of the variance across several decision points of the California and Pennsylvania criminal justice systems, even before controls.

2. *If the DT is valid, why do not disparate outcomes by sex, which are greater than those for race, prove that sexism is more pervasive than racism?* The Appendix points out that the racial gaps were less than the sex gaps at individual decision points of the criminal justice system. For example, in California the sex gap at arrest (7.01:1) was greater than the race gap (5.21:1). Does this indicate that at the point of arrest sexism is greater than racism?

3. *If the DT is proven by an overrepresentation of blacks in prison, how does one explain why a similar overrepresentation occurs at arrest?* In other words, since the black/white gap does not increase significantly across the system from arrest to prison, how can the system be responsible for a gap that began at arrest? The Appendix indicates that the racial gap in California for 1980 increased by only 19 percent from arrest to imprisonment (5.21:1 to 6.18:1), whereas in Pennsylvania the racial gap actually decreased by 9 percent (from 8.1:1 to 7.4:1). Thus the criminal justice systems in these two states did not appear to have increased the racial gap that began at arrest. In short, the racial gap at incarceration is not a cumulative product of an increasing gap as offenders move across the system.

4. *If the DT is valid, how does one explain why many studies have found that blacks receive more lenient treatment than whites at a particular point for a particular crime?* For example, the Appendix shows that blacks tend to receive more lenient treatment at the "front end" of the criminal justice system (for instance, charges dropped by the police and prosecutor, conviction) and harsher treatment at the back end of the system.

5. *If the DT is valid and can be proven in some cases by more lenient treatment and in other cases by more severe treatment, is not the thesis nonfalsifiable?* If not, what results would provide evidence against the thesis? One study, for example, found that the prosecutor was less likely to proceed with cases involving black offenders.[6] This leniency was viewed as being evidence of discrimination, since the result indicated that blacks were more likely to be accused by the police despite flimsy evidence. But if blacks had been more likely to be prosecuted, the author would probably have concluded that this result also indicated discrimination. It is difficult to see what results would disprove the DT.

6. *If the DT is valid, why has the black/white gap in offenses and at each decision point of the criminal justice system not varied over time with the degree of prejudice in society?* The black/white gap in offending and in incarceration is generally greater today than in earlier historical periods when prejudice was more pervasive. How can this fact be explained by the DT? Shouldn't the black/white gaps in offending and incarceration have been greatest when prejudice was greatest? For example, the racial gap for state prisons in the United States for 1932 was

approximately 4:1[7] compared with the 8:1[8] gap for 1979. There is little dissent from the view that the racial gap has grown in recent years.[9] But surely no one would argue that racial prejudice was stronger in 1979 than it was in 1932. How do supporters of the DT explain why the racial gap is increasing over time while prejudice appears to be declining?

7. *If the DT is valid and racial disproportionality indicates racism, why is the black/white incarceration gap lowest in the southern states, where prejudice is allegedly greatest, and highest in some states where prejudice is allegedly less extensive?* In 1979, for example, the states with the highest black/white racial gaps in prison incarceration were Minnesota (23.4:1), Iowa (20.6:1), and Wisconsin (18.6:1); the two states with the lowest racial gap were Mississippi (2.9:1) and New Hampshire (1.2:1).[10] Is anyone prepared to argue that racism in the criminal justice system is far more pervasive in Minnesota than in Mississippi? Furthermore, the Northeast as a region has a racial gap 2.7 times that for the South (14.7:1 compared with 5.5:1).[11] Is anyone prepared to argue that the criminal justice system in the South, where prejudice is allegedly the greatest, is far less racist than the system in the more liberal Northeast? If there is a correlation between degree of prejudice and the extent of racism in the criminal justice system, how can the above results be explained?

8. *If the DT is valid, why do not its adherents also support racial quotas at various decision points of the criminal justice system to correct the racist outcome?* Why are quotas supported in education, housing, and employment but not in criminal justice? How can one support quotas in one area but not in another if racism is equally pervasive in all areas? Or is racism less prevalent in criminal justice than in education, housing, and employment? (See the discussion on this point in Chapter Two.)

9. *If the DT is valid, if blacks are more likely to be punished for attacking whites, and if whites are less likely to be punished for attacking blacks, why do black offenders choose white victims more frequently than black victims, and why do white offenders rarely attack blacks?* Are black and white offenders so irrational that they ignore the facts of punishment that are alleged to exist? (See the discussion on this point in Chapter Two.)

10. *If the DT is valid and disparity in outcome by race is evidence of racism, why are not black assaulters, rapists, and robbers (who are more likely to choose white than black victims) considered racists?* Why is the interracial pattern of rape and assault in prison (predominantly black rapists on white victims) not proof of black racism? And why in today's society (both in and outside of prison), where whites are more likely to be attacked by blacks than blacks are to be attacked by whites, are whites the ones accused of being racist? (See the discussions in Chapters Two and Eight.)

11. *If the DT is valid, what are the prevalence (percentage of blacks affected) and magnitude (extent of extra harshness given to a specific black) of the race effect?* Does the DT mean that all blacks are subjected to extra harshness in decisions? most blacks? 50 percent of blacks? 20 percent of blacks? 5 percent of blacks? 1 percent of blacks? And what is the magnitude of that harshness? At sentencing, for example, are the affected blacks given double the sentence of comparable whites? a sentence 50 percent greater? 20 percent greater? 5 percent greater? And once the size of the prevalence and magnitude factors are specified, how does that greater specification of the DT fit the research evidence that is available and described in this book?

Agenda for Research

Research attempting to validate the DT or the NDT has been seriously deficient. From the materials presented in this book it would appear that the following four-item agenda would lead to future research being more useful in answering the question "Is the criminal justice system racist?"

1. Future research should forgo aggregate studies of decision making and concentrate on studies of individual decision makers. The model used by Uhlman[12] should be followed, so that researchers can determine the extent to which overall group decisions mask racial discrimination by individual members of the group. This method would also allow a determination of the extent to which leniency toward black offenders by some individuals is counterbalanced by harshness to black offenders by other individuals.

2. Future research should examine multiple decision points of the criminal justice system rather than focusing on one particular point, such as sentencing. Though several reviewers of the existing literature have recommended such a strategy, it would appear that little effort has been made to look at the racial gap across the entire system. The study of case processing in California and Pennsylvania for 1980 that is presented in the Appendix examined the cumulative racial gap across the criminal justice system. But it did not use control variables to determine the extent to which the gap at each point, and cumulatively, would decrease if such factors as prior record and type of plea were considered.

3. Future research should carefully define racism and racial discrimination and take into account competing definitions (as Kleck[13] did). Likewise, the researchers should defend their choice of interpretive models from among those listed in Chapter Seven. They should explain, for example, why the remaining variation is interpreted as a race effect rather than as unexplained variation. The model for comparison of interpretive models is the research by Gross and Mauro[14] and Fyfe.[15]

4. Finally, research should attempt to learn why blacks and whites differ so sharply on the DT and to learn the consequences, in terms of behavior, of these differing views. Chapter Three suggests that the belief in a racist criminal justice system by blacks is criminogenic, but little has been done to find whether law-abiding blacks and law-breaking blacks differ in their degree of belief in the DT. There is little research on the extent to which opinion leaders or personal experience shapes the views of blacks and whites with regard to the DT.

Notes

1. Kleck, 1981.
2. Uhlman, 1978, 1979a.
3. Fyfe, 1982a.
4. Uhlman, 1978, p. 885.
5. Kruttschnitt, 1985.
6. Hepburn, 1978.
7. Hall, 1969, p. 556. The ratio in Connecticut was 6:1 in 1880 (Otken, 1984, p. 229) and 15.3 in 1979 (Christianson and Dehais, 1980, p. 17). Several scholars see black crime as rising over time, which may account for the increasing black/white ratio. See Himes, 1938; Silberman, 1978; and Light, 1977a, 1977b.
8. Christianson and Dehais, 1980, p. 15.
9. Christianson and Dehais, 1980, p. 34.
10. Christianson and Dehais, 1980, pp. 15, 17.
11. Christianson and Dehais, 1980, p. 17.
12. Uhlman, 1978, 1979a.
13. Kleck, 1981.
14. Gross and Mauro, 1984.
15. Fyfe, 1982a.

Appendix
Racially Disproportionate Incarceration Rates:
Are They a Product of Cumulative Discrimination
by the Criminal Justice System?

It is often (and correctly) pointed out that blacks in the United States are incarcerated at a much higher rate than are whites. The black/white ratio of prison incarceration rates for all state correctional institutions in the country in 1979 was 7.9:1 (a rate of 368.0 blacks per 100,000 divided by a rate of 46.3 whites per 100,000 = 7.9).[1] This gap means that on a per capita basis 7.9 blacks were incarcerated in state prisons for every white. For jail incarceration rates, the national ratio for 1978 was 4.7:1 for those under sentence of under one year in local facilities and 5.4:1 for those in pretrial detention.[2]

There is considerable disagreement in the literature about the causes of these black/white gaps in incarceration rates. The gaps are the product of gaps at four earlier periods: (1) offense (whether arrested or not), (2) arrest, (3) prosecution and conviction, and (4) sentencing. The relative contribution of the four earlier gaps to the incarceration gap is subject to dispute. Some maintain that the gap in arrest rates is almost totally responsible. Blumstein, for example, found that 80 percent of the racial disproportionality in imprisonment rates could be accounted for by the differential involvement of blacks in arrests.[3] He further argues that if discrimination exists, it could account for a maximum of 20 percent of the racial gap in incarceration; the 20 percent represents a residual variation that may result from discrimination or numerous other factors. He also argues that there could be a strong racial difference in arrest vulnerability and that there is a greater likelihood of racial bias in arrest than in the processing of cases after arrest.

Several other authors, however, point out the similarity in percentages of arrests across crimes for blacks and whites, both in figures from

The data used in this appendix were made available by the Inter-University Consortium for Political and Social Research at the University of Michigan in Ann Arbor. I wish to acknowledge the assistance of Dr. Vicki Schneider in obtaining the data tape and codebook. Perin Patel of Academic Computer Services at Florida International University prepared the data tapes for analysis.

the *Uniform Crime Reports* and in data on the perception of race of offender from victimization surveys.[4] Hindelang found, for example, that victims had reported that 62 percent of all robberies were by blacks and he also found that 62 percent of arrests for robbery had been of blacks.[5] Hindelang also calculated robbery offense rates at arrest (from the *UCR*) and compared them with robbery offense rates (whether arrested or not) from victim surveys.[6] He found almost identical racial gaps. For example, victim survey data and *UCR* data both indicated a 14:1 black/white gap in the offense of robbery for those age 21 and older. Hindelang concluded that arrest data were not seriously biased in that the racial gap at the offense level was similar to that found at the arrest level.

Combining the work of Hindelang and Blumstein, one may conclude that there is little racial bias from offense to incarceration and thus that the racial gap in incarceration is due to a racial gap in offending. But numerous studies have reported bias in arrests, prosecution and conviction, and sentencing. Some have suggested that the discrimination is *cumulative,* in that the racial gap increases as one moves across the criminal justice system from offense to incarceration.[7] Thus a relatively small or nonexistent racial gap at offense "grows" to an 8:1 gap at incarceration.

Several studies have suggested that the racial gap at arrest is much larger than the actual offense gap. McNeely and Pope maintain that self-reports have found "slight or nonexistent" black/white differences in offending and thus conclude that the racial gap found in arrest figures is a product of bias.[8] Hindelang, Hirschi, and Weiss dispute this view and contend that self-reports, if properly constructed and interpreted, do show significant racial differences in offending.[9] They do not claim, however, that the racial differences in self-reports approach the black/white gap found in arrest figures, largely because more trivial behavior is being measured by self-reports than by arrest figures.

Others have suggested that there is evidence of racial discrimination at the prosecution and conviction stage. A few empirical studies[10] have claimed evidence of racial bias at the conviction level, and numerous authors[11] have suggested that blacks are more likely than whites to be convicted for similar offenses. Others have suggested that blacks are less likely to be convicted but blame discrimination, in that blacks are more likely to be arrested on flimsy evidence, and thus their cases are more often dismissed.[12]

Numerous studies suggest that racial discrimination exists at sentencing.[13] By contrast, several recent reviews suggest numerous flaws in research that has claimed to find racial bias in sentencing.[14] These reviews reach a consensus that there is no substantial race effect in sentencing.

Thus researchers disagree on the extent to which the racial gap increases from offense to incarceration. Though some claim to have found evidence of racial bias at various points and cumulative bias across the system, others have reviewed the literature and found little or no evidence of racial discrimination.[15] There are several possible explanations for this disagreement:

1. Most of the studies that claim a significant role for racial discrimination at various points in the system relied on tests of significance rather than measures of association. A difference in outcome by race of offender may be statistically significant and yet be "practically" insignificant, in that little variation in outcome (as indicated by a measure of association) may be accounted for by race of offender. Hagan,[16] Kleck,[17] and Nettler[18] point out the fallacy of total reliance on tests of significance to determine the importance of race as a predictor of outcome.

2. No study has examined the racial gap for all the decision points from arrest to incarceration. Though the black/white gap changes little between arrest and incarceration, this overall stability may mask significant racial gaps in different directions at intervening decision points. It is possible, for example, that the black/white gap decreases at the point of prosecution and conviction and increases at sentencing to produce no overall change from arrest to incarceration. The National Research Council and several researchers have urged that all decision points be studied simultaneously so that the presence or absence of cumulative discrimination can be determined.[19] Only one study, that by Eisenstein and Jacob, has examined differential outcome by race from arrest to sentence.[20] But it did not examine the racial gap and was limited to data in Baltimore, Chicago, and Detroit.

3. No prior study has examined changes in the racial gap from arrest to incarceration for individual offenses. It is possible that the racial gap increases across the criminal justice system for some offenses and decreases for others to produce an overall picture of no change. Also, any racial gap that exists at any decision point may be the result of different proportions of black and white offenders' being charged with particular offenses. For example, if 50 percent of black arrestees but only 25 percent of white arrestees are charged with violent offenses, one would expect a greater proportion of convicted blacks to be incarcerated because of the different mix of offenses among blacks and whites. Goetting and Howsen did find that a greater percentage of black than white prisoners in the United States (62 percent to 49 percent) were incarcerated for violent offenses.[21]

4. Most studies of alleged discrimination have been conducted in one city or criminal court. No study has attempted to use statewide data to determine the extent to which cumulative disadvantage accrues to blacks as they proceed through the criminal justice system. It is possible that there is discrimination in some locales but not in others, and thus the contradictory results reported in the literature may simply represent this disparity in reality.

Present Study and Data Set

This study will examine the black/white gap at three points before incarceration—arrest, prosecution and conviction, and sentencing—to determine the extent to which that gap changes as one moves across the criminal justice system. The Offender Based Transaction System (OBTS) data for California and Pennsylvania trace all 1980 arrests through the system to the eventual outcome at sentencing. The California data set for 1980 was composed of 184,636 felony cases and is considered to be a representative sample of all California cases for 1980 (though the 184,636 cases are estimated to undercount the population by approximately 30 percent). The Pennsylvania data set for 1980 was composed of 59,184 felony cases and is considered to be an almost total approximation of the felony cases processed by the state criminal justice system in that year. These two data sets provide dispositions at the police stage (whether released by the police or forwarded to the prosecutor); prosecution stage (whether nolle prossed or prosecuted, number of charges, whether convicted or not, and number of charges at conviction); and sentencing stage (whether given a jail or prison sentence and, for Pennsylvania only, the length of the sentence).

This study will attempt to overcome the four major shortcomings of prior research listed above:

First, the predictive power of race for outcome at each decision point will be determined by a measure of association that can be interpreted as the proportion of errors reduced by predicting the outcome at each decision point when the race of the offender is known. Tests of significance will also be reported, so that a comparison can be made of the utility of such tests versus a measure of association to gauge the predictive power of race.

Second, the study will trace the size of the black/white gap at three decision points in addition to incarceration. A significant increase in the racial gap from arrest to incarceration would suggest that either legal factors (for example, prior record, strength of evidence, nature of offense) or extralegal factors (for example, discrimination because of race or sex of offender) had produced that increase.

Third, the racial gaps across the same decision points will also be traced for nineteen separate California offenses (the seventeen most frequently charged plus homicide and negligent manslaughter with vehicle) and for sixteen separate Pennsylvania offenses (the fourteen most frequently charged plus homicide and negligent manslaughter with vehicle) to see if the pattern found for all offenses considered together is also found for the individual offenses.

Fourth, the data used will be a representative sample of all cases in two states. As indicated earlier, past studies have relied on data in only one city or court.

Methodology

The crosstabs program of the *Statistical Package for the Social Sciences* (SPSS) was used to obtain crosstabulations of race of offender by outcome at each decision point. Chi-square was chosen as the test of significance, and the asymmetric uncertainty coefficient as the measure of association. The latter was chosen because it is designed for use with nominal level variables and is a proportional reduction in error statistic, so that it can be interpreted as the proportion of variance in the dependent variable (outcome at each decision point) explained by the independent variable (race of offender). Three-way crosstabulations were also obtained for race of offender by outcome for individual offenses.

The racial gaps were obtained by using population figures for blacks and whites in the two states to calculate rates at each decision point. The black rate, which was always larger, was then divided by the white rate to obtain the ratio. For example, 49,389 blacks age 20 and up were arrested in California for all felonies in 1980, for a rate per 100,000 of 4,344.6; the white felony arrest rate was 834.2; and the racial gap was 5.21:1. Arrest rates were also calculated for various subgroups of the California and Pennsylvania populations to determine the variation in rates or relative risk of apprehension by age, sex, and race.

Results

Tables 1 and 2* present the relative risk of apprehension by age, sex, and race subgroups for California and Pennsylvania in 1980. For example, in Table 1 the risk of apprehension of each subgroup is given as a percentage of the overall arrest rate (that of all residents, 969.18 per 100,000 persons 20 and up) for California. Thus the white rate was 86 percent of the overall rate, with whites 20–29 having a rate 228 percent of the overall rate and whites 70 and up having a rate only 1 percent of the overall rate. By contrast, the black rate for those 20 and up was 448 percent of the overall rate, with blacks 20–29 having a rate 880 percent of the overall rate and blacks 70 and up having a rate only 10 percent of the overall rate. The ratios given in Tables 1 and 2 represent the odds of a person in a particular subgroup's being arrested in a given year. For example, the overall California arrest rate for those 20 and up was 969.18 per 100,000, which can be translated into odds of 1:103 (calculated by dividing 100,000 by 969.18). This means that there was one arrest of a person 20 and up for every 103 such people in the California population.

These odds varied greatly by subgroups based on age, sex, and race. Note that one black male 20–29 was arrested for every seven such per-

*All tables appear at the end of the Appendix.

sons in the California population, and one white female 70 and up was arrested for every 41,667 such people in the population. Thus the odds of a black male 20–29 being arrested for a felony were 5,952 times as great as the odds for a white female 70 and up. It should also be noted that the variation in odds of being arrested was much greater across age groups (1:43 for those 20–29 to 1:6,536 for those 70 and up) than between the sexes (1:57 for males to 1:380 for females) or the races (1:23 for blacks to 1:120 for whites). Thus age was the best predictor of arrest probability, followed by sex and then race.

Table 2 presents subgroup percentages and odds of apprehension for Pennsylvania for 1980. Overall the risk of apprehension was less in Pennsylvania (463.1) than in California (969.2), and thus the odds of arrest for a Pennsylvania resident (1:216) were greater than the odds of arrest for a California resident (1:103). However, 10,707 of the 59,184 Pennsylvania cases had no data on race of offender, and thus the Pennsylvania rates are undercounted by approximately 18 percent (Table 2 is based on the 48,477 cases for which race of offender was known). It is interesting that the race gap at arrest in Pennsylvania (9.7:1—532 percent ÷ 55 percent) was greater than that in California (5.2:1—448 percent ÷ 86 percent). Christianson[22] and Christianson and Dehais[23] point out the variation in the racial gap for imprisonment across states but do not note that it might be due to variation in the racial arrest gap. The fact that Christianson and Dehais[24] found the prison racial gap in Pennsylvania to be greater (12.2:1) than that in California (9.5:1) would be consistent with the fact that the racial arrest gap in Pennsylvania was found to be greater than that for California.

Table 3 presents the black/white gaps at eight decision points of the California criminal justice system. Note that the racial gap did increase from 5.21 at arrest to 6.18 at prison incarceration (an increase of 19 percent). When all sentences of incarceration (whether jail or prison) are considered, however, the gap actually narrowed from 5.21 to 4.84 (a decrease of 7 percent). Table 3 also presents the racial gaps across the same eight decision points for black males as opposed to white males, black females as opposed to white females, black males age 20–29 to white males 20–29, and black females 20–29 to white females 20–29. The greatest increase from the arrest gap to the prison incarceration gap occurred for the high-risk subgroups of black males 20–29 (an increase of 68 percent) and black females 20–29 (an increase of 47 percent). But the increase in the racial gap from arrest to prison incarceration was greater for black females (36 percent) than for black males (23 percent). Again, sex appears to be a better predictor of the increase: the black/white gap increased by only 19 percent, compared with a 164 percent increase for the male/female gap.[25]

Table 4 presents racial gaps at ten decision points of the Pennsylvania criminal justice system. The black/white gap from arrest to (prison) incarceration actually declined by 9 percent, with the drop being greatest (-47 percent) for black females as opposed to white females. The sex gap in Pennsylvania increased from arrest to prison (by 174 percent), as it did in California (by 164 percent). Thus if one wants to argue that the 19 percent increase in the black/white gap from arrest to prison in California is indicative of racial discrimination against blacks, one must explain why the 9 percent decrease from arrest to prison in Pennsylvania does not indicate discrimination against whites. Furthermore, if an increase in the black/white gap from arrest to prison suggests racial discrimination, the much greater increases in the male/female gap in the two states suggest that sex discrimination (against males) is greater than racial discrimination (against blacks).

Table 5 examines the black/white ratios at six decision points for nineteen California offenses. The racial gap from arrest to prison actually decreased for seven offenses (homicide, robbery, forgery, selling marijuana, dangerous drugs, fondling children, and driving while intoxicated). The greatest decrease in the black/white gap occurred for driving while intoxicated (1.21 to 0.73—a decline of 40 percent); the greatest increase occurred for weapon offenses (2.35 to 4.53—a rise of 93 percent). Thus if one were to argue that blacks were discriminated against by the criminal justice system as evidenced by the increase in the racial gap for all offenses, one would also have to argue that the system discriminated against blacks charged with weapon offenses but against whites charged with driving while intoxicated. The breakdown in racial gaps across the criminal justice system by offense does not provide evidence of discrimination against all blacks regardless of the charge. From Table 5 one could not even support the view that the more serious offenses most often result in an increase in the racial gap across the system. The table indicates no consistent pattern in this regard.

Table 6 examines black/white gaps at ten decision points for sixteen Pennsylvania offenses. The racial gap from arrest to prison decreased for eight offenses and increased for the remaining eight. Seven of the eight offenses experiencing an increase were violent, and thus it appears that in Pennsylvania there was a general increase in the racial gap from arrest to prison for violent offenses and a decline for property and other offenses.

Table 7 provides another perspective on the attrition of cases from arrest to incarceration. The total number of offenders reaching each stage of the criminal justice system is given for several subgroups of California offenders. (A similar table is not given for Pennsylvania.) Though a greater percentage of black than white arrestees (6.3 percent to 5.2 percent) were incarcerated in prison, a smaller percentage of blacks than whites (42.1 percent to 43.9 percent) were given some type of incarceration (prison or jail). Table 7 indicates that greater attrition of cases (as defined by percentage of all arrestees who are eventually incarcerated) resulted for certain age groups (for example, only 0.7 percent of those 70 and up were given prison terms) and for females (only 2.3 percent of female arrestees were given prison terms) than for blacks (6.3 percent). Again, attrition of cases from arrest to incarceration was better predicted by age and sex than by race.

Tables 8 and 9 present a different perspective on the processing of various subgroups of offenders across the criminal justice systems of California and Pennsylvania. Outcome percentages for several decision points across the system are given for various subgroups of the population by race, sex, and age. In Table 8 the percentage of black arrestees forwarded to the prosecutor in California (86.0 percent) was actually below that for whites (90.4 percent). Also, whereas 85.2 percent of white cases reaching the prosecutor were not dropped (nolle prossed), the figure for blacks was 78.2 percent (meaning that the charges against blacks were more likely to be dropped). The percentage of black cases (that were not dropped) that resulted in a conviction was smaller (72.0 percent) than that for white cases (76.0 percent). By contrast, the percentage of blacks convicted as felons as opposed to misdemeanants was higher (73.2 percent) than that for whites (62.8 percent); and the percentage of blacks sent to prison (of those convicted as felons) was greater (17.8 percent) than that for whites (14.0 percent). Thus at the first three stages blacks received "favored" treatment over whites, and at the last two points the opposite occurred. Certainly there is no evidence here that *the system* discriminated *against* black offenders. The system did not operate in any consistent direction with respect to black and white offenders.

Table 9 presents outcome percentages for nine decision points of the Pennsylvania criminal justice system. At only two of the nine points did blacks receive more favorable treatment; 90.2 percent of white cases were not dropped by the prosecutor, compared with 88.0 percent of black cases, and 12.8 percent of convicted whites received a prison sentence, as opposed to 10.8 percent of blacks. At the remaining seven points blacks had less favorable outcomes than whites. Note especially that 76.6 percent of blacks who received a prison term were given a term of five or more years, compared with 36.4 percent of whites. This seems to have stemmed in part from the tendency of blacks to be convicted of multiple offenses (57.1 percent to 36.1 percent for whites).

Tables 10 and 11 present chi square significance levels and the asymmetric uncertainty coefficients for race and sex (and the asymmetric gamma coefficient for age) as well as outcome at five decision points of the California system and seven decision points of the Pennsylvania system. Since the asymmetric uncertainty coefficient does not have a positive or negative sign to indicate the direction of the relationship, a positive or negative sign is also given to indicate whether blacks, females, and older groups received more favorable treatment (+) or less favorable (-) treatment. In Table 10, for example, the race of arrestee in California is shown to have been only slightly predictive (0.58 percent of the variance in outcome was accounted for by race) at the first decision point. The positive sign below the coefficient indicates that blacks received more favorable treatment than whites at this stage. Though race was not a good predictor of outcome and the influence of race was not in the expected direction (discrimination against blacks), by the measure of association race was a better predictor at each point than sex or age. And yet it appears that race did not even account for 1 percent of the variance at any of the five decision points for California.

Race is statistically significant, however, at the .001 level at each of the five decision points, though it does not explain a "significant" (from a practical as opposed to a statistical viewpoint) amount of the variation in outcome at any point as indicated by the measures of association. Thus it is obvious that the test of significance would not be a good indication here of the predictive power of race. In fact, the two statistics seem contradictory, in that the test of significance would indicate to many that race is a good predictor of outcome but the measure of association would indicate that it is a poor predictor. Since the level of significance is a function of strength of association and sample size, it is obvious that the large sample (184,636) overwhelms, in a statistical sense, the small degree of association.

Table 11 provides chi-square levels of significance and measures of association for seven decision points of the Pennsylvania criminal justice system. Race appears to be a better predictor of outcome than sex or age (as indicated by measures of association) at four of the first five decision points. And yet the only decision point where race accounted for a "significant" amount of variance was whether those convicted were given a term of five or more years (11.6 percent of the variance). Again, level of significance was great at each of the seven points (that is, at .0000), though the measure of association indicated a very small relationship between race and outcome.

Discussion and Conclusion

First, it is clear that the black/white gap does not increase markedly as defendants move across the criminal justice system. Though the gap at prison incarceration was 19 percent greater than at arrest for California, the gap for Pennsylvania actually decreased by 9 percent. Thus there is little evidence here that the black/white prison incarceration gap is a product of cumulative bias across the criminal justice system.

Second, the notion of "systematic" action by the criminal justice system may be inaccurate. The decisions made across the system are made independently, and it appears from the California data that blacks receive more favorable treatment at the front end of the system and less favorable treatment at the back end of the system. This conclusion was also reached by Petersilia, who also utilized California OBTS data.[26]

Third, the racial gaps for individual offenses do not follow a uniform pattern as they are examined at several points across the criminal justice system. Not only is there no "system" with respect to the several stages of the criminal justice system, but it also appears that blacks receive more favorable treatment across the system for some offenses and less favorable treatment for others.[27]

Fourth, since age and sex are better predictors of processing by the criminal justice system (with the exception of sentence length) than race, one could just as easily argue that ageism and sexism are more endemic than racism. Though additional controls (for example, prior record) would be needed before such a conclusion could be drawn, even without such controls the predictive power of race is minimal. Unless blacks actually are *less* likely to have a prior record (or to have other characteristics deemed deserving of more lenient treatment), these results are indicative of no discrimination. In other words, since being black was not a good predictor of outcome in California and Pennsylvania, one must conclude that either (1) there is no discrimination or (2) there is discrimination since blacks got equal treatment though they were unequal (less deserving of punishment) in character, because of a lesser likelihood of a prior record, a lesser likelihood of involvement in a violent as opposed to a property offense, and so on.

Fifth, if the racial gap in prison incarceration is evidence of discrimination, those states with a greater racial gap in their prison populations would have to be viewed as being more discriminatory. Christianson calculated the gaps for 1979 in the United States and found that Wisconsin had the highest figure (22.7:1) and North Dakota the lowest (1.7:1).[28] Surely no one would argue based on these figures that the Wisconsin criminal justice system was 13 times more racist than the system in North Dakota.

Notes

1. Christianson and Dehais, 1980, p. 10.
2. Calculated from figures in Hindelang, Hirschi, and Weiss, 1981, p. 483. For figures on the sex disparity in jail see Weisheit, 1985. This source also discusses the reasons for the sex disparity and concludes that it is due to "legal" factors rather than to discrimination or paternalism.
3. Blumstein, 1982.
4. Hindelang, 1978, 1981; Nettler, 1984, p. 139.
5. Hindelang, 1978, p. 100.
6. Hindelang, 1981, p. 468.

7. Pope, 1984; Balkan, Berger, and Schmidt, 1980; Reiman, 1984, p. 79; Forslund, 1970, p. 99; Korn and McCorkle, 1959, p. 243.
8. McNeely and Pope, 1981b, p. 43.
9. Hindelang et al., 1981, p. 180.
10. See, for example, Bureau of Justice Statistics, 1983b; and National Minority Advisory Council on Criminal Justice, 1982, p. 38.
11. See Peirson, 1977, p. 110; Sutherland and Cressey, 1974, p. 133; and Karmen, 1984, p. 165.
12. See Dehais, 1983, and Hepburn, 1978.
13. See Dehais, 1983; Clayton, 1983; and Radelet, 1981.
14. Kleck, 1981, 1985; Hagan, 1974; Blumstein, Cohen, Martin, and Tonry, 1983, Vol. 1; Hagan and Bumiller, 1983; Klepper, Nagin, and Tierney, 1983.
15. Eisenstein and Jacob, 1977; Williams, 1981a; Nettler, 1984, p. 139; Akers, 1985, p. 17.
16. Hagan, 1974.
17. Kleck, 1981.
18. Nettler, 1984, p. 273.
19. Blumstein et al., 1983, Vol. 1, p. 92; Williams, 1981a; Dannefer and Schull, 1982; Burke and Turk, 1975; Hardy, 1983, p. 196; Zatz and Hagan, 1985, p. 105.
20. Eisenstein and Jacob, 1977.
21. Goetting and Howsen, 1983.
22. Christianson, 1980a, 1980b.
23. Christianson and Dehais, 1980.
24. Christianson and Dehais, 1980, p. 26.
25. One study (Weisheit, 1985) attempted to explain the male/female jail incarceration gap. The author found little support for the DT as an explanation for that gap.
26. Petersilia, 1983, pp. xv, 31–32.
27. Wilbanks (1984c, p. 100) found that Hispanics in Dade County, Florida, who were charged in 1980 homicides received more favorable treatment than did blacks or Anglos. No data on Hispanics and non-Hispanics was available in the Pennsylvania and California OBTS data sets.
28. Christianson, 1982.

Table 1   Probability of arrest and percentage of overall arrest rate for subgroups
          of California for 1980

	All	**20–29**	**30–39**	**40–49**	**50–59**	**60–69**	**70 and up**
				Age group			
All	100%[a]	239%	99%	45%	18%	7%	2%
	1:103[b]	1:43	1:102	1:229	1:572	1:1,475	1:6,536
White	86%	228%	87%	39%	15%	5%	1%
	1:120	1:45	1:118	1:265	1:699	1:1,963	1:8,210
Black	448%	880%	470%	196%	96%	44%	10%
	1:23	1:12	1:22	1:53	1:108	1:235	1:991
Male	181%	416%	176%	80%	34%	14%	4%
	1:57	1:25	1:59	1:129	1:303	1:737	1:2,577
Female	27%	66%	32%	14%	5%	1%	0.2%
	1:380	1:155	1:327	1:761	1:2,245	1:7,194	1:37,313
White male	154%	391%	147%	66%	26%	10%	3%
	1:67	1:26	1:70	1:157	1:390	1:1,027	1:3,531
White female	22%	60%	27%	12%	4%	1%	0.2%
	1:460	1:173	1:389	1:851	1:2,707	1:9,099	1:41,667
Black male	807%	1,517%	837%	351%	180%	89%	25%
	1:13	1:7	1:12	1:29	1:57	1:115	1:409
Black female	119%	245%	131%	46%	20%	7%	1%
	1:87	1:42	1:79	1:222	1:513	1:1,517	1:10,604

[a] The rate for all persons age 20 and up was 969.2 per 100,000 of the population 20 and up. Thus the figure of 100% indicates that the rate for "All" is 100% of the rate of 969.2. Likewise the 86% for whites 20 and up indicates that the rate for this racial group is 86% of the overall rate of 969.2. The 448% for blacks 20 and up indicates that the rate for this racial group is 448% of the overall rate of 969.2.

[b] The ratio of 1:103 indicates that one resident 20 and up in 103 was arrested (calculated by dividing 100,000 by the rate for the group—in this case, a rate of 969.2). The ratio of 1:7 for black males age 20–29 indicates that one was arrested for every seven in the population. These figures should be interpreted as the odds of a member of a particular population group's being arrested in 1980. However, it should be noted that these odds assume that no offender was arrested several times in 1980 (a questionable assumption).

Table 2 Probability of arrest and percentage of overall arrest rate for subgroups of Pennsylvania for 1980

| | All | Age group | | | | | |
		20–29	30–39	40–49	50–59	60–69	70 and up
All[a]	100%[b] 1:216[c]	276% 1:78	117% 1:185	51% 1:421	19% 1:1,129	8% 1:2,801	2% 1:11,236
White	55% 1:394	161% 1:134	57% 1:376	27% 1:801	10% 1:2,101	4% 1:5,051	1% 1:17,857
Black	532% 1:41	1,185% 1:18	668% 1:32	267% 1:81	112% 1:193	49% 1:443	11% 1:2,016
Male	192% 1:112	502% 1:43	211% 1:102	93% 1:231	37% 1:591	15% 1:1,397	5% 1:4,566
Female	20% 1:1,098	54% 1:402	27% 1:806	13% 1:1,686	4% 1:5,814	1% 1:15,385	0.2% 1:89,286
White male	107% 1:203	296% 1:73	105% 1:207	50% 1:436	19% 1:1,125	8% 1:2,551	3% 1:7,519
White female	9% 1:2,304	27% 1:808	12% 1:1,825	6% 1:3,731	2% 1:9,434	1% 1:25,000	0.2% 1:100,000
Black male	1,060% 1:20	2,269% 1:10	1,303% 1:17	526% 1:41	230% 1:94	103% 1:209	28% 1:779
Black female	117% 1:184	263% 1:82	158% 1:136	68% 1:319	18% 1:1,203	8% 1:2,584	0% ——

[a] The table is based on 48,477 cases that included race of offender.

[b] The rate for all persons 20 and up was 463.1 per 100,000 of the population 20 and up. Thus the figure of 100% indicates that the rate for "All" is 100% of the rate of 463.1. Likewise the 55% for whites 20 and up indicates that the rate for this racial group is 55% of the overall rate of 463.1. The 532% for blacks 20 and up indicates that the rate for this racial group is 532% of the overall rate of 463.1.

[c] The ratio of 1:216 indicates that one resident 20 and up in 216 was arrested in 1980 (calculated by dividing 100,000 by the rate for the group—in this case, a rate of 463.1). The ratio of 1:10 for black males 20-29 indicates that one was arrested for every ten in the population. These figures should be interpreted as the odds of a member of a particular population group's being arrested in 1980.

Table 3 Gaps by race, sex, and selected age groups at 8 decision points of the California criminal justice system in 1980

	Arrest	Sent to pros.[a]	Not dropped[b]	Conv.[c]	Conv. as fel.[d]	Incar. prison[e]	% change arrest to prison[f]	Jail m./fel.[g]	Prison or jail m./fel.[h]
Black/white	5.21:1	4.79:1	4.40:1	4.17:1	4.86:1	6.18:1	+ 19%	4.66:1	4.84:1
Male/female	7.01:1	6.90:1	6.86:1	7.10:1	7.56:1	18.59:1	+164%	8.90:1	9.57:1
Black male/ white male	5.05:1	4.79:1	4.40:1	4.13:1	4.78:1	6.19:1	+ 23%	4.62:1	4.81:1
Black female/ white female	5.13:1	4.98:1	4.59:1	4.64:1	5.65:1	6.99:1	+ 36%	5.29:1	5.31:1
Black male 20–29/white male 20–29	3.88:1	3.67:1	3.38:1	3.21:1	3.74:1	6.52:1	+ 68%	4.60:1	4.83:1
Black female 20–29/white female 20–29	4.10:1	3.97:1	3.67:1	3.73:1	4.42:1	6.02:1	+ 47%	5.71:1	5.60:1
20–59/60 and up	26.96:1	26.23:1	25.65:1	25.18:1	27.86:1	38.94:1	+ 44%	34.13:1	34.73:1

[a] Indicates those forwarded by the police to the prosecutor.
[b] Indicates that the cases at this point were not dropped by the prosecutor before a court disposition.
[c] Indicates cases where a conviction resulted.
[d] Indicates that the conviction (or at least one if multiple convictions) was for a felony.
[e] Indicates that a prison sentence was given.
[f] Indicates the percentage increase in the gap from arrest to incarceration in prison.
[g] Indicates incarceration in jail whether the offender was ultimately convicted of a felony or misdemeanor.
[h] Indicates incarceration in prison or jail whether the offender was convicted of a felony or misdemeanor. (All were initially charged with felonies.)

Table 4 Gaps by race, sex, and selected age groups at 10 decision points of the Pennsylvania criminal justice system in 1980

	Arrest & sent to pros. [a]	Not dropped [b]	Pros. as fel. [c]	2 or more chgs. [d]	Conv. [e]	2 or more convs. [f]	Conv. as fel. [g]	Incar. prison [h]	5 or more years [i]	Incar. jail or prison [j]	% change arrest to incar. [k]
Black/white	8.1:1	7.9:1	8.1:1	9.6:1	8.7:1	13.5:1	8.4:1	7.4:1	15.5:1	8.8:1	− 9%
Male/female	8.6:1	8.6:1	8.5:1	9.6:1	12.2:1	14.8:1	8.3:1	23.6:1	38.2:1	23.7:1	+174%
Black male/white male	8.4:1	8.2:1	8.4:1	9.9:1	9.0:1	14.1:1	8.8:1	8.0:1	16.6:1	9.3:1	− 4%
Black female/white female	9.7:1	9.3:1	9.4:1	11.5:1	11.1:1	16.7:1	9.7:1	5.1:1	11.5:1	8.3:1	− 47%
Black male 20–29/ white male 20–29	7.7:1	7.6:1	7.8:1	8.9:1	7.9:1	12.1:1	8.2:1	6.4:1	14.0:1	8.4:1	− 17%
Black female 20–29/ white female 20–29	9.9:1	9.4:1	9.6:1	10.2:1	9.1:1	12.1:1	6.0:1	4.0:1	12.6:1	5.7:1	− 60%
20–59/60 and up	26.2:1	26.8:1	26.3:1	28.7:1	29.1:1	30.2:1	26.4:1	67.5:1	130.6:1	52.6:1	+157%

[a] Indicates those arrested by the police and forwarded to the prosecutor. (In Pennsylvania no cases were released by the police, as was the case in California).

[b] Indicates that the cases at this point were not dropped by the prosecutor before a court disposition.

[c] Indicates that the original felony charge was prosecuted as a felony.

[d] Indicates that those at this point were charged with two or more offenses by the prosecutor.

[e] Indicates cases where a conviction resulted.

[f] Indicates a conviction for two or more offenses.

[g] Indicates that the conviction (or at least one if multiple convictions) was for a felony.

[h] Indicates that a prison sentence was given.

[i] Indicates prison term of 5 or more years.

[j] Indicates that a term of incarceration (whether jail or prison) resulted.

[k] Indicates the percentage increase or decrease in the gap from arrest to incarceration in prison.

Table 5 Black/white gaps at 6 decision points of the California criminal justice system for 19 offenses in 1980

Offense	Arrest	Sent to pros.[a]	Not dropped[b]	Conv.[c]	Conv. as fel.[d]	Incar. prison[e]	% change arrest to prison[f]
Negligent manslaughter—vehicle (909[g])	1.41:1	1.40:1	1.43:1	1.53:1	1.69:1	1.72:1	+22%
Homicide (999)	6.47:1	6.32:1	6.09:1	5.76:1	5.83:1	5.69:1	-12%
Abduction (1008)	5.68:1	5.19:1	6.54:1	4.56:1	5.22:1	5.96:1	+ 4%
Rape (1103)	7.27:1	7.22:1	6.12:1	5.82:1	6.39:1	9.12:1	+25%
Robbery (1299)	9.42:1	8.95:1	8.56:1	8.18:1	8.49:1	8.32:1	-12%
Aggravated assault—weapon (1315)	5.14:1	4.88:1	4.52:1	4.05:1	5.27:1	7.70:1	+50%
Assault (1399)	3.59:1	3.50:1	3.16:1	2.74:1	3.52:1	5.47:1	+52%
Burglary (2299)	4.34:1	4.16:1	4.03:1	3.81:1	4.03:1	5.39:1	+24%
Larceny (2399)	5.51:1	5.32:1	4.99:1	4.75:1	5.10:1	6.35:1	+15%
Motor vehicle theft (2404)	5.84:1	5.40:1	5.16:1	5.02:1	5.48:1	6.16:1	+ 5%
Forgery (2589)	6.06:1	5.83:1	5.68:1	5.62:1	5.62:1	5.47:1	-10%
Fraud (2699)	5.53:1	5.36:1	5.22:1	5.28:1	5.59:1	6.67:1	+21%
Selling marijuana (3560)	6.00:1	5.76:1	5.10:1	4.60:1	3.46:1	5.70:1	- 5%
Possessing marijuana (3562)	3.33:1	3.19:1	2.55:1	2.85:1	2.78:1	5.18:1	+56%
Dangerous drugs (3599)	5.68:1	5.52:1	4.77:1	4.62:1	6.11:1	5.47:1	- 4%
Fondling children (3601)	2.02:1	1.99:1	1.71:1	1.49:1	1.69:1	1.93:1	- 4%
Weapon offense (5299)	2.35:1	2.25:1	2.10:1	1.94:1	2.13:1	4.53:1	+93%
Driving while intoxicated (5404)	1.21:1	1.21:1	1.19:1	1.20:1	1.22:1	0.73:1	-40%
Public order (7399)	4.05:1	3.96:1	3.18:1	3.12:1	3.55:1	4.23:1	+ 4%
All offenses	5.21:1	4.79:1	4.40:1	4.17:1	4.86:1	6.18:1	+19%

[a] Indicates those arrested by the police and forwarded to the prosecutor.
[b] Indicates that the cases at this point were not dropped by the prosecutor before a court disposition.
[c] Indicates conviction in court.
[d] Indicates conviction as a felony rather than as a misdemeanor.
[e] Indicates a prison sentence.
[f] Indicates the percentage of change in the black/white gap from arrest to prison.
[g] Numbers in parentheses are National Crime Information Center offense codes.

Table 6 Black/white gaps for 16 offense categories at 10 decision points of the Pennsylvania criminal justice system in 1980

Offense	Arrest & sent to pros.[a]	Not dropped[b]	Pros. as fel.[c]	2 or more chgs.[d]	Conv.[e]	2 or more convs.[f]	Conv. as fel.[g]	Incar, prison[h]	5 or more years[i]	Incar. jail or prison[j]	% change arrest to incar.[k]
Negligent manslaughter (909[l])	1.0:1	1.0:1	1.1:1	0.9:1	0.8:1	0.3:1	1.0:1	1.9:1	—m	1.31:1	+ 9%
Homicide (999)	14.1:1	1.2:1	15.8:1	19.6:1	18.9:1	37.6:1	16.6:1	30.8:1	34.8:1	24.6:1	+118%
Rape (1103)	21.8:1	21.7:1	22.9:1	24.6:1	22.0:1	38.4:1	23.9:1	26.8:1	47.5:1	23.0:1	+ 23%
Sexual assault (1199)	2.5:1	2.5:1	2.5:1	3.1:1	2.8:1	4.9:1	2.5:1	5.5:1	12.2:1	3.4:1	+120%
Robbery (1299)	30.5:1	29.4:1	29.8:1	31.6:1	31.6:1	47.6:1	30.5:1	18.0:1	26.5:1	32.8:1	- 41%
Simple assault (1313)	6.4:1	6.1:1	6.3:1	7.5:1	7.6:1	13.4:1	6.6:1	8.9:1	25.1:1	9.1:1	+ 39%
Assault (1399)	11.0:1	10.6:1	10.9:1	11.6:1	12.6:1	19.8:1	11.4:1	16.3:1	27.3:1	15.1:1	+ 48%
Burglary (2299)	2.4:1	2.4:1	2.5:1	2.3:1	1.8:1	1.4:1	2.4:1	1.4:1	2.0:1	2.1:1	- 42%
Shoplifting (2303)	29.7:1	29.1:1	30.2:1	34.2:1	40.0:1	53.6:1	30.3:1	8.5:1	—m	47.6:1	- 71%
Auto theft (2411)	10.7:1	10.0:1	10.0:1	11.6:1	8.4:1	10.1:1	10.4:1	3.0:1	4.9:1	7.0:1	- 72%
Fraud (2699)	4.6:1	4.5:1	4.5:1	7.9:1	4.7:1	6.8:1	4.5:1	2.4:1	4.5:1	4.5:1	- 48%
Stolen property (2899)	7.5:1	7.6:1	7.6:1	10.4:1	7.4:1	12.8:1	7.7:1	3.7:1	8.8:1	6.8:1	- 51%
Resisting arrest (4801)	5.1:1	4.9:1	5.2:1	4.9:1	4.1:1	5.4:1	6.3:1	1.9:1	—m	4.0:1	- 63%
Weapon offense (5299)	18.1:1	18.6:1	19.3:1	23.9:1	20.7:1	33.2:1	20.6:1	12.5:1	14.2:1	14.6:1	- 31%
On person (7099)	5.1:1	4.7:1	4.8:1	5.1:1	4.5:1	5.0:1	4.8:1	7.3:1	5.7:1	5.9:1	+ 43%
Public order (7399)	4.7:1	4.3:1	4.0:1	4.6:1	4.4:1	4.2:1	3.9:1	6.7:1	15.7:1	6.7:1	+ 43%
All 16 above[n]	8.3:1	6.7:1	8.3:1	9.8:1	9.0:1	13.9:1	8.6:1	7.9:1	15.7:1	9.2:1	- 5%
All offenses[o]	8.1:1	7.9:1	8.1:1	9.6:1	8.7:1	13.5:1	8.4:1	7.4:1	15.5:1	8.8:1	- 9%

[a]Indicates those arrested by the police and forwarded to the prosecutor. (In Pennsylvania no cases were released by the police, as was the case in California.) [b]Indicates that the cases at this point were not dropped by the prosecutor before a court disposition. [c]Indicates that the initial felony charge was prosecuted as a felony. [d]Indicates that those at this point were charged with two or more offenses by the prosecutor. [e]Indicates cases where a conviction resulted. [f]Indicates a conviction for two or more offenses. [g]Indicates that the conviction (or at least one if multiple convictions) was for a felony. [h]Indicates that a prison sentence was given. [i]Indicates prison term of 5 or more years. [j]Indicates a term of incarceration (whether in jail or prison) resulted. [k]Indicates the percentage increase or decrease in the gap or rate ratio from arrest to incarceration in prison. [l]Numbers in parentheses are National Crime Information Center offense codes. [m]Cannot calculate, since one or fewer cases for either or both races. [n]Indicates the total figures for the 16 offenses. [o]Indicates all felony offenses for which charges were placed against blacks and whites.

Table 7 Attrition of California felony cases from arrest to incarceration by subgroups of the population in 1980

	Arrest	Sent to pros. [a]	Not dropped [b]	Conv. [c]	Conv. as fel. [d]	Prison [e] and % of arrests [f]	Jail and % of arrests [g]	Prison [e] or jail and % of arrests [h]
All	181,197	161,423	134,137	100,379	65,820	9,969 / 5.5%	68,470 / 37.8%	78,439 / 43.3%
White	124,608	112,624	95,862	72,846	45,760	6,418 / 5.2%	48,181 / 38.7%	54,599 / 43.9%
Black	55,046	47,354	37,015	26,637	19,507	3,484 / 6.3%	19,697 / 35.8%	23,181 / 42.1%
Indian	1,029	952	826	612	386	48 / 4.7%	441 / 42.9%	489 / 47.6%
Asian	514	493	434	284	167	19 / 3.7%	151 / 29.4%	170 / 33.1%
Male	160,328	142,664	118,445	89,085	58,911	9,669 / 6.0%	62,267 / 38.8%	71,936 / 44.8%
Female	24,308	21,981	18,357	13,333	8,283	553 / 2.3%	7,439 / 30.6%	7,992 / 32.9%
White male	108,362	97,832	83,228	63,694	40,407	6,081 / 5.6%	43,233 / 39.9%	49,314 / 45.5%
White female	16,149	14,710	12,561	9,093	5,321	330 / 2.0%	4,905 / 30.4%	5,235 / 32.4%
Black male	47,674	40,835	31,876	22,879	16,831	3,276 / 6.9%	17,381 / 36.5%	20,657 / 43.4%
Black female	7,324	6,479	5,104	3,733	2,658	204 / 2.8%	2,296 / 31.3%	2,500 / 34.1%
20–29	109,122	96,929	80,422	60,397	39,977	6,135 / 5.6%	42,364 / 38.8%	48,499 / 44.4%
30–39	35,964	32,632	27,302	19,682	13,059	2,672 / 7.4%	13,529 / 37.6%	16,201 / 45.0%
40–49	10,963	10,053	8,539	6,211	3,999	749 / 6.8%	3,938 / 35.9%	4,687 / 42.7%

	Arrest	Sent to pros.[a]	Not dropped[b]	Conv.[c]	Conv. as fel.[d]	Prison[e] and % of arrests[f]	Jail and % of arrests[g]	Prison[e] or jail and % of arrests[h]
50–59	4,364	4,035	3,432	2,527	1,547	242 / 5.5%	1,527 / 35.0%	1,769 / 40.5%
60–69	1,285	1,187	1,016	773	467	64 / 5.0%	414 / 32.2%	476 / 37.2%
70 and up	261	237	197	145	79	2 / 0.7%	58 / 22.2%	60 / 22.9%
Black male 20–29	27,726	23,585	18,459	13,435	10,004	2,040 / 7.4%	10,547 / 38.0%	12,587 / 45.4%
White male 20–29	64,533	58,130	49,356	37,852	24,179	3,592 / 5.6%	26,329 / 41.8%	29,921 / 47.4%
Black female 20–29	4,494	3,938	3,083	2,235	1,584	125 / 2.8%	1,457 / 32.4%	1,582 / 35.2%
White female 20–29	9,486	8,590	7,267	5,191	3,099	194 / 2.0%	2,940 / 31.0%	3,134 / 33.0%
20–59	160,413	143,649	119,695	88,817	58,582	9,798 / 6.1%	61,358 / 38.3%	71,156 / 44.4%
60 and up	1,546	1,424	1,213	918	546	66 / 4.3%	472 / 30.5%	538 / 34.8%

[a] Indicates those arrested by the police and forwarded to the prosecutor.
[b] Indicates that the cases at this point were not dropped by the prosecutor before a court disposition.
[c] Indicates conviction in court.
[d] Indicates conviction as a felony rather than as a misdemeanor.
[e] Includes 24 death sentences (14 were given to white males, 8 to black males, 1 to an Asian male, and 1 to a male of unknown race).
[f] Indicates those sentenced to prison and the percentage of those arrested that this figure represents.
[g] Does the same for jail incarceration.
[h] Combines the two previous columns.

Table 8 Percentage outcome at 5 points of the California criminal justice system by race, sex, and age in 1980

	Sent to pros.[a]	Not dropped[b]	Conv.[c]	Conv. as fel.[d]	Sentenced as a felon		
					Prison sentence	Jail sentence	Probation or fine
All	89.1%	83.1%	74.8%	65.6%	15.1%	61.4%	23.5%
White	90.4	85.2	76.0	62.8	14.0	61.6	24.4
Black	86.0	78.2	72.0	73.2	17.8	60.9	21.3
Asian	95.9	88.0	65.4	58.8	11.4	53.9	34.7
Indian	92.5	86.8	74.1	63.1	12.4	66.8	20.8
Male	89.0	83.0	75.2	66.1	16.4	61.8	21.8
Female	90.4	83.5	72.6	62.1	6.7	56.9	36.4
White male	90.3	85.1	76.5	63.4	15.0	62.2	22.8
White female	91.1	85.4	72.4	58.5	6.2	57.2	36.6
Black male	85.7	78.1	71.8	73.8	19.4	61.6	19.0
Black female	88.7	78.8	73.1	71.2	7.7	56.8	35.5
20–29	88.8	83.0	75.1	66.2	15.3	63.2	21.5
30–39	90.7	83.7	72.1	66.3	20.4	57.3	22.3
40–49	91.7	84.9	72.7	64.4	18.8	53.7	27.5
50–59	92.5	85.1	73.6	61.2	15.6	54.1	30.2
60–69	92.4	85.6	76.1	60.4	13.7	50.3	36.0
70 and up	90.8	83.1	73.6	54.5	2.5	38.0	59.5
White male 20–29	90.1	84.9	76.7	63.9	14.8	64.1	21.1
Black male 20–29	85.1	78.3	72.8	74.5	20.3	63.3	16.4
White female 20–29	90.6	84.6	71.4	59.7	6.3	59.6	34.1
Black female 20–29	87.6	78.3	72.5	70.9	7.9	60.7	31.4
60 and up	92.1	85.2	75.6	59.6	12.0	48.9	39.1
20–59	89.5	83.3	74.2	66.0	16.7	61.0	22.3

[a] Indicates the percentage of those arrested by the police who were forwarded to the prosecutor.

[b] Indicates the percentage of the cases at this point that were not dropped by the prosecutor before a court disposition.

[c] Indicates the percentage of those cases that were not dropped that resulted in a conviction in court.

[d] Indicates conviction as a felony rather than as a misdemeanor.

Table 9   Percentage outcome at 9 decision points of the Pennsylvania criminal justice system by race, sex, and age in 1980

	Arrests	Not dropped [a]	Pros. as fel. [b]	2 or more chgs. [c]	Conv. [d]	2 or more convs. [e]	Incar. prison [f]	5 or more years [g]	Incar. jail or prison % of conv. [h]	Incar. jail or prison % of arr. [i]
All	48,477	89.3%	96.0%	69.4%	47.7%	45.5%	11.9%	52.2%	38.1%	16.0%
White	28,288	90.2	95.5	64.3	46.1	36.6	12.8	36.4	37.9	15.5
Black	20,189	88.0	96.7	76.8	50.0	57.1	10.8	76.6	38.2	16.7
Male	51,500	89.2	95.8	67.2	46.7	44.7	12.5	51.2	39.9	16.4
Female	6,915	88.6	97.5	60.1	33.0	36.8	6.4	31.5	20.4	5.9
White male	25,371	90.2	95.3	64.9	47.6	37.1	13.1	37.1	39.1	16.5
White female	2,912	90.1	97.0	58.4	33.2	30.6	9.0	22.4	23.0	6.8
Black male	17,567	88.3	96.5	77.4	51.5	58.3	11.5	77.7	40.5	18.3
Black female	2,618	86.0	98.1	71.8	39.3	46.2	4.1	50.0	17.3	5.8
Black male 20–29	9,053	90.1	96.1	78.9	54.6	59.9	11.3	76.4	43.0	21.0
White male 20–29	12,172	91.1	94.5	68.1	53.1	39.1	14.1	34.7	40.3	19.2
Black female 20–29	1,237	87.0	98.0	71.1	39.5	44.9	5.0	47.6	17.9	6.1
White female 20–29	1,109	91.3	96.1	65.6	40.5	33.8	11.8	14.9	28.9	10.6

[a] Indicates the percentage of the cases at this point that were not dropped by the prosecutor before a court disposition.

[b] Indicates that the initial felony charge was prosecuted as a felony.

[c] Indicates the percentage of those at this point who were charged with two or more offenses by the prosecutor.

[d] Indicates the percentage of those cases that were not dropped that resulted in a conviction in court.

[e] Indicates a conviction for two or more offenses.

[f] Indicates that a prison sentence was given.

[g] Indicates prison term of 5 or more years.

[n] Indicates the percentage of those convicted who were sentenced to a term of incarceration (whether in jail or prison).

[i] Indicates the percentage of those arrested who were eventually incarcerated.

Table 10   Level of significance and measure of association for race, sex, and age
subgroups at 5 decision points of the California criminal justice system
in 1980

	Sent to prosecutor		Not dropped		Convicted		Convicted as felon		Sentenced as felon	
	Sig.	Assoc.	Sig.	Assoc.	Sig.	Assoc.	Sig.	Assoc.	Sig.	Assoc.
Race[a]	.0000	.0061	.0000	.0076	.0000	.0016	.0000	.0075	.0000	.0017
Black vs. white	.0000	.0058 (+)[b]	.0000	.0075 (+)	.0000	.0015 (+)	.0000	.0075 (-)	.0000	.0015 (-)
Sex	.0000	.0004 (-)	.0728	.0000 (-)	.0000	.0004 (+)	.0000	.0006 (+)	.0000	.0116 (+)
Age[c]	.0000	.0000 (-)	.0000	.0000 (-)	.0000	.0000 (+)	.0000	.0000 (+)	.0000	.0000 (+)
60 and up vs. 20-59	.0014	.0001 (-)	.0641	.0000 (-)	.2833	.0000 (-)	.0001	.0001 (+)	.0000	.0007 (+)

[a] Includes black, white, Indian, and Asian.

[b] The (+) indicates favorable treatment for blacks, women, and older groups. The (-) indicates unfavorable treatment for the same groups. For example, blacks were less likely to be sent to the prosecutor by the police (more favorable treatment), more likely to be nolle prossed, and less likely to be convicted. But blacks were more likely to be convicted as felons rather than misdemeanants (less favorable treatment) and more likely to be given prison sentences.

[c] The measure of association used for age was the asymmetric lambda, since the six age categories represent the ordinal scale. The measure of association for race, black vs. white, sex, and 60 and up vs. 20-59 was the uncertainty coefficient.

Table 11   Level of significance and measure of association for race, sex, and age subgroups at 7 decision points of the Pennsylvania criminal justice system in 1980

	Not dropped[a]	Pros. as fel.[b]	2 or more chgs.[c]	Conv.[d]	2 or more convs.[e]	Incar. prison[f]	5 or more years[g]
	Sig. Assoc.	Sig. Assoc.	Sig. Assoc.	Sig. Assoc.	Sig. Assoc.	Sig. Assoc.	Sig. Assoc.
Race	.0000	.0000	.0000	.0000	.0000	.0000	.0000
	.0017	.0028	.0149	.0011	.0302	.0013	.1161
	(+)[h]	(−)	(−)	(−)	(−)	(+)	(−)
Sex	.1587	.0000	.0000	.0000	.0000	.0000	.0000
	.0001	.0027	.0018	.0059	.0015	.0043	.0051
	(+)	(−)	(+)	(+)	(+)	(+)	(+)
Age	.0000	.0001	.0063	.0000	.5322	.0017	.0000
(6 groups)	.0000[i]	.0000	.0000	.0206	.0000	.0000	.0533
	(+)	(−)	(+)	(+)	(−)	(+)	(+)
60 and up	.1608	.0734	.0410	.1099	.6786	.0035	.0021
vs. 20–59	.0001	.0004	.0001	.0001	.0000	.0009	.0012
	(+)	(−)	(+)	(+)	(+)	(+)	(+)

[a] Indicates that the cases at this point were not dropped by the prosecutor before a court disposition.

[b] Indicates that the initial felony charge was prosecuted as a felony.

[c] Indicates that those at this point were charged with two or more offenses by the prosecutor.

[d] Indicates cases where a conviction resulted.

[e] Indicates a conviction for two or more offenses.

[f] Indicates that a prison sentence was given.

[g] Indicates prison term of 5 or more years.

[h] The (+) indicates favorable treatment for blacks, women, older age groups, and those 60 and up. The (−) indicates unfavorable treatment for the same groups. For example, blacks were more likely to receive favorable treatment at only two points (more likely to have case dropped by the prosecutor and less likely to receive a prison sentence if convicted), as indicated by (+).

[i] The asymmetric lambda is used for age, since the six categories of age represent an ordinal scale.

Bibliography

The letters at the beginning of each entry refer to the topics covered by the book or article, using the following key: **A** = all or most topics; **D** = defining racism; **F** = crime figures or statistics; **I** = introduction; **J** = jail or prison; **P** = police; **R** = criminological theory; **S** = sentencing; **T** = trial and prosecution; **W** = origin of beliefs; and **X** = methodological issues.

W, F   Abbot, D., & Calonico, J. Black man, white woman—the maintenance of a myth: Rape and the press in New Orleans. In M. Reidel & T. Thornberry (Eds.), *Crime and Delinquency: Dimensions of Deviance*. New York: Praeger, 1974.

J   Adamson, C. R. Punishment after slavery: Southern state penal systems, 1865-1890, *Social Problems*, 1983, *30*(5), 554-569.

T   Adler, F. Empathy as a factor in determining jury verdicts. *Criminology*, 1974, *12*(1), 127-128.

R   Akbar, N. *Chains and Images of Psychological Slavery*. Jersey City, NJ: New Mind Production, 1984.

P   Akers, R. L. *Deviant Behavior* (3rd ed.). Belmont, CA: Wadsworth, 1985.

P   Alex, N. *Black in Blue*. New York: Appleton-Century-Crofts, 1969.

S   Alexander, H. T., & Washington, M. Black judges in white America. *Black Law Journal*, 1971, *1*(3), 245-248.

P   Alexander, J. T. *Blue Coats, Black Skin: The Black Experience in New York City Police Department since 1891*. Hicksville, NY: Exposition Press, 1978.

T   Alker, H. L., Hoslicka, C., & Mitchell, M. Jury selection as a biased social process. *Law and Society Review*, 1976, *11*(1), 9-41.

D   Allport, G. W. *The Nature of Prejudice*. Garden City, NY: Doubleday, 1954.

D   Allport, G. W., Pettigrew, T. F., & Williams, J. Prejudice: A symposium. In M. M. Smythe (Ed.), *The Black American Reference Book*. Englewood Cliffs, NJ: Prentice-Hall, 1976, pp. 515-536.

J   Alpert, G. P. Patterns of change in prisonization: A longitudinal analysis. *Criminal Justice and Behavior*, 1979, *6*(2), 112-130.

D, P   Alpert, G. P. Civilian attacks on police. Dade County Police Benevolent Association's *Union Heat*, 1985, *3*(12), 7, 10.

A   Alpert, G. P., & Hicks, D. A. Prisoners' attitudes toward components of the legal and judicial system. *Criminology*, 1977, *14*(4), 461-482.

P   Anson, R. H. Validation of Niederhoffer's cynicism scale: The case for black officers. *International Journal of Comparative and Applied Criminal Justice*, 1983, 7, 35-48.

X, S   Arkin, S. D. Discrimination and arbitrariness in capital punishment: An analysis of post-Furman murder cases in Dade County, Florida, 1973–1976. *Stanford Law Review*, 1980, *33*(1), 75-101.

T   Arnold, W. R. Race and ethnicity relative to other factors in juvenile court dispositions. *American Journal of Sociology*, 1971, 77(2), 211-227.

F, R   Austin, R. L. Race, father-absence and female delinquency. *Criminology*, 1978, *15*(4), 487-504.

S   Austin, R. L. Unconvincing rejection of the hypothesis of racial discrimination in sentencing: A commentary on Kleck. Unpublished manuscript, Pennsylvania State University, 1981.

S   Austin, R. L. The court and sentencing of black offenders. In D. Georges-Abeyie (Ed.), *The Criminal Justice System and Blacks*. New York: Clark Boardman, 1984, pp. 167-193.

J   Bacchus, J. Shackles in the sunshine. *Orlando Sentinel Star*, Florida Magazine, June 17, 24, and 29, 1973.

J   Bailey, D. Inequalities of the parole system in California. *Howard Law Journal*, 1973, *17*, 797-804.

S   Baldus, D. C., Pulaski, C., & Woodworth, G. Comparative review of death sentences: An empirical study of the Georgia experience. *Journal of Criminal Law and Criminology*, 1983, *74*, 661-725.

F   Baldwin, J. A. Theory and research concerning the notion of black self-hatred: A review and reinterpretation. *Journal of Black Psychology*, 1979, *5*(2), 51-77.

I   Balkan, S., Berger, R. J., & Schmidt, J. *Crime and Deviance in America: A Critical Approach*. Belmont, CA: Wadsworth, 1980.

P, W   Banfield, E. *The Unheavenly City*. Boston: Little, Brown, 1970.

A   Banks, T. L. Discretionary decision-making in the criminal justice system and the black offender: Some alternatives. *Black Law Journal*, 1975, *5*(1), 20-29.

D, W   Banks, W. M. The changing attitudes of black students. *Personnel and Guidance Journal*, 1970, *48*, 739-745.

P   Bannon, J. D., & Wilt, G. M. Black policemen: A study of self-images. *Journal of Police Science Administration*, 1973, *1*(1), 23-29.

X   Barnett, S. Researching black justice: Description and implication. In C. E. Owens & J. Bell (Eds.), *Blacks and Criminal Justice*. Lexington, MA: D. C. Heath, 1977, pp. 25-33.

F   Barnhart, E. Negro homicides in the U.S. *Opportunity*, 1932, *10*, 212-214, 225.

D, F   Bart, P. B., & O'Brien, P. H. *Stopping Rape: Successful Survival Strategies*. New York: Pergamon Press, 1985.

D, J   Bartollas, C., & Sieverdes, C. M. The victimized white in a juvenile correctional system. *Crime and Delinquency*, 1981, 27(4), 534-543.

P   Beard, E. The black police in Washington, D.C. *Journal of Police Science Administration*, 1977, *5*(1), 48-52.

A   Bell, W. Bias, probability and prison populations: A future for affirmative action. *Futurics*, 1983, 7(1), 18-25.

T   Benokraitis, N. Racial exclusion in juries. *Journal of Applied Behavioral Science*, 1982, *18*(1), 29-47.

T   Benokraitis, N., & Griffin-Keene, J. A. Prejudice and jury selection. *Journal of Black Studies*, 1982, *12*(4), 427-449.

F   Berger, B. Black culture or lower-class culture. In L. Rainwater (Ed.), *Soul.* Chicago: Aldine, 1970, pp. 117–128.

S   Berk, R. *Racial Discrimination in Capital Sentencing: A Review of Recent Research.* Paper presented at the meeting of the American Society of Criminology, Cincinnati, November 1984.

A   Berman, J. J. Parolees' perceptions of the justice system: Black–white differences. *Criminology*, 1976, *13*(4), 507–520.

T, S   Bernstein, B. Since the Moynihan report. *New Perspectives*, 1984, *16*(2), 2–7.

A   Bernstein, I. N., Kelly, W. R., & Doyle, P. A. Societal reaction to deviants: The case of criminal defendants. *American Sociological Review*, 1977, *42*, 743–755.

T   Bernstein, I. N., Kick, E., Leung, J. T., & Schulz, B. Charge reduction: An intermediate stage in the process of labeling criminal defendants. *Social Forces*, 1977, *56*(2), 362–383.

J   Black, A. The role of education in prison and the black inmate. In D. Georges-Abeyie (Ed.), *The Criminal Justice System and Blacks.* New York: Clark Boardman, 1984, pp. 307–314.

F   Black, D. Crime as social control. *American Sociological Review*, 1973, *48*, 34–45.

P   Black, D. J., & Reiss, A. J., Jr. Police control of juveniles. *American Sociological Review*, 1970, *35*, 63–77.

F, R   Black on black crime: The consequences, the causes, the cures. *Ebony*, 1979, *34*(10), 32–146 (Entire issue).

P   Black police officers: Do they really make a difference?—the empirical evidence. *Blacks in Criminal Justice: Quarterly News Magazine*, Spring/Summer 1985, pp. 37–39.

P   Blacks in blue: Black police officers then and now, do they really make a difference? *Blacks in Criminal Justice: Quarterly News Magazine*, Spring/Summer 1985, pp. 11–13.

F, R   Blau, J. R., & Blau, P. M. The cost of inequality: Metropolitan structures and violent crime. *American Sociological Review*, 1982, *47*, 114–129.

F   Blauner, R. Black culture: Lower class result or ethnic creation. In L. Rainwater (Ed.), *Soul.* Chicago: Aldine, 1970, pp. 129–166.

F   Block, C. R. Race/ethnicity and patterns of Chicago homicide, 1865–1981. *Crime and Delinquency*, 1985, *31*(1), 104–116.

F   Block, C. R., & Block, R. L. *Patterns of Change in Chicago Homicides: The Twenties, the Sixties and the Seventies.* Chicago: Illinois Law Enforcement Commission, 1980.

F, J   Blumstein, A. On the racial disproportionality of United States prison populations. *Journal of Criminal Law and Criminology*, 1982, *73*(3), 1259–1281.

F   Blumstein, A., & Cohen, J. Estimation of individual crime rates from arrest records. *Journal of Criminal Law and Criminology*, 1979, *70*(4), 561–585.

S   Blumstein, A., & Cohen, J. Sentencing of convicted offenders: An analysis of the public's view. *Law and Society Review*, 1980, *14*(2), 223–261.

S, X   Blumstein, A., Cohen, J., Martin, S. E., & Tonry, M. H. (Eds.). *Research on Sentencing: The Search for Reform* (2 vols.). Washington, DC: National Academy Press, 1983.

F, J   Blumstein, A., & Graddy, E. Prevalence and recidivism in index arrests: A feedback model. *Law and Society Review*, 1982, *16*(2), 265–290.

D   Blumstein, J. F. Defining discrimination: Intent vs. impact. *New Perspectives*, 1984, *16*(1), 29–33.

P Boggs, S. L., & Galliher, J. F. Evaluating the police: A comparison of black street and household respondents. *Social Problems*, 1975, *22*, 393–406.

F Boland, B. Patterns of urban crime. In W. Skogan (Ed.), *Sample Surveys of Crime*. Cambridge, MA: Ballinger, 1976, pp. 27–41.

F Bonger, W. A. *Race and Crime*. Montclair, NJ: Patterson Smith, 1972.

F Boone, S. L., & Montare, A. Tests of the language-aggression hypothesis. *Psychological Reports*, 1976, *39*(3), 851–857.

T, S Boris, S. B. Stereotypes and dispositions for criminal homicide. *Criminology*, 1979, *17*(2), 139–158.

T, S Bowers, W. J. The pervasiveness of arbitrariness and discrimination under post-Furman capital statutes. *Journal of Criminal Law and Criminology*, 1983, *74*(3), 1067–1100.

T, S Bowers, W. J. *Legal Homicide: Death as Punishment in America, 1864–1982*. Boston: Northeastern University Press, 1984.

A Box, S. *Deviance, Reality and Society* (2nd ed.). New York: Holt, Rinehart & Winston, 1981.

F Braithwaite, J. Paradoxes of class bias in criminal justice. In H. E. Pepinsky (Ed.), *Rethinking Criminology*. Beverly Hills, CA: Sage, 1982, pp. 61–84.

S Bramwell, H. Alternative sentencing or part-time imprisonment is discriminatory. *Howard Law Journal*, 1983, *26*, 1265–1267.

F Brantingham, P., & Brantingham, P. *Patterns in Crime*. New York: Macmillan, 1984.

D Brigham, J. C., & Barkowitz, P. Do "they all look alike"?: The effect of race, sex, experience, and attitudes on the ability to recognize faces. *Journal of Applied Social Psychology*, 1978, *8*(4), 306–318.

D Brigham, J. C., & Giesbrecht, L. W. All in the family: Racial attitudes. *Journal of Communication*, 1976, *26*(4), 69–74.

D, T Broeder, D. W. The Negro in court. *Duke Law Journal*, 1965, *19*, 19–31.

A Brown, L. *The Administration of Criminal Justice: A View From Black America* (Occasional Paper, Vol. 2, No. 2). Washington, DC: Institute for Urban Affairs and Research, Howard University, 1974.

P Brown, L. P. Bridge over troubled waters: A perspective on policing in the black community. In R. L. Woodson (Ed.), *Black Perspectives on Crime and the Criminal Justice System*. Boston: G. K. Hall, 1977, pp. 79–105.

J Brown, R. M., & Steiner, J. F. *The North Carolina Chain Gang: A Study of County Convict Road Work*. Montclair, NJ: Patterson Smith, 1969.

F Brown, W. K. Black gangs as family extensions. *International Journal of Offender Therapy and Comparative Criminology*, 1978, *22*(1), 39–45.

F Browning, F. Life on the margin: Atlanta is not the only city where black children are dying. *The Progressive*, September 1981, pp. 34–37.

P Browning, F., & Gerassi, J. *The American Way of Crime*. New York: Putnam, 1980.

F Brownmiller, S. *Against Our Will: Men, Women and Rape*. New York: Simon & Schuster, 1971.

P Bryce, H. J. *Black Crime: A Police View*. Washington, DC: Police Foundation, 1977.

F Budros, A. The ethnic vice industry revisited. *Ethnic and Racial Studies*, 1983, *6*(4), 438–456.

S Bullock, H. A. Significance of the racial factor in the length of prison sentences. *Journal of Criminal Law, Criminology and Police Science*, 1961, *52*, 411–417.

F   Bureau of Justice Statistics. *Report to the Nation on Crime and Justice: The Data.* Washington, DC: U.S. Department of Justice, 1983a.

F, T   Bureau of Justice Statistics. *Tracking Offenders.* Washington, DC: U.S. Department of Justice, 1983b.

D, F   Bureau of Justice Statistics. *Criminal Victimization in the United States, 1983.* Washington, DC: U.S. Department of Justice, 1985.

X, T, S   Burke, P., & Turk, A. Factors affecting post arrest dispositions: A model for analysis. *Social Problems,* 1975, *22,* 313–332.

P, F   Burnham, D. F. B. I. arrest data found inaccurate: Study says local law officials fail to follow the bureau's complex instructions. *New York Times,* July 29, 1984, p. 17.

T   Bynum, T. Release on recognizance. *Criminology,* 1982, *20*(1), 67–82.

J   Cahalan, M. Trends in incarceration in the U.S. since 1880: A summary of reported rates and distribution of offenses. *Crime and Delinquency,* 1979, *25*(1), 9–41.

I, D   Caldwell, L., & Greene, H. E. T. Implementing a black perspective in criminal justice. In A. W. Cohn & B. Ward (Eds.), *Improving Management in Criminal Justice.* Beverly Hills, CA: Sage, 1980, pp. 143–156.

P   Campbell, V. Double marginality of black policemen: A reassessment. *Criminology,* 1980, *17*(4), 477–484.

J   Carper, N. G. *The Convict-Lease System in Florida, 1866–1923.* Doctoral dissertation, Florida State University, 1964.

J   Carroll, L. *Hacks, Blacks and Cons: Race Relations in a Maximum Security Prison.* Lexington, MA: D. C. Heath, 1974.

D, J   Carroll, L. Humanitarian reform and biracial sexual assault in a maximum security prison. *Urban Life,* 1977, *5,* 417–437.

J   Carroll, L. Race, ethnicity and the social order of prison. In R. Johnson and H. Toch (Eds.), *The Pains of Imprisonment.* Beverly Hills, CA: Sage, 1982.

F, J   Carroll, L., & Doubet, M. B. U.S. social structure and imprisonment. *Criminology,* 1983, *21*(3), 449–456.

J   Carroll, L., & Mondrick, M. E. Racial bias in the decision to grant parole. *Law and Society Review,* 1976, *11*(1), 93–107.

P   Center for Research on Criminal Justice. *The Iron Fist and the Velvet Glove: An Analysis of the U.S. Police.* Berkeley, CA: Author, 1975.

T   Center for the Study of Race, Crime and Social Policy. *Observations of Charging* (Report No. 103, Working Paper). Oakland, CA: Author, 1983.

T   Center for the Study of Race, Crime and Social Policy. *Observations of Plea Negotiation* (Report No. 101, Working Paper). Oakland, CA: Author, 1983.

F, R   Centerwall, B. S. Socioeconomic status and domestic homicide, Atlanta, 1971–72. *American Journal of Public Health,* 1984, *74*(8), 813–815.

T   Chambliss, W. J. The saints and the roughnecks. *Society,* 1973, *11*(11), 24–31.

A   Chambliss, W. J., & Seidman, R. B. *Law, Order and Power.* Reading, MA: Addison-Wesley, 1971.

D   Chang, E. C., & Ritter, E. H. Ethnocentrism in black college students. *The Journal of Social Psychology,* 1976, *100,* 89–98.

P   Chevigny, P. *Police Power: Police Abuse in New York City.* New York: Vintage Books, 1969.

A   Chiricos, T. G., Jackson, P. D., & Waldo, G. P. Inequality in the imposition of a criminal label. *Social Problems,* 1972, *19*(4), 553–572.

S Chiricos, T. G., & Waldo, G. P. Socioeconomic status and criminal sentencing. *American Sociological Review*, 1975, *40*, 753-772.

J Christianson, S. Legal implications of racially disproportionate incarceration rates. *Criminal Law Bulletin*, 1980a, *16*(1), 59-63.

J Christianson, S. Racial discrimination and prison confinement: A follow-up. *Criminal Law Bulletin*, 1980b, *16*(6), 616-621.

J Christianson, S. *Disproportionate Imprisonment of Blacks in the U.S.: Policy, Practice, Impact and Change.* Albany: State University of New York, Center on Minorities and Criminal Justice, 1982.

J Christianson, S., & Dehais, R. *The Black Incarceration Rate in the U.S.: A Nationwide Problem.* Albany: State University of New York, School of Criminal Justice, 1980.

F Clark, G. A. Corporate homicide: A new assault on corporate decision-making. *Notre Dame Lawyer*, 1979, *54*(5), 911-924.

S Clarke, S. H., & Koch, G. The influence of income and other factors on whether criminal defendants go to prison. *Law and Society Review*, 1976, *11*(1), 57-92.

S Clayton, O. A reconsideration of the effect of race in criminal sentencing. *Criminal Justice Review*, 1983, *8*(2), 15-20.

T Cohen, L. E., & Kluegel, J. P. Selecting delinquents for adjudication. *Journal of Research in Crime and Delinquency*, 1979, *16*(1), 143-163.

F Coles, R. The question of Negro crime. *Harper's Magazine*, 1964, *228*, 134-139.

R, X Comer, J. P. Black violence and public policy. In L. A. Curtis (Ed.), *American Violence and Public Policy: An Update of the National Commission on the Causes and Prevention of Violence.* New Haven, CT: Yale University Press, 1985.

D Condran, J. G. Change in white attitudes toward blacks, 1963-1977. *Public Opinion Quarterly*, 1979, *43*(4), 463-476.

P Conyers, J., Jr. Police violence and riots. *Black Scholar*, 1981, *12*(1), 2-5.

T Cooke, G., Pogany, E., & Johnston, N. G. A comparison of blacks and whites committed for evaluation of competency to stand trial on criminal charges. *Journal of Psychiatry and Law*, 1974, *2*(3), 319-337.

T Costantini, E., Mallery, M., & Yadpundich, D. M. Gender and juror partiality: Are women more likely to prejudge guilt? *Judicature*, 1983, *67*(3), 120-133.

P Crawford, T. J. Police overperception of ghetto hostility. *Journal of Police Science Administration*, 1973, *1*(2), 168-174.

P Cray, E. *The Enemy in the Streets: Police Malpractice in America.* New York: Doubleday, 1972.

S Crockett, G. W., Jr. Challenge for the judicial system: Economic and racial equality. In C. E. Owens & J. Bell (Eds.), *Blacks and Criminal Justice.* Lexington, MA: D. C. Heath, 1977, pp. 47-52.

S Crockett, G. W., Jr. The role of the black judge. In D. Georges-Abeyie (Ed.), *The Criminal Justice System and Blacks.* New York: Clark Boardman, 1984, pp. 195-204.

P, W Cross, D. W. *Mediaspeak: How Television Makes Up Your Mind.* New York: Putnam, 1983.

F Curtis, L. A. *Violence, Race and Culture.* Lexington, MA: D. C. Heath, 1975.

D, W Da Costa Nunes, R. Public opinion, crime and race: A congressional response to law and order in America. *Political Studies*, 1980, *28*(3), 420-430.

P, T   Dannefer, D., & Schull, R. K. Race and juvenile justice processing in court and police agencies. *American Journal of Sociology*, 1982, *87*(5), 1113-1132.

J   Davis, A. J. Sexual assaults in the Philadelphia prison system and sheriff's vans. *TransAction*, 1968, *6*, 8-16.

I, F   Davis, J. A. Justification for no obligation: Views of black males toward crime and the criminal law. *Issues in Criminology*, 1974, *9*(2), 69-87.

T   Davis, K. C. *Discretionary Justice*. Urbana, IL: University of Illinois Press, 1977.

P   Dean, A. W. Black police officers: An interview with Alfred W. Dean, director of public safety, City of Harrisburg, Pennsylvania. In D. Georges-Abeyie (Ed.), *The Criminal Justice System and Blacks*. New York: Clark Boardman, 1984, pp. 161-166.

A   Dehais, R. J. *Racial Disproportionality in Prison and Racial Discrimination in the Criminal Justice Process: Assessing the Empirical Evidence.* Paper presented at the meeting of the American Society of Criminology, Denver, November, 1983.

X   Del Olmo, R. Limitations for the prevention of violence: The Latin American reality and its criminological theory. *Crime and Social Justice*, Summer 1975, 21-29.

T   Denno, D. Psychological factors for the black defendant in a jury trial. *Journal of Black Studies*, 1981, *11*(3), 313-326.

F   Dertke, M. C., Penner, L. A., & Ulrich, K. Observer's reporting of shoplifting as a function of thief's race and sex. *Journal of Social Psychology*, 1974, *94*, 213-221.

J   Dobbins, D. A., & Bass, B. M. Effects of unemployment on white and Negro prison admission in Louisiana. *Journal of Criminal Law, Criminology and Police Science*, 1958, *48*(15), 522-525.

F   Doleschal, E. Crime—some popular beliefs. *Crime and Delinquency*, 1979, *25*(1), 1-8.

I, F, S   Dorin, D. D. Two different worlds: Criminologists, justices, and racial discrimination in the imposition of capital punishment in rape cases. *Journal of Criminal Law and Criminology*, 1981, *72*(4), 1667-1679.

F   Dubois, W. E. B. *The Philadelphia Negro*. New York: Schocken Books, 1899/1967.

F   Dubois, W. E. B. (Ed.). *Some Notes on Negro Crime Particularly in Georgia*. Atlanta: Atlanta University Press, 1904.

D, S, P   Ducassi, J. Women lawyers' pay is lagging. *Miami Herald*, December 31, 1985, p. 3D.

J   Duffy, B. Drug trade thrives at prison, court told. *Miami Herald*, December 4, 1985, p. 2B.

W   Dulaney, W. L. Identification of race in newspaper crime stories. *Journalism Quarterly*, 1969, *46*(3), 603-605.

D   Duncan, B. L. Differential social perception and attribution of intergroup violence: Testing the lower limits of stereotyping of blacks. *Journal of Personality and Social Psychology*, 1976, *34*(4), 590-598.

D   Dutton, D. G., & Lake, R. A. Threat of own prejudice and reverse discrimination in interracial situations. *Journal of Personality and Social Psychology*, 1973, *28*(1), 94-100.

D   Eastland, T., & Bennett, W. J. *Counting by Race: Equality from the Founding Fathers to Bakke and Weber*. New York: Basic Books, 1979.

R   Echols, A. E. Deadline, vengeance and tribute: A prescription for black juvenile delinquency. *Crime and Delinquency*, 1970, *16*(4), 357-362.

W, T, S   Eisenstein, J., & Jacob, H. *Felony Justice: An Organizational Analysis of Criminal Courts.* Boston: Little, Brown, 1977.

J   Elion, V. H., & Megargee, E. I. Racial identity, length of incarceration and parole decision-making. *Journal of Research in Crime and Delinquency,* 1979, *16*(2), 232–245.

F   Elliott, D. S., & Ageton, S. S. Reconciling race and class differences in self-reported and official estimates of delinquency. *American Sociological Review,* 1980, *45,* 95–100.

P, D   Engel, K., & Rothman, S. Prison violence and the paradox of reform. *The Public Interest,* 1983, *73*(Fall), 91–105.

I, F   Enright, R. D., Enright, W. F., Manheim, L. A., & Harris, B. E. Distributive justice development and social class. *Developmental Psychology,* 1980, *16*(6), 555–563.

I, T, S   Epstein, B. S. *Patterns of Sentencing and Their Implementation in Philadelphia City and County, 1795–1829.* Doctoral dissertation, University of Pennsylvania, 1981, pp. 218–220.

D, W   Estep, R., & MacDonald, P. T. How prime-time crime evolved on TV, 1976–1983. In R. Surette (Ed.), *Justice and the Media.* Springfield, IL: Charles C Thomas, 1984, pp. 110–123.

F   Farley, F. H., & Sewell, T. Attribution and achievement motivation differences between delinquent and non-delinquent black adolescents. *Adolescence,* 1975, *10*(34), 391–397.

F   Farley, F. H., & Sewell, T. Test of an arousal theory of delinquency: Stimulation-seeking in delinquent and non-delinquent black adolescents. *Criminal Justice and Behavior,* 1976, *3*(4), 315–320.

F   Farley, R. Homicide trends in the U.S. *Demography,* 1980, *17*(2), 177–188.

S   Farnworth, M., & Horan, P. M. Separate justice: An analysis of race differences in court processes. *Social Science Research,* 1980, *9,* 381–399.

T, S   Farrell, R. H., & Swigert, V. L. Legal disposition of inter-group and intra-group homicides. *Sociological Quarterly,* 1978a, *19,* 565–576.

X, P, S   Farrell, R. A., & Swigert, V. L. Prior offense record as a self-fulfilling prophecy. *Law and Society Review,* 1978b, *12,* 437–454.

D   Feagin, J. R., & Feagin, C. B. *Discrimination American Style: Institutional Racism and Sexism.* Englewood Cliffs, NJ: Prentice-Hall, 1978.

T   Feild, H. S. Rape trials and jurors' decisions: A psycholegal analysis of the effects of victim, defendant, and case characteristics. *Law and Human Behavior,* 1979, *3*(4), 261–284.

D   Feldman, J. M. Stimulus characteristics and subject prejudice as determinants of stereotype attribution. *Journal of Personality and Social Psychology,* 1972, *21*(3), 333–340.

T   Feuerverger, A., & Shearing, C. D. An analysis of the prosecution of shoplifters. *Criminology,* 1982, *20*(2), 273–289.

W   Fisher, P. L., & Lowenstein, R. L. (Eds.). *Race and the News Media.* New York: Praeger, 1967.

D   Fishkin, J. S. *Justice, Equal Opportunity and the Family.* New Haven, CT: Yale University Press, 1983.

D   Foley, L. Personality characteristics and interracial contact as determinants of black prejudices toward whites. *Human Relations,* 1977, *30*(8), 701–720.

T   Foley, L., & Chamblin, M. H. The effect of race and personality on mock jurors' decisions. *Journal of Psychology,* 1982, *112,* 47–51.

D   Foley, L., & Kranz, P. L. Black stereotypes of other ethnic groups. *Journal of Mind and Behavior,* 1981, *2*(4), 435–449.

T, S Foley, L., and Powell, R. S. The discretion of prosecutors, judges, and juries in capital cases. *Criminal Justice Review*, 1982, 7(2), 16–22.

T, S Foley, L., & Rasche, C. E. The effect of race on sentence, actual time served and final disposition of female offenders. In J. A. Conley (Ed.), *Theory and Research in Criminal Justice: Current Perspectives.* Cincinnati: Anderson, 1979, pp. 93–106.

F Forslund, M. A. A comparison of Negro and white crime rates. *Journal of Criminal Law, Criminology and Police Science*, 1970, 61, 214–217.

T, S Forst, B. Prosecution and sentencing. In J. Q. Wilson (Ed.), *Crime and Public Policy*. San Francisco: Institute for Contemporary Studies, 1983, pp. 165–182.

S Forst, M. L. Sentencing disparity: An overview of research and issues. In M. L. Forst (Ed.), *Sentencing Reform: Experiments in Reducing Disparity*. Beverly Hills, CA: Sage, 1982, pp. 9–34.

P Foster, H. *Ribbin', Jivin' and Playin' the Dozens*. Cambridge, MA: Ballinger, 1974.

X, S Frazier, C. E., & Bock, E. W. Effects of court officials on sentencing severity: Do judges make a difference? *Criminology*, 1982, 20(2), 257–272.

T Frazier, C. E., Bock, E. W., & Henretta, J. C. Pretrial release and bail decisions: The effects of legal, community, and personal variables. *Criminology*, 1980, 18(2), 162–181.

F Frazier, E. F. *The Negro in the United States*. New York: Macmillan, 1949.

T Freedberg, S. P. Report shows more blacks on Dade juries. *Miami Herald*, April 12, 1984a, p. 1C.

T Freedberg, S. P. Report shows race a factor in verdicts. *Miami Herald*, May 11, 1984b, p. 1C.

T Freedberg, S. P., & Macari, A. Circuit court jury system is racially balanced. *Miami Herald*, July 15, 1984, pp. 1A, 10–11A.

J French, L. Elitism: Perpetuation through incarceration. In C. E. Owens & J. Bell (Eds.), *Blacks and Criminal Justice*. Lexington, MA: D. C. Heath, 1977, pp. 53–65.

J French, L. The incarcerated black female: The case of social double jeopardy. *Journal of Black Studies*, 1978, 8(3), 321–335.

T Friday, P. C., Malzahn-Bass, K. R., & Harrington, D. K. Referral and selection criteria in deferred prosecution. *British Journal of Criminology*, 1981, 21(2), 166–172.

J Fuller, D., & Orsagh, T. Violence and victimization within a state prison system. *Criminal Justice Review*, 1977, 2(2), 35–55.

P Fyfe, J. Who shoots? A look at officer race and police shooting. *Journal of Police Science and Administration*, 1981, 9(4), 367–382.

P Fyfe, J. Blind justice: Police shootings in Memphis. *Journal of Criminal Law and Criminology*, 1982a, 73(2), 707–722.

P Fyfe, J. (Ed.). *Readings on Police Use of Deadly Force*. Washington, DC: Police Foundation, 1982b.

D Gaertner, S. L. The role of racial attitudes in helping behavior. *Journal of Social Psychology*, 1975, 97, 95–101.

D Gaertner, S. L., & Davidio, J. F. The subtlety of white racism, arousal and helping behavior. *Journal of Personality and Social Psychology*, 1977, 35(10), 691–707.

G Gaertner, S. L., & McLaughlin, J. P. Racial stereotypes: Associations and ascriptions of positive and negative characteristics. *Social Psychology Quarterly*, 1983, 46(1), 23–30.

W Gans, H. J. *More Equality*. New York: Pantheon, 1973.

X, S Garber, S., Klepper, S., & Nagin, D. The role of extralegal factors in determining criminal case disposition. In A. Blumstein, J. Cohen, S. E. Martin, & M. H. Tonry (Eds.), *Research on Sentencing: The Search for Reform* (Vol. 2). Washington, DC: National Academy Press, 1983, pp. 129–183.

F Gary, L. E. Role of alcohol and drug abuse in homicide. *Public Health Reports*, 1980, *95*(6), 553–554.

F Gary, L. E. Substance abuse, homicide and the black male. *Black Caucus Journal*, 1982, *12*, 13–18.

A Gary, L. E., & Brown, L. P. (Eds.). *Crime and Its Impact on the Black Community*. Washington, DC: Howard University, 1975.

F Geis, G. Statistics concerning race and crime. In R. Knudten (Ed.), *Crime, Criminology and Contemporary Society*, 1970, pp. 27–33.

P Geller, W. A. Deadly force: What we know. *Journal of Police Science and Administration*, 1982, *10*, 152–177.

T Geller, W. A. Officer restraint in the use of deadly force: The next frontier in police shooting research. *Journal of Police Science and Administration*, 1985, *13*(2), 153–166.

R, X Genovese, E. D. *Roll, Jordan, Roll: The World the Slaves Made*. New York: Vintage, 1976.

D Gentry, W. D. Biracial aggression: Effect of verbal attack and sex of victim. *Journal of Social Psychology*, 1972, *88*, 75–82.

A George, P. S. *Criminal Justice in Miami, 1896–1930*. Doctoral dissertation, Florida State University, 1975.

P George, P. S. Policing Miami's black community, 1896–1930. *Florida Historical Quarterly*, 1979, *57*(4), 434–450.

A Georges-Abeyie, D. (Ed.). *The Criminal Justice System and Blacks*. New York: Clark Boardman, 1984a.

I, X Georges-Abeyie, D. The criminal justice system and minorities—a review of the literature. In D. Georges-Abeyie (Ed.), *The Criminal Justice System and Blacks*. New York: Clark Boardman, 1984b, pp. 125–150.

F Georges-Abeyie, D. Definitional issues: Race, ethnicity, and official crime/victimization statistics. In D. Georges-Abeyie (Ed.), *The Criminal Justice Statistics and Blacks*. New York: Clark Boardman, 1984c, pp. 5–13.

S Gibson, J. L. Race as a determinant of criminal sentences: A methodological critique and a case study. *Law and Society Review*, 1978, *12*(3), 455–478.

D Glazer, N. *Ethnic Dilemmas, 1964–1982*. Cambridge, MA: Harvard University Press, 1983.

F Godwin, J. *Murder, U.S.A.* New York: Ballantine Books, 1978.

J Goetting, A. Racism, sexism and ageism in the prison community. *Federal Probation*, 1985, *49*(3), 10–22.

J Goetting, A., & Howsen, R. M. Blacks in prison: A profile. *Criminal Justice Review*, 1983, *8*(2), 21–31.

P Goldcamp, J. S. Minorities as victims of police shooting: Interpretations of racial disproportionality and police use of deadly force. *Justice System Journal*, 1976, *2*, 169–183.

J Goodstein, L., & MacKenzie, D. L. Racial differences in adjustment patterns of prison inmates—prisonization, conflict, stress, and control. In D. Georges-Abeyie (Ed.), *The Criminal Justice System and Blacks*. New York: Clark Boardman, 1984, pp. 271–306.

D Gossett, T. F. *Race: The History of an Idea in America*. New York: Schocken Books, 1965.

F   Graham, F. P. Black crime: The lawless image. *Harper's Magazine*, 1970, *241*(1444), 64–71.

P   Green, E. Race, social status and criminal arrest. *American Sociological Review*, 1970, *35*, 476–490.

P   Griswald, D. B. Police discrimination: An elusive question. *Journal of Police Science and Administration*, 1978, *6*(1), 61–66.

S, X Gross, S. R., & Mauro, R. Patterns of death: An analysis of racial disparities in capital sentencing and homicide victimization. *Stanford Law Review*, 1984, *37*, 27–120.

D   Guichard, C. P. Ethnic group stereotypes: A new look at an old problem. *Journal of Negro Education*, 1977, *46*(3), 344–357.

F, X Gurr, T. R. Historical trends in violent crime: A critical review of the literature. In M. Tonry & N. Morris (Eds.), *Crime and Justice*. Chicago: University of Chicago Press, 1981, pp. 295–353.

X, S Hagan, J. Extra-legal attributes and criminal sentencing: An assessment of a sociological viewpoint. *Law and Society Review*, 1974, *8*, 357–383.

T   Hagan, J. Parameters of criminal prosecution: An application of path analysis to a problem of criminal justice. *Journal of Criminal Law and Criminology*, 1975a, *65*, 536–544.

T   Hagan, J. The social and legal construction of criminal justice: A study of the pre-sentence process. *Social Problems*, 1975b, *22*, 620–637.

I, D Hagan, J., & Albonetti, C. Race, class and the perception of criminal injustice in America. *American Journal of Sociology*, 1982, *88*(2), 329–355.

X, S Hagan, J., & Bumiller, K. Making sense of sentencing: A review and critique of sentencing research. In A. Blumstein, J. Cohen, S. E. Martin, & M. H. Tonry (Eds.), *Research on Sentencing: The Search for Reform* (Vol. 2). Washington, DC: National Academy Press, 1983, pp. 1–54.

T   Hagan, J., Hewitt, J. D., & Alwin, D. F. Ceremonial justice: Crime and punishment in a loosely coupled system. *Social Forces*, 1979, *58*, 506–527.

T, S Hagan, J., Nagel, I. H., & Albonetti, C. The differential sentencing of white-collar offenders in ten federal district courts. *American Sociological Review*, 1980, *45*, 802–820.

F   Hall, C. F. *Negroes in the United States, 1920–1932*. Washington, DC: U.S. Department of Commerce, 1969, pp. 555–567.

T   Hampton, E. Court ruling on black jury will have impact on cases in Miami. *Miami News*, February 22, 1985, p. 6A.

F   Haran, J. F., & Martin, J. M. The armed urban bank robber: A profile. *Federal Probation*, 1984, *48*(4), 47–53.

S   Hardy, K. A. Equity in court dispositions. In G. P. Whitaker & C. D. Phillips (Eds.), *Evaluating Performance in Criminal Justice Agencies*. Beverly Hills, CA: Sage, 1983, pp. 183–207.

F   Harries, K. D. Black crime and criminal victimization. In D. Georges-Abeyie (Ed.), *The Criminal Justice System and Blacks*. New York: Clark Boardman, 1984, pp. 37–49.

F   Harris, A. R. Race, commitment to deviance and spoiled identity. *American Sociological Review*, 1976, *41*, 432–442.

D   Hawkins, D. F. Black and white homicide differentials: Alternatives to an inadequate theory. *Criminal Justice and Behavior*, 1983, *10*(4), 407–440.

F, R Hawkins, D. F. Black homicide: The adequacy of existing research for devising prevention strategies. *Crime and Delinquency*, 1985, *31*(1), 83–103.

J   Hawkins, K. Assessing evil: Decision behavior and parole board justice. *British Journal of Sociology*, 1983, *23*(2), 101-127.

T, S Hawkinson, T. The effect of pre-trial release, race and prior arrest on conviction and sentencing. *Creighton Law Review*, 1975, *8*, 930-937.

F   Headley, B. D. "Black on black" crime: The myth and the reality. *Crime and Social Justice*, 1983, *20*, 50-62.

F   Heilbrun, A. B., Jr., & Cross, J. M. An analysis of rape patterns in white and black rapists. *Journal of Social Psychology*, 1979, *108*(1), 83-87.

F, R Heilbrun, A. B., Jr., & Heilbrun, K. S. The black minority criminal and violent crime: The role of self-control. *British Journal of Criminology*, 1977, *17*(4), 270-277.

J, R Heilbrun, K. L., Heilbrun, A. B., Jr., & Heilbrun, L. C. Impulsive and premeditated homicide: An analysis of subsequent parole risk of the murderer. *Journal of Criminal Law, Criminology and Police Science*, 1978, *69*(1), 108-114.

D, P Heiligman, A. C. Racism in U.S. drug legislation and the trade-off behind it. *Drug Forum*, 1978-79, *7*(1), 19-26.

J   Held, B. S., Levine, D., & Swartz, V. D. Interpersonal aspects of dangerousness. *Criminal Justice and Behavior*, 1979, *6*(1), 49-58.

W   Helmreich, W. *What They Say Behind Your Back*. Garden City, NY: Doubleday, 1982.

S, D Henderson, J., & Taylor, J. Racial justice: Discrimination even in death. *Dallas Times Herald*, Nov. 17, 1985, pp. 1, 16-18.

D   Hepburn, C., & Locksley, A. Subjective awareness of stereotyping: Do we know when our judgments are prejudiced? *Social Psychology Quarterly*, 1983, *46*(4), 311-318.

P   Hepburn, J. Race and the decision to arrest: An analysis of warrants issued. *Journal of Research in Crime and Delinquency*, 1978, *15*(1), 54-73.

D, P Hershey, M. R., & Hill, D. B. Is pollution a "white thing"? Racial differences in preadults' attitudes. *Public Opinion Quarterly*, 1977-78, *41*, 439-458.

P, X Hilliard, T. O. Applications of psychology and the criminal justice system: A black perspective. *Journal of Black Psychology*, 1977, *4*(1), 65-81.

F   Himes, J. S. Crime in Negro Columbus. *Opportunity*, 1938, *16*(9), 302-305.

S   Hindelang, M. J. Equality under the law. *Journal of Criminal Law, Criminology and Police Science*, 1969, *60*, 306-313.

F, P Hindelang, M. J. Race and involvement in common law personal crimes. *American Sociological Review*, 1978, *43*, 93-109.

F   Hindelang, M. J. Variation in sex-race-age-specific incidence rates of offending. *American Sociological Review*, 1981, *46*, 461-474.

T   Hindelang, M. J., Gottfredson, M. R., & Flanagan, T. J. *Sourcebook of Criminal Justice Statistics—1980*. Washington, DC: U.S. Department of Justice, 1981.

F, P Hindelang, M. J., Hirschi, T., & Weiss, J. G. Correlates of delinquency: The illusion of discrepancy between self-report and official measures. *American Sociological Review*, 1979, *44*, 995-1014.

F, P Hindelang, M. J., Hirschi, T., & Weiss, J. G. *Measuring Delinquency*. Beverly Hills, CA: Sage, 1981.

P   Hinds, L. S. The police use of excessive and deadly force: Racial implications. In R. N. Brenner & M. Kravitz (Eds.), *A Community Concern: Police Use of Deadly Force*. Washington, DC: U.S. Department of Justice, 1979.

A   Hindus, M. S. Black justice under white law—criminal prosecution of blacks in antebellum South Carolina. *Journal of American History*, 1976, *63*(3), 575–599.

A   Hindus, M. S. *Prison and Plantation: Crime, Justice and Authority in Massachusetts and South Carolina, 1767–1878.* Chapel Hill: University of North Carolina Press, 1980.

D   Hines, B. L. Uproar over Harms firing hints at racism. *Miami Herald*, February 13, 1984, p. 1B.

F   Hirschi, T., & Gottfredson, M. Age and the explanation of crime. *American Journal of Sociology*, 1983, *89*(3), 552–583.

D   Hoffman, F. L. *Race Traits and Tendencies of the American Negro.* New York: Macmillan, 1896.

S   Hogarth, J. *Sentencing as a Human Process.* Toronto: University of Toronto Press, 1971.

P   Hollinger, R. C. Race, occupational status, and pro-active arrest for drinking and driving. *Journal of Criminal Justice*, 1984, *12*(2), 173–183.

S, X   Holmes, M., & Daudistel, H. C. Ethnicity and justice in the Southwest: The sentencing of Anglo, black and Mexican origin defendants. *Social Science Quarterly*, 1984, *65*(2), 265–277.

D   Hook, S. Rationalizations for reverse discrimination. *New Perspectives*, 1985, *17*(1), 8–11.

J   Hopper, C. B. *Sex in Prison: The Mississippi Experiment with Conjugal Visiting.* Baton Rouge: Louisiana State University Press, 1969.

T   Horney, J. *Effects of Race on Plea Bargaining Decisions.* Paper presented at the meeting of the American Society of Criminology, San Francisco, November 1980.

D, T   Howard, C. What colour is the "reasonable man"? *Criminal Law Review*, 1961, 41–48.

W   Howard, J., & Hammond, R. Rumors of inferiority: The hidden obstacles to black success. *New Republic*, September 9, 1985, pp. 17–21.

S   Howard, J. C. Racial discrimination in sentencing. *Judicature*, 1975, *59*(3), 120–125.

F, R   Hulbary, W. E. Race, deprivation and adolescent self-image. *Social Science Quarterly*, 1975, *56*(1), 105–114.

F, R   Hunt, L. L., & Hunt, J. G. Race and the father-son connection: The conditional relevance of father absence for the orientation and identities of adolescent boys. *Social Problems*, 1975, *23*(1), 35–52.

J   Hussey, F. A. *The Decision to Parole: A Study of the Parole Process with Juveniles.* Doctoral dissertation, Brandeis University, 1974.

P   Inn, A., Wheeler, A. C., & Sparling, C. L. The effects of suspect race and situation hazard on police officer shooting behavior. *Journal of Applied Social Psychology*, 1977, *7*(1), 27–37.

W   Jacob, H. Black and white perceptions of justice in the city. *Law and Society Review*, 1971, *6*(1), 69–90.

J   Jacobs, J. B. Race relations and the prisoner subculture. In N. Morris & M. Tonry (Eds.), *Crime and Justice: An Annual Review of the Research* (Vol. 1). Chicago: University of Chicago Press, 1979, pp. 1–28.

J   Jacobs, J. B. The limits of racial integration in prison. *Criminal Law Bulletin*, 1982, *18*, 117–153.

J   Jacobs, J. B. *New Perspectives on Prisons and Imprisonment.* Ithaca, NY: Cornell University Press, 1983.

P   Jacobs, J. B., & Cohen, J. The impact of racial integration on the police. *Journal of Police Science and Administration*, 1978, *6*(2), 168–183.

J   Jacobs, J. B., & Kraft, L. J. Integrating the keepers: A comparison of black and white prison guards in Illinois. *Social Problems*, 1978, *25*, 304–318.

W   Jacobson, C. K. Black support for affirmative action programs. *Phylon*, 1983, *44*(4), 299–310.

X, F   Jason, J., Strauss, L. T., & Tyler, C. W. A comparison of primary and secondary homicides in the United States. *American Journal of Epidemiology*, 1983, *117*(3), 309–319.

W   Jencks, C. *Inequality: A Reassessment of the Effect of Family and Schooling in America.* New York: Basic Books, 1972.

F, R   Jensen, G. F. Race, achievement and delinquency: A further look at delinquency in a birth cohort. *American Journal of Sociology*, 1976, *82*(2), 379–387.

F, R   Jensen, G. F., White, C. S., & Galliher, J. M. Ethnic status and adolescent self-evaluation: An extension of research on minority self-esteem. *Social Problems*, 1982, *30*(2), 226–239.

A   Johnson, G. B. The Negro and crime. In M. E. Wolfgang, L. Savitz, & N. Johnson (Eds.), *The Sociology of Crime and Delinquency*. New York: Wiley, 1970, pp. 419–429.

J   Johnson, R. *Culture and Crisis in Confinement.* Lexington, MA: D. C. Heath, 1976.

I, W   Johnson, S. Luncheon speaker. In R. L. Woodson (Ed.), *Black Perspectives on Crime and the Criminal Justice System*. Boston: G. K. Hall, 1977, pp. 161–168.

P   Johnson, S. L. Race and the decision to detain a suspect. *Yale Law Journal*, 1983, *93*(2), 214–258.

P   Johnson, W. T., Petersen, R. E., & Wells, L. E. Arrest probabilities for marijuana users as indicators of selective law enforcement. *American Journal of Sociology*, 1977, *83*(3), 681–699.

X   Jones, A. *Women Who Kill.* New York: Holt, Rinehart & Winston, 1980.

I   Jones, C. B. Criminal justice/racial justice nexus. In R. G. Iacovetta & D. H. Chang (Eds.), *Critical Issues in Criminal Justice*. Chapel Hill: University of North Carolina Press, 1979.

D   Jones, E. E., & Nisbett, R. E. The actor and the observer: Divergent perception of the causes of behavior. In E. E. Jones et al. (Eds.), *Attribution: Perceiving the Causes of Behavior*. Morristown, NJ: General Learning Press, 1971, pp. 79–94.

A   Jones, H. *Crime, Race and Culture: A Study in a Developing Country.* New York: Wiley, 1981.

D   Jones, J. M. *Prejudice and Racism.* Reading, MA: Addison-Wesley, 1972.

S   Jones, M. E. Racism in special courts. *Journal of Public Law*, 1971, *20*, 401–406.

A   Jones, T. Blacks in the American criminal justice system: A study of sanctioned deviance. *Journal of Sociology and Social Welfare*, 1978, *5*(3), 356–373.

T   Jorgenson, J. R. Back to the laboratory with peremptory challenges: A Florida response. *Florida State University Law Review*, 1984, *12*(3), 559–582.

S   Joyner, I. Legal theories for attacking racial disparity in sentencing. *Criminal Law Bulletin*, 1982, *18*, 101–116.

I, D, R Justice, B. *Violence in the City.* Ft. Worth, TX: Christian University Press, 1969.

T, S, J Karmen, A. *Crime Victims: An Introduction to Victimology.* Monterey, CA: Brooks/Cole, 1984.

I, D   Keith, D. J. Should color blindness and representativeness be a part of American justice? *Howard Law Journal*, 1983, *26*, 1–7.

T, S   Kelly, H. E. A comparison of defense strategy and race as influences in differential sentencing. *Criminology*, 1976, *14*(2), 241–249.

D, F   Kelman, M. G. The politics of explaining crime. *Stanford Law Review*, 1979, *31*(3), 527–539.

D   Kendall, D., & Feagin, J. R. Blatant and subtle patterns of discrimination: Minority women in medical schools. *Journal of Intergroup Relations*, 1983, *11*(2), 8–33.

F   Kephart, W. M. The Negro offender: An urban research project. *American Journal of Sociology*, 1954, *60*, 46–50.

D   Kilpatrick, J. J. Literacy isn't a racial issue. *Miami Herald*, January 6, 1981, p. 7A.

P   Kirkham, G. On the etiology of police aggression in the black communities. In J. Kinton (Ed.), *Police Roles in the Seventies*. Aurora, IL: Social Science and Sociological Resources, 1975, pp. 167–194.

F   Klebba, A. J. Homicide trends in the U.S., 1900–1974. *Public Health Reports*, 1975, *90*(3), 195–204.

X, S   Kleck, G. Racial discrimination in criminal sentencing: A critical evaluation of the evidence with additional data on the death penalty. *American Sociological Review*, 1981, *46*, 783–805.

X, S   Kleck, G. Life support for ailing hypotheses: Modes of summarizing the evidence for racial discrimination in sentencing. *Law and Human Behavior*, 1985, *9*(3), 271–285.

X   Klepper, S., Nagin, D., & Tierney, L. Discrimination in the criminal justice system: A critical appraisal of the literature. In A. Blumstein, J. Cohen, S. E. Martin, & M. H. Tonry (Eds.), *Research on Sentencing: The Search for Reform* (Vol. 2). Washington, DC: National Academy Press, 1983, pp. 55–128.

W   Kluegel, J. R., & Smith, E. R. Whites' beliefs about blacks' opportunity. *American Sociological Review*, 1982, *47*, 518–542.

W   Knopf, T. A. Media myths on violence. *New Society*, 1970, *12*, 856–859.

D   Knowles, L. L., & Prewitt, K. *Institutional Racism in America*. Englewood Cliffs, NJ: Prentice-Hall, 1969.

P   Kochman, T. *Black and White: Styles in Conflict*. Chicago: University of Chicago Press, 1981.

J   Korn, R. R., & McCorkle, L. W. *Criminology and Penology*. New York: Holt, Rinehart & Winston, 1959.

D   Kranz, P. L., & Foley, L. Current racial myths: Similarities between two southern samples, college students and prison inmates. *Negro Educational Review*, 1978, *39*(1), 52–56.

I   Krohn, M., & Stratton, J. A sense of injustice. *Criminology*, 1980, *17*(4), 495–504.

J   Kruttschnitt, C. Race relations and the female inmate. *Crime and Delinquency*, 1983, *29*(4), 579–592.

X, S   Kruttschnitt, C. Legal outcomes and legal agents: Adding another dimension to the sex-sentencing controversy. *Law and Human Behavior*, 1985, *9*(3), 287–303.

T, S   Kulig, F. H. Plea bargaining, probation and other aspects of conviction and sentencing. *Creighton Law Review*, 1975, *8*, 938–954.

I, T, S Kuntz, W. F., II. *Criminal Sentencing in Three Nineteenth Century Cities: A Social History of Punishment in New York, Boston, and Philadelphia, 1830–1880*. Doctoral dissertation, Harvard University, 1978, pp. 402–416.

F   LaFree, G. D. The effect of sexual stratification by race on official reac-
           tion to rape. *American Sociological Review*, 1980a, *45*, 842–854.

T   LaFree, G. D. Variables affecting guilty pleas and convictions in rape
           cases: Toward a social theory of rape processing. *Social Forces*,
           1980b, *58*(3), 833–850.

D, F, R   LaFree, G. D. Male power and female victimization: Toward a theory of in-
           terracial rape. *American Journal of Sociology*, 1982, *88*(2), 311–328.

F   Lalli, M. D., & Turner, S. Suicide and homicide: A comparative analysis
           by race and occupational levels. *Journal of Criminal Law, Criminol-
           ogy and Police Science*, 1968, *59*, 191–200.

F, R   Lane, R. *Violent Death in the City: Suicide, Accident and Murder in
           Nineteenth Century Philadelphia.* Cambridge, MA: Harvard Univer-
           sity Press, 1979.

A   Lane, R. *Roots of Violence in Black Philadelphia, 1860–1900.* Cambridge,
           MA: Harvard University Press, 1986.

J   Langan, P. A., & Greenfeld, L. A. *The Prevalence of Imprisonment.* Wash-
           ington, DC: U.S. Department of Justice, 1985.

T   Langbein, J. H. Understanding the short history of plea bargaining. *Law
           and Society Review*, 1979, *13*(2), 261–272. (This issue also contains
           two other histories of plea bargaining.)

F, W   Langer, E. J. *The Psychology of Control.* Beverly Hills, CA: Sage, 1983.

D   Lapchick, R. E. *Broken Promises: Racism in American Sport.* New York:
           St. Martin's Press, 1984.

F   Laub, J. H. Urbanism, race and crime. *Journal of Research in Crime and
           Delinquency*, 1983, *20*(2), 183–198.

P, F   Laub, J. H., & McDermott, M. J. An analysis of serious crime by young
           black women. *Criminology*, 1985, *23*(1), 81–98.

D, J   Leger, R. G. Race, class and conflict in a custodial setting: Toward the de-
           velopment of a theory of minority group politicalization. *Human Re-
           lations*, 1983, *36*(9), 841–862.

P   Leinen, S. *Black Police, White Society.* New York: New York University
           Press, 1984.

D, P   Lester, D. The murder of police officers in American cities. *Criminal Jus-
           tice and Behavior*, 1984, *11*(1), 101–113.

T, S   Lewis, D. O., Balla, D. A., & Shanak, S. S. Some evidence of race bias in
           the diagnosis and treatment of the juvenile offender. *American Jour-
           nal of Orthopsychiatry*, 1979, *49*(1), 53–61.

T, S   Lewis, D. O., Shanak, S. S., Cohen, J., Kligfield, M., & Frisone, G. Race
           bias in the diagnosis and disposition of violent adolescents. *American
           Journal of Psychiatry*, 1980, *137*(10), 1211–1216.

W   Lichter, L. S. Who speaks for black America? *Public Opinion*, 1985, *8*(4),
           41–44.

D, W   Lichter, L. S., & Lichter, S. R. *Prime Time Crime.* Washington, DC: The
           Media Institute, 1983.

X   Lieber, A. L. *The Lunar Effect: Biological Tides and Human Emotions.*
           Garden City, NY: Doubleday, 1978.

F   Lief, H. I., & Savitz, L. D. Negro and white sex crime rates. In R. Slovenko
           (Ed.), *Sexual Behavior and the Law.* Springfield, IL: Charles C Thom-
           as, 1965, pp. 210–220.

R   Light, I. *Ethnic Enterprise in America: Business and Welfare Among
           Chinese, Japanese and Blacks.* Berkeley: University of California Press,
           1972.

F   Light, I. Numbers gambling among blacks: A financial institution. *Ameri-
           can Sociological Review*, 1977a, *42*, 892–904.

F   Light, I. The ethnic vice industry. *American Sociological Review*, 1977b, *42*, 464-479.

D, W   Lillyquist, J. J. *Understanding and Changing Criminal Behavior.* Englewood Cliffs, NJ: Prentice-Hall, 1980.

I, P, T, S Liska, A. F., & Tausig, M. Theoretical interpretations of social class and racial differentials in legal decision-making for juveniles. *Sociological Quarterly*, 1979, *20*, 197-208.

D   Liss, M. B. Children's television selection: A study of indicators of same-race preferences. *Journal of Cross-Cultural Psychology*, 1981, *12*(1), 103-110.

T, S   Lizotte, A. J. Extra-legal factors in Chicago's criminal courts: Testing the conflict model of criminal justice. *Social Problems*, 1978, *25*(5), 564-580.

D, J   Lockwood, D. *Prison Sexual Violence.* New York: Elsevier, 1980.

T   Loftus, E. F. *Eyewitness Testimony.* Cambridge, MA: Harvard University Press, 1979.

I, W   Long, E., Long, J., Leon, W., & Weston, P. *American Minorities: The Justice Issue.* Englewood Cliffs, NJ: Prentice-Hall, 1975.

D, W   Loury, G. C. The need for moral leadership in the black community. *New Perspectives*, 1984, *16*(1), 14-19.

D, W   Loury, G. C. The moral quandary of the black community. *Public Interest*, 1985, *79*(Spring), 9-22.

F   Luckenbill, D. F. Criminal homicide as a situated transaction. *Social Problems*, 1977, *25*(2), 176-186.

P   Lundman, R. S., Sykes, R. E., & Clark, J. P. Police control of juveniles: A replication. *Journal of Research in Crime and Delinquency*, 1978, *15*(1), 74-91.

R   Lundsgaarde, H. P. *Murder in Space City: A Cultural Analysis of Houston Homicide Patterns.* New York: Oxford University Press, 1977.

F   MacAndrew, C., & Edgerton, R. B. *Drunken Comportment: A Social Explanation.* Chicago: Aldine, 1969.

D   Mackie, M. Arriving at "truth" by definition: The case of stereotype and accuracy. *Social Problems*, 1972/73, *20*, 431-447.

J   Mancini, M. J. Race, economics and the abandonment of convict leasing. *The Journal of Negro History*, 1978, *63*(4), 339-352.

T   Mar, L. Probing racial prejudice on voir dire: The Supreme Court provides illusory justice for minority defendants. *Journal of Criminal Law and Criminology*, 1981, *72*(4), 1444-1460.

P   Margarita, M. Killing the police: Myths and motives. *Annals of the American Academy of Political and Social Science*, 1980, *452*(November), 63-71.

P   Martin, S. E. *Breaking and Entering: Police Women on Patrol.* Berkeley: University of California Press, 1980.

D, P   Matulia, K. J. *A Balance of Forces.* Gaithersburg, MD: International Association of Chiefs of Police, 1982.

D, W   Mayas, J. B. *Perceived Criminality: The Attribution of Criminal Race from News-Reported Crime.* Doctoral dissertation, University of Michigan, 1977.

X, T, S   Maynard, D. W. Defendant attributes in plea bargaining: Notes on the modeling of sentencing decisions. *Social Problems*, 1982, *29*(4), 347-360.

X, T, S   Maynard, D. W. *Inside Plea Bargaining: The Language of Negotiation.* New York: Plenum, 1984.

F   McClain, P. D. Cause of death—homicide: A research note on black females as homicide victims. *Victimology*, 1982, *7*(1-4), 204*ff.*

F   McClain, P. D. Determinants of black and white attitudes toward gun regulation. *Journal of Research in Criminal Justice*, 1983, *11*(1), 77–82.

T   McGonigle, S., & Timms, E. Race bias pervades jury selection: Prosecutors routinely bar blacks, study finds. *The Dallas Morning News*, March 9, 1986, pp. 1A, 28A–30A; March 10, 1986, pp. 1A, 10A–11A.

P   McLeary, R., O'Neill, M. J., Epperlein, T., Jones, C., & Gray, R. H. Effects of legal education and work experience on perception of crime seriousness. *Social Problems*, 1981, *28*(3), 276–289.

F   McMurray, H. L. *The Criminal Victimization of the Elderly* (Occasional Paper No. 22). Washington, DC: Institute for Urban Affairs and Research, Howard University, 1983.

A   McNeely, R. L., & Pope, C. E. (Eds.). *Race, Crime and Criminal Justice.* Beverly Hills, CA: Sage, 1981a.

P   McNeely, R. L., and Pope, C. E. Socio-economic and racial issues in the measurement of criminal involvement. In R. L. McNeely and C. E. Pope (Eds.), *Race, Crime and Criminal Justice.* Beverly Hills, CA: Sage, 1981b, pp. 31–47.

W   Meeker, J. W. Criminal appeals over the last 100 years: Are the odds of winning increasing? *Criminology*, 1984, *22*(4), 551–571.

A   Mendoza de Arce, D., & Peraza, O. L. Institutional discrimination in criminal justice processes. In R. Alvarez & K. G. Lutterman (Eds.), *Discrimination in Organizations.* San Francisco: Jossey-Bass, 1979, pp. 291–299.

F   Mercy, J. A., Smith, J. C., & Rosenberg, M. L. *Homicide among Young Black Males: A Descriptive Assessment.* Paper presented at the meeting of the American Society of Criminology, Denver, November 1983.

D, W   Meriwether, H. Deciding when race is relevant to a news story. *Miami Herald*, October 2, 1983, p. 4E.

R   Messner, S. F. Regional and racial effects on the urban homicide rate: The subculture of violence revisited. *American Journal of Sociology*, 1983a, *88*(5), 997–1007.

F, R   Messner, S. F. Regional differences in the economic correlates of the urban homicide rate: Some evidence on the importance of cultural context. *Criminology*, 1983b, *21*(4), 477–488.

I, J   Meyers, S. L., Jr. The incidence of "justice." In C. M. Gray (Ed.), *The Costs of Crime.* Beverly Hills, CA: Sage, 1979, pp. 61–84.

D   Middleton, R. Regional differences in prejudice. *American Sociological Review*, 1976, *41*, 94–117.

S, X   Miethe, T. D., & Moore, C. A. *Racial discrimination in criminal court sentencing decisions: A comparison of aggregate and race-specific models of criminal processing.* Paper presented at the meeting of the American Society of Criminology, Cincinnati, November 1984. Forthcoming in *The Sociological Quarterly*, 1986, *27*.

D   Miller, A. S. The court and racial bias: The second reconstruction is ending. *Miami Herald*, May 24, 1981, p. 4E.

X, T   Miller, G. *Invitation to a Lynching.* Garden City, NY: Doubleday, 1975.

T   Miller, M., & Hewitt, J. Conviction of a defendant as a function of juror-victim racial similarity. *Journal of Social Psychology*, 1978, *105*(1), 159–160.

P, J   Mobley, L. A waste of taxpayers' money . . . construction of new prisons: Increased oppression of minorities. *The Crisis*, 1982, *89*(4), 13.

D, W   Moe, J. L., Nacoste, R. W., & Insko, C. A. Belief vs. race as determinants of discrimination: A study of southern adolescents in 1966 and 1969. *Journal of Personality and Social Psychology*, 1981, *41*(6), 1031–1050.

F, X   Monkkonen, E. H. *The Dangerous Class: Crime and Poverty in Columbus, Ohio, 1860-1885.* Cambridge, MA: Harvard University Press, 1975.

X   Montero, D. Research among racial and cultural minorities: An overview. *Journal of Social Issues,* 1977, *33*(4), 1-10.

I, P   Moore, H., Jr. Does justice have a color: Law—is it a skin game? *North Carolina Central Law Journal,* 1973, *5*, 2-14.

I, D   Morales, A. Institutional racism in mental health and criminal justice. *Social Casework,* 1978, *59*(7), 387-395.

F   Moses, E. Negro and white crime rates. In M. E. Wolfgang, L. Savitz, & N. Johnston (Eds.), *The Sociology of Crime and Delinquency.* New York: Wiley, 1970, pp. 430-439.

T, S   Myers, M. A. Offended parties and official reactions: Victims and the sentencing of criminal defendants. *Sociological Quarterly,* 1979, *20,* 529-540.

X, T   Myers, M. A., & Hagan, J. Private and public trouble: Prosecutors and the allocation of court resources. *Social Problems,* 1979, *26,* 439-451.

R, J   Myers, S. L. Racial differences in postprison employment. *Social Science Quarterly,* 1983, *64*(3), 655-669.

T   Nagel, I. H. The legal/extra-legal controversy: Judicial decisions in pretrial release. *Law and Society Review,* 1983, *17*(3), 481-515.

X, T, S Nagel, S., & Neef, M. Racial disparities that supposedly do not exist: Some pitfalls in analysis of court records. *Notre Dame Lawyer,* 1976, *52,* 87-94.

P   Napper, G. Perception of crime: Problems and implications. In R. L. Woodson (Ed.), *Black Perspectives on Crime and the Criminal Justice System.* Boston: G. K. Hall, 1977, pp. 5-22.

R   Nassi, A. J., & Abramowitz, S. I. From phrenology to psychosurgery and back again: Biological studies in criminality. *American Journal of Orthopsychiatry,* 1976, *46,* 591-607.

D   National Advisory Commission on Civil Disorders. *Report of the National Advisory Commission on Civil Disorders.* New York: Bantam Books, 1968.

A   National Minority Advisory Council on Criminal Justice. *The Inequality of Justice: A Report on Crime and the Administration of Justice.* Washington, DC: U.S. Government Printing Office, 1982.

I, T, S Naylor, T. J. *Crime, Criminals, and Punishment in Philadelphia, 1866-1916.* Doctoral dissertation, University of Chicago, 1979, pp. 161-167.

T   Neil v. State, 433 So. 2d 51 (Fla. App. 3 Dist. 1983).

A   Nettler, G. *Explaining Crime* (3rd ed.). New York: McGraw-Hill, 1984.

J   New York State Special Commission on Attica. *Attica.* New York: Praeger, 1972.

F   Nichols, W. W., Jr. Community safety and criminal activity in black suburbs. *Journal of Black Studies,* 1979, *9*(3), 311-334.

R   Norland, S., Wessell, R. C., & Shover, N. Masculinity and delinquency. *Criminology,* 1981, *19*(3), 421-433.

F   O'Brien, R. M. *Crime and Victimization Data.* Beverly Hills, CA: Sage, 1985.

D, W   Official: Blacks led into political suicide. *Miami Herald,* November 20, 1984, p. 5A.

R   Oglesby, J. Tolerant views an invitation to black crime. *Miami Herald,* July 7, 1984, p. 23A.

D, W   O'Gorman, H. J. White and black perceptions of racial values. *Public Opinion Quarterly,* 1979, *43*(1), 48-59.

P   Ostrom, E. Equity in police services. In G. P. Whitaker & C. D. Phillips (Eds.), *Evaluating Performance in Criminal Justice Agencies.* Beverly Hills, CA: Sage, 1983, pp. 99-124.

D   Otken, C. H. *The Ills of the South.* New York: Putnam, 1984.

D, J   Owen, B. A. Race and gender relations among prison workers. *Crime and Delinquency,* 1985, *31*(1), 147-159.

J   Owens, C. E. Classifying black inmates: The Alabama prison classification project. In C. E. Owens & J. Bell (Eds.), *Blacks and Criminal Justice.* Lexington, MA: D. C. Heath, 1977, pp. 129-142.

A   Owens, C. E. *Mental Health and Black Offenders.* Lexington, MA: D. C. Heath, 1980.

A   Owens, C. E., & Bell, J. *Blacks and Criminal Justice.* Lexington, MA: D. C. Heath, 1977.

P   Palmer, E. Black police in America. *Black Scholar,* 1973, *5*(2), 19-27.

X   Parisi, N. Are females treated differently? In N. H. Rafter & E. A. Stanko (Eds.), *Judge Lawyer Victim Thief.* Boston: Northeastern University Press, 1982, pp. 205-220.

I, R   Parker, J. A., & Brownfield, A. C. *What the Negro Can Do about Crime.* New York: Arlington House, 1974.

R   Parker, R. N., & Smith, M. D. Deterrence, poverty and type of homicide. *American Journal of Sociology,* 1979, *85*(3), 614-624.

D   Patchen, M. Students' own racial attitudes and those of peers of both races as related to interracial behaviors. *Sociology and Social Research,* 1983, *68*(1), 58-77.

S   Paternoster, R. Race of victim and location of crime: The decision to seek the death penalty in South Carolina. *Journal of Criminal Law and Criminology,* 1983, *74*(3), 754-788.

D, W   Patterson, O. The moral crisis of the black American. *Public Interest,* 1973, *32*(Summer), 43-69.

D   Pearson, L. The rescue in Goulds: Second thoughts. *Miami Herald,* September 25, 1983, p. 1E.

T   Peirson, G. Institutional racism and crime clearance. In R. L. Woodson (Ed.), *Black Perspectives on Crime and the Criminal Justice System.* Boston: G. K. Hall, 1977, pp. 107-122.

D, T   Pekkanen, J. *Victims: An Account of a Rape.* New York: Popular Library, 1977.

F, T, S Pepinsky, H. E., & Jesilow, P. *Myths That Cause Crime.* Cabin John, MD: Seven Locks Press, 1984.

R   Perry, A. M., & Hokanson, J. E. Race factors in responses to interpersonal stress among young adult offenders. *Criminal Justice and Behavior,* 1977, *4*(1), 45-61.

S   Perry, R. W. *Racial Discrimination and Military Justice.* New York: Praeger, 1977a.

S   Perry, R. W. The justice system and sentencing: The importance of race in the military. *Criminology,* 1977b, *15*(2), 225-234.

S, J   Petersen, D. M., & Friday, P. Early release from incarceration: Race as a factor in the use of shock probation. *Journal of Criminal Law and Criminology,* 1975, *66*, 79-97.

J   Petersilia, J. *The Prison Experience of Career Criminals.* Santa Monica, CA: Rand Corporation, 1980.

A   Petersilia, J. *Racial Disparities in the Criminal Justice System.* Santa Monica, CA: Rand Corporation, 1983.

A   Petersilia, J. Racial disparities in the criminal justice system: A summary. *Crime and Delinquency,* 1985, *31*(1), 15-34.

S   Petersilia, J., & Turner, S. *Guideline-Based Justice: The Implications for Racial Minorities.* Santa Monica, CA: Rand Corporation, 1985.

X, S   Peterson, R. D., & Hagan, J. Changing conceptions of race: Towards an account of anomalous findings of sentencing research. *American Sociological Review,* 1984, *49,* 56-70.

D   Pettigrew, T. F. Racism and the mental health of white Americans: A social psychological view. In C. V. Willie, B. M. Kramer, & B. S. Brown (Eds.), *Racism and Mental Health.* Pittsburgh: University of Pittsburgh Press, 1973, pp. 269-285.

F   Pettigrew, T., & Spier, R. B. Ecological pattern of Negro homicide. *American Journal of Sociology,* 1972, *67*(6), 621-629.

F, R   Pettiway, L. E. Mobility of robbery and burglary offenders: Ghetto and non-ghetto space. *Urban Affairs Quarterly,* 1982, *18*(2), 255-270.

D, J   Pfefferbaum, A., & Dishotsky, N. I. Racial intolerance in a correctional institution: An ecological view. *Psychiatry,* 1981, *138*(8), 1057*ff.*

R   Phillips, D. P. The impact of mass media violence on U.S. homicides. *American Sociological Review,* 1983, *48,* 560-568.

F, R   Phillips, L., & Votey, H. L., Jr. Black women, economic disadvantage, and incentives to crime. *American Economic Review,* 1984, *74*(2), 293-297.

R   Picou, J. S., et al. Occupational choice and perception of attainment blockage: A study of lower class delinquent and non-delinquent black males. *Adolescence,* 1974, *9*(34), 289-298.

F   Pinkney, A. A. The statistics—social deviance. In R. Endo & W. Strawbridge (Eds.), *Perspectives on Black America.* Englewood Cliffs, NJ: Prentice-Hall, 1970, pp. 124-142.

D, J   Pisciotta, A. W. Race, sex and rehabilitation: A study of differential treatment in the juvenile reformatory, 1825-1900. *Crime and Delinquency,* 1983, *29*(2), 254-269.

J   Poole, E. D., & Regoli, R. M. Race, institutional rule breaking and disciplinary response: A study of discretionary decision-making in prison. *Law and Society Review,* 1980, *14,* 931-946.

S   Pope, C. E. The influence of social and legal factors on sentence dispositions: A preliminary analysis of offender-based transaction statistics. *Journal of Criminal Justice,* 1976, *4,* 203-221.

P   Pope, C. E. Post-arrest release decision: An empirical examination of social and legal criteria. *Journal of Research in Crime and Delinquency,* 1978, *15*(1), 35-53.

P   Pope, C. E. Race and crime revisited. *Crime and Delinquency,* 1979, *25,* 347-357.

I   Pope, C. E. Blacks and juvenile crime: A review. In D. Georges-Abeyie (Ed.), *The Criminal Justice System and Blacks.* New York: Clark Boardman, 1984, pp. 75-94.

A   Porter, B., & Dunn, M. *The Miami Riot of 1980: Crossing the Bounds.* Lexington, MA: D. C. Heath, 1984.

D   Poskocil, A. Encounters between blacks and liberals: The collusion of stereotypes. *Social Forces,* 1977, *55*(3), 715-727.

D, T   Potash, D. Mandatory inclusion of racial minorities on jury panels. *Black Law Journal,* 1973, *3*(1), 80-95.

F, R   Poussaint, A. F. Black on black homicide: A psychological-political perspective. *Victimology,* 1983, *8*(3-4), 161-169.

F, R   Poussaint, A. *Why Blacks Kill Other Blacks.* New York: Emerson Hall, 1972.

D, P   Powell, D. D. Race, rank and police discretion. *Journal of Police Science and Administration,* 1981, *9*(4), 383-389.

J   Powell, J. C. *The American Siberia: Fourteen Years' Experience in a South-
         ern Convict Camp.* Philadelphia: H. J. Smith, 1891.

D   Press, A. A law for racist killers. *Newsweek,* February 23, 1981, p. 80.

R   Price-Williams, D. R., & Ramirez, M. Ethnic differences in delay of gratifi-
         cation. *Journal of Social Psychology,* 1974, *93,* 23–30.

S, X   Pruitt, C. R., & Wilson, J. Q. A longitudinal study of the effect of race on
         sentencing. *Law and Society Review,* 1983, *17*(4), 613–635.

D, J   Racism and imprisonment internationally. *Jericho,* 1984, *34*(9), 1–2.

X, S   Radelet, M. L. Racial characteristics and the imposition of the death pen-
         alty. *American Sociological Review,* 1981, *46*(6), 918–927.

T   Radelet, M. L., & Pierce, G. L. Race and prosecutorial discretion in homi-
         cide cases. *Law and Society Review,* 1985, *19*(4), 587–621.

P   Rafky, D. M. Police race attitudes and labeling. *Journal of Police Science
         and Administration,* 1973, *1*(1), 65–86.

I, J   Rafter, N. H. *Partial Justice: Women in State Prisons, 1800-1935.* Boston:
         Northeastern University Press, 1985.

R   Rainwater, L., & Yancey, W. L. *The Moynihan Report and the Politics of
         Controversy.* Cambridge, MA: MIT Press, 1967.

J   Ramirez, J. Race and apprehension of inmate misconduct. *Journal of
         Criminal Justice,* 1983, *2,* 413–427.

R   Raspberry, W. New black leadership has a new challenge. *Miami Herald,*
         December 24, 1983, p. 15A.

R   Raspberry, W. Black families face the truth. *Miami Herald,* February 4,
         1984a, p. 27A.

D   Raspberry, W. Question for blacks: Is it just racism? *Miami Herald,* Octo-
         ber 12, 1984b, p. 23A.

D   Raspberry, W. Who is Harold Brown anyway? *Miami Herald,* February 6,
         1985a, p. 15A.

W   Raspberry, W. Conservative blacks disserved by Pendleton blasts. *Miami
         Herald,* March 14, 1985b, p. 31A.

J   Reasons, C. Racism, prison and prisoners' rights. *Issues in Criminology,*
         1974, *9*(2), 3–20.

A   Reasons, C. E., & Kuykendall, J. L. (Eds.). *Race, Crime and Justice.*
         Pacific Palisades, CA: Goodyear, 1972.

J   Reid, I. D. A. The Negro goes to Sing Sing. *Journal of Negro Life,* 1932,
         215–217.

A   Reiman, J. H. *The Rich Get Rich and the Poor Get Prison* (2nd ed.). New
         York: Wiley, 1984.

P   Reiss, A. J., Jr. *The Police and the Public.* New Haven, CT: Yale University
         Press, 1971.

P   Reiss, A. J., Jr. Police brutality. In R. J. Lundman (Ed.), *Police Behavior:
         A Sociological Perspective.* New York: Oxford University Press, 1980,
         pp. 274–296.

P   Remmington, P. W. *Policing: The Occupation and the Introduction of
         Female Officers.* Washington, DC: University Press of America, 1981.

X, S   Rhodes, W. M. Study of sentencing in Hennepin County and Ramsey
         County district courts. *Journal of Legal Studies,* 1977, *6*(2), 333–353.

I, D, P Ridenour, R. Who is a black political prisoner? *Black Law Journal,* 1971,
         1(1), 16–26.

S   Riedel, M. Discrimination in the imposition of the death penalty: A com-
         parison of the characteristics of offenders sentenced pre-Furman and
         post-Furman. *Temple Law Quarterly,* 1976, *49,* 261–287.

F   Riedel, M. Blacks and homicide. In D. Georges-Abeyie (Ed.), *The Crimi-
         nal Justice System and Blacks.* New York: Clark Boardman, 1984,
         pp. 51–74.

F   Riedel, M., Zahn, M. A., Mock, L. F., & Tech, E. *The Nature and Patterns of American Homicide*. Washington, DC: U.S. Government Printing Office, 1985.

R   Robins, L. N., West, P. A., & Herjanic, B. L. Arrests and delinquency in two generations: A study of black urban families and their children. *Journal of Child Psychology and Psychiatry*, 1975, *16*(2), 125–140.

R   Robins, L. N., & Wish, E. Childhood deviance as a developmental process: A study of 223 urban black men from birth to 18. *Social Forces*, 1977, *56*, 448–473.

R   Roizen, J. Alcohol and criminal behavior among blacks: The case for research on special populations. In J. J. Collins (Ed.), *Drinking and Crime*. New York: Guilford Press, 1981.

F   Rose, H. M. *Black Homicide and the Urban Environment* (Final Report). Washington, DC: National Institute of Mental Health, 1981.

F   Rose, H. M. Black-on-black homicides: Overview and recommendations. In D. Georges-Abeyie (Ed.), *The Criminal Justice System and Blacks*. New York: Clark Boardman, 1984, pp. 61–74.

W, S   Rossi, P. H., Simpson, J. E., & Miller, J. L. Beyond crime seriousness: Fitting the punishment to the crime. *Journal of Quantitative Criminology*, 1985, *1*(1), 91–102.

X   Rotton, J., & Kelly, I. W. Much ado about the full moon: A meta-analysis of lunar-lunacy research. *Psychological Bulletin*, 1985, *97*(2), 286–306.

J   Rowe, A. R. Race, age and conformity in prison. *Psychological Reports*, 1983, *52*, 445–446.

P   Rudwick, E. M. The southern Negro policeman and the white offender. *Journal of Negro Education*, 1961, *30*, 426–431.

W   Rudwick, E. M. Race labeling and the press. *Journal of Negro Education*, 1962, *31*, 177–181.

F   Rushforth, N. B., et al. Violent death in a metropolitan county: Changing patterns in homicide, 1958–74. *New England Journal of Medicine*, 1977, *297*, 531–538.

D   Ryan, W. *Equality*. New York: Pantheon, 1981.

T   Sample, B. C., & Philip, M., Jr. Perspectives on race and crime in research and planning. In D. Georges-Abeyie (Ed.), *The Criminal Justice System and Blacks*. New York: Clark Boardman, 1984, pp. 21–35.

F   Sampson, R. J. Race and criminal violence: A demographically disaggregated analysis of urban homicide. *Crime and Delinquency*, 1985, *31*(1), 47–82.

F, R   Savitz, L. D. Black crime. In K. S. Miller & R. M. Dreger (Eds.), *Comparative Studies of Blacks and Whites in the U.S.* New York: Seminar Press, 1973, pp. 467–516.

J   Scacco, A. M. *Rape in Prison*. Springfield, IL: Charles C Thomas, 1975.

P   Scharf, P., et al. Deadly force: The moral reasoning and education of police officers faced with the option of lethal legal violence. *Policy Studies Journal*, 1978, *7*, 450–454.

D, W   Schulman, G. I. Race, sex and violence: A laboratory test of the sexual threat of the black male hypothesis. *American Journal of Sociology*, 1974, *79*(5), 1260–1277.

R   Schultz, L. G. Why the Negro carries weapons. *Journal of Criminal Law, Criminology and Police Science*, 1962, *53*(4), 476–583.

D, W   Schuman, H., & Hatchett, S. *Black Racial Attitudes: Trends and Complexities*. Ann Arbor, MI: Institute for Social Research, 1974.

J   Scott, J. F. The use of discretion in determining the severity of punish-
       ment for incarcerated offenders. *Journal of Criminal Law and Crimi-
       nology*, 1974, *65*(2), 214-224.

P   Sealy, L. The dilemma of the black police executive. In H. J. Bryce (Ed.),
       Black Crime: A Police View. Washington, DC: Police Foundation,
       1977, pp. 141-154.

D   Sedlacek, W. E., & Brooks, G. C., Jr. *Racism in American Education*.
       Chicago: Nelson-Hall, 1976.

J   Sellin, J. T. *Slavery and the Penal System*. New York: Elsevier, 1976.

D, S   Shade, O. D. Determinate sentencing: A racist reform. *Corrections Today*,
       1982, *44*(5), 62-65.

D, W   Shaver, K. G. *An Introduction to Attribution Processes*. Hillsdale, NJ:
       Erlbaum, 1983.

P   Sherman, L. W. Causes of police behavior: The current state of quanti-
       tative research. *Journal of Research in Crime and Delinquency*, 1980,
       17(1), 69-100.

F, P   Sherman, L. W., & Glick, B. D. *The Quality of Police Arrest Statistics*.
       Washington, DC: Police Foundation, 1984.

P   Sherman, L. W., & Langworthy, R. H. Measuring homicide by police
       officers. *Journal of Criminal Law and Criminology*, 1979, *70*(4),
       546-560.

F   Shin, Y., Jedlicka, D., & Lee, E. S. Homicide among blacks. *Phylon*, 1977,
       38, 398-407.

R   Silberman, C. E. *Criminal Violence, Criminal Justice*. New York: Random
       House, 1978.

R   Silverman, I. J., & Dinitz, S. Compulsive masculinity and delinquency: An
       empirical investigation. *Criminology*, 1974, *11*(4), 498-515.

S   Skene, Neil. Death penalty in Florida. *St. Petersburg Times*, November
       13-15, 1983, pp. 1A*ff*.

F   Slotkin, R. Narratives of Negro crime in New England, 1775-1880. *Ameri-
       can Quarterly*, 1973, *25*, 3-31.

P   Smith, D. A., & Klein, J. R. Police agency characteristics and arrest deci-
       sions. In G. P. Whitaker & C. D. Phillips (Eds.), *Evaluating Performance
       in Criminal Justice Agencies*. Beverly Hills, CA: Sage, 1983, pp. 63-95.

P   Smith, D. A., & Visher, C. A. Street-level justice: Situational determinants
       of police arrest decisions. *Social Problems*, 1981, *29*(2), 167-177.

W   Smith, E. R., & Kluegel, J. R. Beliefs and attitudes about women's oppor-
       tunity: Comparisons with beliefs about blacks and a general perspec-
       tive. *Social Psychology Quarterly*, 1984, *47*(1), 81-95.

D   Sowell, T. Are quotas good for blacks? *Commentary*, 1978, *65*(6), 39-43.

W, R   Sowell, T. *Ethnic America: A History*. New York: Basic Books, 1981.

W, R   Sowell, T. *The Economics and Politics of Race: An International Perspec-
       tive*. New York: Morrow, 1983.

D   Sowell, T. *Civil Rights: Rhetoric or Reality*. New York: Morrow, 1984.

S   Spohn, C., Gruhl, J., & Welch, S. The effect of race on sentencing: A re-
       examination of an unsettled question. *Law and Society Review*,
       1981-1982, *16*(1), 71-88.

D, R   Staples, R. White racism, black crime and American justice: An applica-
       tion of the colonial model to explain crime and race. *Phylon*, 1975,
       36, 14-22.

P   Stark, R. *Police Riots: Collective Violence and Law Enforcement*. Bel-
       mont, CA: Wadsworth, 1972.

D   Stasz, C. *The American Nightmare: Why Inequality Persists*. New York:
       Schocken Books, 1983.

S Stecher, B. A., & Sparks, R. Removing the effects of discrimination in sentencing guidelines. In M. L. Forst (Ed.), *Sentencing Reform Experiments in Reducing Disparity.* Beverly Hills, CA: Sage, 1982, pp. 113-129.

I, T, S Steinberg, A. R. *The Criminal Courts and the Transformation of Criminal Justice in Philadelphia.* Doctoral dissertation, Columbia University, 1983, pp. 177-180.

D, W Stephan, W. G. Stereotyping: The role of in-group and out-group difference in causal attribution for behavior. *Journal of Social Psychology,* 1977, *101,* 255-266.

T Stewart, H. A black district attorney's view of criminal court: An interview with Mr. Howard Stewart, assistant district attorney, Dauphin County, Pennsylvania. In D. Georges-Abeyie (Ed.), *The Criminal Justice System and Blacks.* New York: Clark Boardman, 1984, pp. 219-223.

W Suarez, E. M., & Mills, R. C. *Sanity, Insanity and Common Sense: The Missing Link in Understanding Mental Health.* West Allis, WI: Med-Psych Publications, 1983.

T Sutherland, E. H., & Cressey, D. R. *Criminology.* Philadelphia: Lippincott, 1974.

J Swan, A. L. Successful passage of black parolees: From prison to prison. In L. E. Gary & L. P. Brown (Eds.), *Crime and Its Impact on the Black Community.* Washington, DC: Howard University, Institute for Urban Affairs and Research, 1975, pp. 195-205.

P Swan, A. L. Improving police relations in the black community. In C. E. Owens & J. Bell (Eds.), *Blacks and Criminal Justice.* Lexington, MA: D. C. Heath, 1977, pp. 119-127.

R Swan, L. A. A methodological critique of the Moynihan report. *Black Scholar,* 1974, *5*(9), 18-24.

X Swartz, J. Silent killers at work. *Crime and Social Justice,* Summer 1975, 15-20.

X, S Swigert, V. L., & Farrell, R. A. *Murder, Inequality and the Law.* Lexington, MA: D. C. Heath, 1976.

T Swigert, V. L., & Farrell, R. A. Speedy trial and the legal process. *Law and Human Behavior,* 1980, *4*(3), 135-146.

J, R Sylvester, S. F., Reed, J. H., & Nelson, D. O. *Prison Homicide.* New York: Spectrum, 1977.

W Taft, A. Leaders out of step with public's concerns. *Miami Herald,* March 31, 1981, p 1C.

P Takagi, P. A garrison state in a "democratic" society. *Crime and Social Justice,* 1974, *5*(Spring-Summer), 27-33.

F, R Taub, R. P., Taylor, D. G., & Dunham, J. D. *Paths of Neighborhood Change: Race and Crime in Urban America.* Chicago: University of Chicago Press, 1984.

D, R, X Tavris, C. *Anger: The Misunderstood Emotion.* New York: Simon & Schuster, 1982.

W, R Taylor, H., & Dozier, C. Television violence, African-Americans and social control, 1950-1976. *Journal of Black Studies,* 1983, *14*(2), 107-135.

P Teahan, J. E. A longitudinal study of attitude shifts among black and white police officers. *Journal of Social Issues,* 1975a, *31*(1), 47-56.

P Teahan, J. E. Role playing and group experience to facilitate attitude and value changes among black and white police officers. *Journal of Social Issues,* 1975b, *31*(1), 35-46.

P Teplin, L. A. Criminalizing mental disorder: The comparative arrest rate of the mentally ill. *American Psychologist,* 1984, *39*(7), 794-803.

T, S   Thomas, C., & Cage, R. The effect of social characteristics in juvenile court dispositions. *Sociological Quarterly*, 1977, *18*, 237-252.

X, S   Thompson, R. J., & Zingraff, M. T. Detecting sentencing disparity: Some problems and evidence. *American Journal of Sociology*, 1981, *86*(4), 869-880.

S   Thornberry, T. P. Race, socioeconomic status and sentencing in the juvenile justice system. *Journal of Criminal Law and Criminology*, 1973, *64*, 90-98.

F, R   Thornberry, T. P., & Farnsworth, M. Social correlates of criminal involvement: Further evidence on the relationship between status and criminal behavior. *American Sociological Review*, 1982, *47*, 505-518.

S   Tiffany, L. P., Avichai, Y., & Peters, G. W. A statistical analysis of sentencing in federal courts: Defendants convicted after trial, 1967-1968. *Journal of Legal Studies*, 1975, *4*(2), 369-389.

F, R   Tittle, C. R. Social class and criminal behavior: A critique of the theoretical foundation. *Social Forces*, 1983, *62*(2), 334-355.

F, R   Tittle, C. R., Villemez, W., & Smith, D. A. The myth of social class and criminality: An empirical assessment of the empirical evidence. *American Sociological Review*, 1978, *43*, 643-656.

P   Toch, H. *Violent Men: An Inquiry into the Psychology of Violence.* Chicago: Aldine, 1969.

J   Toch, H. *Living in Prison: The Ecology of Survival.* New York: Free Press, 1977.

P   Toch, H., Grant, J. D., & Galvin, R. T. *Agents of Change: A Study in Police Reform.* New York: Wiley, 1975.

P   Townsey, R. D. Black women in policing: An advancement display. *Journal of Criminal Justice*, 1982, *10*(6), 455-468.

P, W   Trojanowicz, R. C., & Banas, D. W. *The Impact of Foot Patrol on Black and White Perceptions of Policing.* East Lansing, MI: Michigan State University, National Neighborhood Foot Patrol Center, School of Criminal Justice, 1985.

D, W   Tunteng, P. Ideology, racism and black political culture. *British Journal of Sociology*, 1976, *27*(2), 237-249.

I, W   Turk, A. The mythology of crime in America. *Criminology*, 1971, *8*(4), 397-411.

W   Turner, C. B., & Wilson, W. J. Dimensions of racial ideology: A study of urban black attitudes. *Journal of Social Issues*, *32*(2), 139-152.

D, T   Ugwuegbu, D. C. E. Racial and evidential factors in juror attribution of legal responsibility. *Journal of Experimental and Social Psychology*, 1979, *15*, 133-146.

X, T, S   Uhlman, T. M. Black elite decision making: The case of trial judges. *American Journal of Political Science*, 1978, *4*(22), 884-895.

X, T, S   Uhlman, T. M. *Racial Justice: Black Judges and Defendants in an Urban Trial Court.* Lexington, MA: D. C. Heath, 1979a.

T, S   Uhlman, T. M. A plea is no bargain: The impact of case disposition on sentencing. *Social Science Quarterly*, 1979b, *60*(2), 213-234.

X, S   Unnever, J. D. Direct and organizational discrimination in the sentencing of drug offenders. *Social Problems*, 1982, *30*(2), 212-225.

S   Unnever, J. D., Frazier, C. E., & Henretta, J. C. Race differences in criminal sentencing. *The Sociological Quarterly*, 1980, *21*, 197-205.

F   Van den Haag, E. Could successful rehabilitation reduce the crime rate? *Journal of Criminal Law and Criminology*, 1982, *73*(3), 1022-1035.

P   Van Maanen, J. Street justice. In R. J. Lundman (Ed.), *Police Behavior: A Sociological Perspective.* New York: Oxford University Press, 1980, pp. 274-296.

P   Waegel, W. B. Case routinization in investigative police work. *Social Problems*, 1981, *28*(3), 263–275.

I, D   Walker, S. *Popular Justice: A History of American Criminal Justice.* Oxford University Press, 1980.

W   Walker, S. *Sense and Nonsense about Crime: A Policy Guide.* Monterey, CA: Brooks/Cole, 1985.

W   Warr, M. The accuracy of public beliefs about crime. *Criminology*, 1982, *20*(2), 185–204.

S   Washington, M. Black judges in white America. *The Black Law Journal*, 1971, *1*(3), 173–179.

T   Wasserman, D. T., & Robinson, J. N. Extra-legal influences, group processes and jury decision-making: A psychological perspective. *North Carolina Central Law Journal*, 1980, *12*, 96–159.

F, R   Watts, A. D., & Watts, T. M. Minorities and urban crime: Are they the cause or the victims? *Urban Affairs Quarterly*, 1981, *16*(4), 423–436.

P   Watts, J. G. "It just ain't righteous": On witnessing black crooks and white cops. *Dissent*, 1983, *30*(3), 347–353.

P   Webster, D. NAACP police-citizen violence project aimed at curbing abuses. *The Crisis*, 1982, *89*(10), 39.

P   Weiner, N. L., & Willie, C. V. Decisions by juvenile officers. *American Journal of Sociology*, 1971, *77*(2), 199–210.

X, S, J   Weisheit, R. A. Sex differences in the jail population: Competing explanations. *Criminal Justice Review*, 1985, *10*(1), 47–51.

X, S   Welch, S., Gruhl, J., & Spohn, C. Sentencing: The influence of alternative measures of prior record. *Criminology*, 1981, *22*(2), 215–228.

R   Wells, E. E. *The Mythical Negative Black Self-Concept.* Saratoga, CA: R & E Publishers, 1978.

R   Wells, L. E., & Rankin, J. H. Self-concept as a mediating factor in delinquency. *Social Psychology Quarterly*, 1983, *46*(1), 11–22.

P   Wesley, W. A. *Violence and the Police: A Sociological Study of Law, Custom and Morality.* Cambridge, MA: MIT Press, 1970.

D   West, S. G., Whitney, C., & Schnedler, R. Helping a motorist in distress: The effects of sex, race and neighborhood. *Journal of Personality and Social Psychology*, 1975, *31*(4), 691–698.

D, R   Weyl, N. Race, nationality and crime. *Mankind Quarterly*, 1973, *14*, 41–48.

R   Weyl, N. The geography of stupidity in the U.S.A. *Mankind Quarterly*, 1974, *15*(2), 117–123.

T   Wheeler, G. R., & Wheeler, C. L. Reflections on legal representation of the economically disadvantaged: Beyond assembly line justice: Type of counsel, pretrial detention, and outcomes in Houston. *Crime and Delinquency*, 1980, *26*(3), 319–332.

R   Wideman, J. E. *Brothers and Keepers.* New York: Holt, Rinehart, & Winston, 1984.

F   Wilbanks, W. Homicide and the criminal justice system in Dade County, Florida. *Journal of Crime and Justice*, 1979, *2*, 58–74.

R   Wilbanks, W. Does alcohol cause homicide? *Journal of Crime and Justice*, 1981, *4*, 149–170.

D   Wilbanks, W. Racism and double standards. *Miami Herald*, October 2, 1983, p. 1E.

F   Wilbanks, W. The elderly offender: Sex and race variations in frequency and patterns. In W. Wilbanks & P. Kim (Eds.), *Elderly Criminals.* Washington, DC: University Press of America, 1984a, pp. 41–52.

D   Wilbanks, W. Miami's had enough loose talk. *Miami Herald*, February 22, 1984b, p. 19A.

F, T, S   Wilbanks, W. *Murder in Miami: An Analysis of Homicide Patterns and Trends in Dade County (Miami), Florida, 1917-1983.* Washington, DC: University Press of America, 1984c.

F, R   Wilbanks, W. Is violent crime intraracial? *Crime and Delinquency,* 1985a, *31*(1), 117-128.

F   Wilbanks, W. *Criminal Homicide in the U.S.: Black vs. White.* Unpublished manuscript, 1985b.

D   Wilbanks, W. *Interracial vs. Intraracial Crime in Miami.* Unpublished manuscript, 1985c.

T   Wilbanks, W. *Does Type of Counsel Make a Difference?* Unpublished manuscript, 1985d.

D, P   Wilbanks, W., & Lewis, R. G. *Racial Bias in the Processing of Complaints about Excessive Force by Police Officers: An Empirical Examination of Data from Two Police Departments in Dade County, Florida, 1974-1980.* Paper presented at the meeting of the American Society of Criminology, Washington, DC, November 1981. (Available through NCJRS, No. 84369.)

I   Wilkins, L. T. *Consumerist Criminology.* Totowa, NJ: Rowman & Allanheld, 1984.

F, R   Willcox, W. R. *Negro Criminality: An Address Delivered Before the American Social Science Association at Saratoga, Sept. 6, 1899.* Boston: G. H. Ellis, 1899.

I, T, S   Williams, F. P., III. Conflict theory and differential processing: An analysis of the research literature. In J. Inciardi (Ed.), *Radical Criminology: The Coming Crisis.* Beverly Hills, CA: Sage, 1981a, pp. 213-231.

X, T   Williams, F. P., III. Keeping defendants out of jail: An analysis of a release on recognizance project. *California Sociologist,* 1981b, *4*(2), 206-218.

All   Williams, G. C. *The Negro Offender.* New York: Russell Sage Foundation, 1922.

I, D   Williams, W. E. *The State Against Blacks.* New York: McGraw-Hill, 1982.

F, R   Willie, C. V., & Gershenowitz, A. Juvenile delinquency in racially mixed areas. *American Sociological Review,* 1964, *29*, 740-744.

I, W   Wilson, J. Q. Luncheon speaker and reaction. In R. L. Woodson (Ed.), *Black Perspectives on Crime and the Criminal Justice System.* Boston: G. K. Hall, 1977, pp. 37-54.

S   Wilson, J. Q. *Thinking about Crime* (2nd ed.). New York: Vintage, 1985.

R   Wilson, J. Q., & Herrnstein, R. J. *Crime and Human Nature.* New York: Simon & Schuster, 1985.

D, R   Wilson, L., & Rogers, R. W. The fire this time: Effects of race of target, insult, and potential retaliation on black aggression. *Journal of Personality and Social Psychology,* 1975, *32*(5), 857-864.

I   Wilson, W. J. *The Declining Significance of Race: Blacks and Changing American Institutions.* Chicago: University of Chicago Press, 1978.

I   Wilson, W. J. The black community in the 1980's: Questions of race, class and public policy. *Annals of the American Academy of Political and Social Science,* 1981, *454*, 26-41.

F   Wiltz, C. J. Fear of crime, criminal victimization and elderly blacks. *Phylon,* 1982, *43*(4), 283-294.

R   Wolfgang, M. E. Suicide by means of victim-precipitated homicide. *Quarterly Review of Psychiatry and Neurology,* 1959, *20*(4), 335-349.

A   Wolfgang, M. E. Race and crime. In H. J. Klare (Ed.), *Changing Concepts of Crime and Its Treatment.* Oxford: Pergamon Press, 1977.

A   Wolfgang, M. E., & Cohen, B. *Crime and Race: Conceptions and Misconceptions.* New York: Institute of Human Relations Press, 1970.

S Wolfgang, M. E., & Riedel, M. Race, judicial discretion and the death penalty. *Annals of the American Academy of Political and Social Science*, 1973, *407*, 119-133.

S Wolfgang, M. E., & Riedel, M. Rape, race and the death penalty in Georgia. *American Journal of Orthopsychiatry*, 1975, *45*(4), 658-688.

F, J Wolfson, W. P. *The Pattern of Prison Homicide.* Doctoral dissertation, University of Pennsylvania, 1978.

A Woodson, R. L. (Ed.). *Black Perspectives on Crime and the Criminal Justice System.* Boston: G. K. Hall, 1977.

D, S Wright, B. M. A black brood on black judges. *Judicature*, 1973, *57*(1), 22-23.

A Wright, B. M. A view from the bench. In D. Georges-Abeyie (Ed.), *The Criminal Justice System and Blacks.* New York: Clark Boardman, 1984a, 205-218.

T Wright, B. M. Interview with Judge Bruce McM. Wright. In D. Georges-Abeyie (Ed.), *The Criminal Justice System and Blacks.* New York: Clark Boardman, 1984b, pp. 345-350.

T Wynne, D. F., & Hartnagel, T. F. Race and plea negotiation: An analysis of some Canadian data. *Canadian Journal of Sociology*, 1975, *1*(2), 147-155.

F Young, V. Women, race and crime. *Criminology*, 1980, *18*(1), 36-54.

J Young, W. Retaining black staff in correctional institutions. *Corrections Today*, 1982, *44*(1), 40-41.

S Zalman, M., Ostrom, C. W., Guilliams, P., & Peaslee, G. *Sentencing in Michigan: Report of the Michigan Felony Sentencing Project.* Lansing, MI: State Court Administrative Office, 1979.

X, S Zatz, M. S. Race, ethnicity and determinate sentencing: A new dimension to an old controversy. *Criminology*, 1984, *22*(2), 147-172.

X, S Zatz, M. S., & Hagan, J. Crime, time, and punishment: An exploration of selection bias in sentencing research. *Journal of Quantitative Criminology*, 1985, *1*(1), 103-126.

S Zeisel, H. Race bias in the administration of the death penalty: The Florida experience. *Harvard Law Review*, 1981, *95*(2), 456-468.

S Zimmerman, S., & Frederick, B. C. Discrimination and the decision to incarcerate. In D. Georges-Abeyie (Ed.), *The Criminal Justice System and Blacks.* New York: Clark Boardman, 1984, pp. 315-329.

S Zimring, F. E., Eigen, J., & O'Malley, S. Punishing homicide in Philadelphia: Perspective on the death penalty. *University of Chicago Law Review*, 1976, *43*(2), 227-252.

Name Index

Adamson, C. R., 12, 140
Akbar, N., 39
Akers, R. L., 55, 159
Alex, N., 82
Allport, G. W., 28
Alpert, G. P., 39
Alwin, D. F., 100, 123–125
Arkin, S. D., 123
Austin, R. L., 55, 106, 122–123
Avichai, Y., 55–56, 112, 123

Bacchus, J., 140
Bailey, D., 140–141
Baldus, D. C., 123–125
Balkan, S., 159
Balla, D. A., 11
Banas, D. W., 81
Banks, T. L., 97, 102
Banks, W. M., 28, 29
Bannon, J. D., 81
Bart, P. B., 28
Bartollas, C., 141
Bass, B. M., 140
Beard, E., 81–82
Bell, W., 23, 29, 60, 80, 87, 97, 100, 102, 122
Bennett, W. J., 29
Benokraitis, N., 100
Berger, R. J., 159
Berk, R., 122–124
Berman, J. J., 39
Bernstein, I. N., 99, 100, 102
Black, D. J., 69, 81
Blumstein, A., 56, 80, 101, 122, 140, 141, 149–150, 158, 159
Bock, E. W., 99–100
Bowers, W. J., 101, 110, 122–123
Box, S., 80
Bramwell, H., 122
Brigham, J. C., 39
Brooks, G. C., 28
Brown, L. P., 80, 81, 100

Brown, R. M., 12, 140
Brownmiller, S., 28
Bullock, H. A., 55, 111, 123–124
Bumiller, K., 105–106, 122–124, 159
Burke, P., 100, 102, 123, 125, 159
Burnham, D., 80
Bynum, T., 99, 100

Cahalan, M., 12
Campbell, V., 81–82
Carper, N. G., 12, 140
Carroll, Leo, 29, 135, 140–141
Carroll, Lewis, 28
Chamblin, M. H., 101
Chevigny, P., 81
Chiricos, T. G., 55, 101, 123, 124
Christianson, S., 122, 140, 148, 154, 158–159
Clarke, S. H., 101, 113, 115, 123
Clayton, O., 110, 123–124, 159
Cohen, J., 11, 56, 81–82, 122, 129, 140–141, 159
Comer, J. P., 124
Condran, J. G., 29
Conyers, J., 81
Cray, E., 81
Cressey, D. R., 122, 159
Crockett, G. W., 11, 29, 80–81

Dannefer, D., 123, 159
Daudistel, H. C., 122–123
Davis, A. J., 29, 141
Davis, J. A., 2, 11
Davis, K. C., 99
Dean, A. W., 81–82
Dehais, R. J., 102, 122–123, 140, 148, 154, 158–159
Del Olmo, R., 55
Denno, D., 100
Dobbins, D. A., 140
Doyle, P. A., 99, 100, 102
Ducassi, J., 122

Subject Index

Credits

CHAPTER 1. **7,** quote from *Brothers and Keepers,* by J. E. Wideman. Copyright © 1984 by John Edgar Wideman. Reprinted by permission of Henry Holt and Company.

CHAPTER 2. **21,** quote from "The Moral Crisis of the Black American," by O. Patterson, *The Public Interest,* No. 32 (Summer 1973). Copyright © 1973 by National Affairs, Inc. Reprinted by permission. **25,** quote from *The Miami Riot of 1980: Crossing the Bounds,* by B. Porter and M. Dunn. Copyright © 1984 by D. C. Heath and Company. Reprinted by permission of the publisher.

CHAPTER 3. **34,** quote from *Brothers and Keepers,* by J. E. Wideman. Copyright © 1984 by John Edgar Wideman. Reprinted by permission of Henry Holt and Company.

CHAPTER 5. **58,** quote from *Myths That Cause Crime,* by H. E. Pepinsky and P. Jesilow. (Cabin John, M.D.: Seven Locks Press, 1984). **69,** quote from *The Police and the Public,* by A. J. Reiss. Copyright © 1971 by Yale University Press. Reprinted by permission. **69,** quote from *The Police and the Public,* by A. J. Reiss. Copyright © 1971 by Yale University Press. Reprinted by permission.

CHAPTER 7. **104–105,** quotes from "Racial Discrimination in Criminal Sentencing: A Critical Evaluation of the Evidence with Additional Data on the Death Penalty," by G. Kleck, *American Sociological Review,* 1981, *46,* 798–799. Reprinted by permission. **105,** quotes from *Research on Sentencing: The Search for Reform,* by National Research Council, Panel on Sentencing Research, 1983. Reprinted by permission.

CHAPTER 8. **129,** quotes from "The Limits of Racial Integration in Prison," by J. Jacobs, *Criminal Law Bulletin,* 1982, *18,* 118, 143. Copyright © 1982 by Warren, Gorham & Lamont, Inc., 210 South Street, Boston, MA 02111. All rights reserved. **130, 131,** and **137,** quotes from *Racial Disparities in the Criminal Justice System,* by J. Petersilia. Copyright © 1983 by The Rand Corporation. Reprinted by permission.